The Spokane Valley
Volume 2
A History of the Growing Years
1921-1945

Best wishes!
Florence Boutwell

EIGHTH NATIONAL APPLE SHOW

The silver medal was awarded to the Growers Union, the largest shipping agency in the Valley during the '20s. It handled the crops of 243 growers and had 355 stockholders. The packing house at Opportunity was 320 feet by 60 feet and was valued at $110,000 with equipment. The packing and sorting equipment, unique in the country, was designed by Ed Peirce who held the patent. The Union was organized in 1911 and by 1922 had packed 309,769 boxes of apples for the growers members.

Photo courtesy of Robert Nelson.

The Spokane Valley

Volume 2
A History of the Growing Years
1921-1945

---

compiled by
Florence Boutwell

UNITED LITHOGRAPHERS INC.
Spokane, Washington
2001

LIBRARY OF CONGRESS CATALOG CARD NUMBER 94-79244
ISBN 0-87062-245-5 (cloth)
ISBN 0-87062-246-3 (paper)

Third Printing, 2001

First Printing, 1995, The Arthur H. Clark Company
Second Printing, 1996, The Arthur H. Clark Company

Other Books by Florence Boutwell
The Teresa Series for middle school readers
The Spokane Valley Years (Poems)
Those Pheasants (for Little Folks)

DEDICATION:

"...let us honor all the Americans who lost their lives in World War II. They were the fathers we never knew, the uncles we never met, the friends who never returned, the heroes we can never repay. They gave us our world and those simple sounds of freedom we hear today are their voices speaking across the years."

PRESIDENT BILL CLINTON
June 6, 1994, D-Day Speech at Colleville-Sur-Mer, France.

It is to those voices from the Spokane Valley speaking across the years that this book is dedicated.

FLORENCE BOUTWELL

Contents

Illustrations

PINES ROAD NORTH OF PRESENT VALLEYWAY IN 1906.
The road went around a low place where water stood when it rained.
Left: Wilson (Talarico) House; Right: Modern Electric tank.
Courtesy of Patricia Smith Goetter.

Preface:
The Story Thus Far and a Hint of What's to Come

In the 1800s most travelers who passed through the Spokane Valley did not tarry—unless it was to admire the scenery or rest their horses. The rocky character of the soil was not friendly and coupled with the dry summers and the abundance of bunch grass, the Valley gave little promise of providing a means of making a living.

In the early 1900s however, the picture changed. Visionaries successfully brought water to the area from nearby lakes, the Spokane River, and by drilling wells into the abundant aquifer.

By 1901 sixteen miles of main and branch ditches were bringing small amounts of water from Liberty Lake to 560 acres offered for sale in Greenacres. This was the beginning of what has been termed the "blooming" of the Valley. It was not long before some 20,000 acres of land were irrigated and carved into saleable parcels by surveyors' lines, and the Valley was advertised as prime fruit growing country.

Meanwhile, in 1903 the Spokane and Inland Empire Railway Company built a line on the south side of the Valley from Coeur d'Alene to Spokane when developer W.L. Benham offered a right-of-way through Greenacres. For people interested in farming and fruit growing, the railway added incentive to settle in the Valley. It connected the newly irrigated tracts with city markets, using electric by day to haul passengers and freight, and steam at night to haul lumber.

Three thousand acres on the north side of the Spokane River known as East Greenacres was developed and watered from Twin Lakes. Crops, especially apple trees, produced abundantly and the profits to be made from farming the Valley were touted by developers and the railroads throughout the east and midwest. Speculators and farmers who had questioned whether or not rocky Valley soil could hold water were convinced.

City residents eager for the "freedom" of country life in the West came in droves. By 1905 there were no parcels in all of Greenacres left unsold.

As far back as 1886 settlers around Newman Lake had constructed a ditch of sorts to drain the rich flatlands around the lake. In 1903 Mark F. Mendenhall and Laughlin MacLean contracted to convert the old ditch into a canal to serve water to 2750 acres of Valley land north of the river. This area became known as Otis Orchards. These tracts soon filled with midwesterners when booklets such as "Irrigation Is King" circulated in the Chicago area, the hub for marketing apples at apple auctions.

South across the river at what is now Pines Road and Broadway the first big well was dug. The Modern Irrigation Company opened up the 3000-acre Opportunity tract six miles from the Spokane city limits. Here the water was secured from wells through underground wooden and (later) concrete pipelines as it was for the nearby 1885-acre development called Vera. A spur of the electric railroad that served Greenacres was built to serve Opportunity, Vera and two communities along the east-west highway known first as Harrington's and Hutchinson's additions, but later as Dishman.

Because the east-west highway was abundant with apple blooms, people began to call the eastern extension of Sprague Avenue "The Appleway."* The beauty of the Valley in blossom time was said to have been a sight whose splendor could not be surpassed. Growers' Unions were formed and marketing was at its peak.

The Valley Chamber of Commerce was formed in 1921 by the communities of Dishman, Opportunity, Greenacres, Otis Orchards, Millwood, Pasadena, Trentwood-Irvin and University Place for the purposes of promoting the Valley and providing a unified effort to improve facilities and plan conven-

*Early in Spokane history James Glover named Sprague Avenue for General J.W. Sprague, superintendent of the western division of the Northern Pacific Railroad. The Appleway also became Sprague Avenue when the east-west roads in the Valley were made to correspond with names of City streets. At that time Shelleyway, McCanna, Campus and Saltese were changed to Fourth, Eighth, Twelfth, and Sixteenth respectively. University Road, early in history, was known as Apple Center. Argonne Road was first known as Millwood Road north of Appleway and Chester Road south of Appleway.

iences. Millwood was and remains the only incorporated town in the Valley. It was developed by the Inland Empire Paper Company as a hometown for its workers. University Place developed as a site for Spokane University and its employees. Dishman's location as the first community east of Spokane on the Appleway made it the ideal place for business growth. All of the other communities owed their existence totally to irrigation and originated as irrigation districts.

Valley population increased rapidly. It soon became evident that the lakes could not supply enough water to meet irrigation demands—especially since there were many extensive commercial orchards in the Valley.

From 1906-1910 an unlined, two-foot-wide ditch and a box flume almost five miles long were constructed to bring water from the Spokane River to supplement the water being drawn from various lakes, chiefly Liberty and Newman. The south branch watered Greenacres, Corbin Addition and small tracts as far west as Millwood. The north branch helped supply water to East Farms, Otis Orchards, West Farms and Pasadena Park areas.

The added water from the river eased the increasing water supply problems but did not solve other problems that were arising. Equipment, canals and ditches were deteriorating because very little provision had been made for maintaining them. Financial problems were becoming serious because fees for water usage were based on acreage rather than amount used; and so income was lagging.

Soon small water companies and even the large Spokane Canal Company became insolvent. The growers, too, began to experience financial problems due in some cases to inexperience and in others to unseasonable weather and poor growing conditions. Some growers came into the market in 1912 when apple production began to exceed demand. They could not compete with the experienced growers of Wenatchee and Yakima.

Fruit trees were pulled out and farmers turned to truck farming. Berries became an especially profitable crop.

With collapsing canals needing repairs and old wooden flumes rotting, the people formed their own irrigation districts (the first in the county) for the purpose of maintaining ditches and equipment. In 1923 and '24 state loans also helped pay for renovations to canals. The loans, although not a permanent answer to maintenance problems, extended the life of the irrigation services to Valley farmers.

When severe early frosts hit the Valley in 1927 and '28, and a pest known as the leaf roller damaged a large portion of the trees in the Valley, the death knell was sounded for the apple industry.

The early twentieth century Valley built on agriculture began to disappear, but the Valley did not collapse. Fortunately there was a tax base of city workers living in the Valley who were not dependent on agriculture for an income. Business hubs with stores and shops at crossroads and along the highways had developed at Millwood, Dishman and Opportunity. There were established schools and churches, banks and postal routes, a paper mill and a cement plant for jobs. There was a newspaper that provided communication and a network of roads that provided transportation beyond Valley boundaries.

The Valley was able to cope with change and able to start life anew.

1930-1945

Growth continued and the population of 7,648 in 1920 increased to 15,831 in 1940 and 24,500 by October 1946. Dynamic outside influences which would have been unimaginable to the early settlers—inventions, the Depression, government intervention, World War II—left indelible marks. This is the story of 1921-1945.

Volume II of the history of the Spokane Valley continues the format of Volume I. As in Volume I, the make-up of the book allows for blank pages at the end of chapters. Many who purchased Volume I used these pages to insert their own Valley memories, photos and experiences. This made their copies personal and exceedingly valuable as family keepsakes. I highly recommend this practice.

And now my thanks—to Robert A. Clark of the Arthur Clark Company to whom goes all the credit for the book design and for helping me with countless details. Thanks also to so many other people that I cannot enumerate them all: those who allowed me to excerpt their autobiographies, those who loaned photos, those who volunteered research materials and scrap books and clippings, those who wrote or told me of their reminiscences—you are all part of these two books of Valley history. As you read and enjoy them, know that they could not have been accomplished without you.

FLORENCE BOUTWELL

Synopsis of Early Spokane Valley History

...Continued

[From *History of the Spokane Valley Chamber of Commerce* by Tom M. Smith, published by the Chamber of Commerce, October 1, 1971. Earlier years are found in VOLUME I of this history.]

1921-1945

It was decided to form the Spokane Valley Chamber of Commerce in 1921 with Terry T. Grant as the first president. Ray Kelley was secretary. The directors were to consist of three members from each of the Valley Community Clubs. It was suggested that each club have its president as one of the representatives. Dues were to be $10 per year per club. In most years to follow, ten clubs were represented. [Dishman, Greenacres, Trentwood-Irvin, Millwood, Otis Orchards, Opportunity, Orchard Avenue, Veradale, Liberty Lake and University Place.] Meetings were held once a month or more often, if necessary. The first meetings are said to have been held in the office of the bank in Opportunity. Meetings were also held in the *Valley Herald* building and in the office of Sidney E. Smith. (See "Sidney Smith," Volume I.)

With little money available and with only volunteer, unpaid members, the organization could not handle much of a project by itself. Members could be, however, the leaders that the Valley needed. They gave much of their time to the discussion and planning of needed Valley projects. These plans were then brought before the people and with the backing of the merchants, various other organizations and the people as a whole, many projects were carried out. Sometimes credit was given to the Chamber as such; other times people did not realize the hard work of a few and just assumed that things "just happened."

One of the first All-Valley projects was the Apple Show at Otis Orchards. An Apple Blossom Day was held there in 1921. It is said that 5000 people attended and that 1000 apple pies were consumed. This event was also held in 1922. In 1923 the first of many All-Valley picnics was held at Liberty Lake. These popular picnics were well attended and the tradition continued about twenty years. Every place of business was supposed to close on that day. Most of them did and everyone went to the picnic. People met old friends there and also made new ones. One of the objects of the picnics was to get people acquainted, interested in each other's problems and thus tie the Valley communities together. (See article, "6351 Attend Big Picnic.")

TWO DECADES OF GROWING YEARS

Terry Grant served as president of the Chamber two years, 1921 and 1922. He was followed by M.J. Luby in 1923. Both of these men were Spokane attorneys and lived in the Valley. J.B. Felts, a successful orchardist at Opportunity, followed and served 1924 and 1925. In 1926 Harry E. Nelson held office. Nelson was an orchardist when he first came to the Valley. In later years he was interested in the apple packing business and was also associated with government fruit inspection. (See "Harry E. Nelson, 'Mr. Spokane Valley,'" Volume I.)

Ray Kelley was president during 1927 and 1928. He was in the advertising business. He was secretary of the Chamber most of the time after it started, but Buell Felts served part of the time until his death in 1927. Felts was editor of the *Valley Herald* and was killed in an airplane crash in May 1927. (See "Felts Field," Volume I.)

Oscar Reinemer, a Dishman merchant, was president in 1929, followed by A.H. Syverson of Orchard Avenue in 1930. Syverson was in advertising with Ray Kelley. Earl Z. Smith, editor of the *Valley Herald*, served through 1931.

A Yard and Garden Contest was sponsored in 1925 and was continued for several years. Winners could enter a national contest and Valley homes did win awards in the contest. All of these things helped the relations of people with each other but one of the most popular and rewarding events was the Community Club Dinner.

An early committee of five men, including Buell Felts, Reinemer and William Moore met at Moore's home on Orchard Avenue to talk over building community relations and public interest in the Valley. They came up with the happy idea of a public dinner once a month held by each community in turn. There were ten clubs and ten months from September until June. July would be given over to a dance at Liberty Lake and August would be Valley Picnic. The dinner project was to be in the form of a contest for the clubs to see which one could put on the best dinner. A speaker or other entertainment was provided and the event was so popular that tickets to the affair were often at a premium. Oscar Reinemer says that the early charge to dinner was 60¢. The club gave the Chamber 10¢ and kept the rest. Prices were low in those days and as the club had most of the food and all of the work donated, it was a money raiser as well as a good time for all.

Apple growing was a gamble as is most farming, and fruit was a perishable product and could only be stored for a limited time. The cost of production was expensive and some years the price for apples was too low to pay those costs. Also, new tree diseases, as well as insects, came to attack the trees. By 1925 many trees were being removed and cantaloupes and tomatoes became the leading crops. (See "George W. Pierce and the Rise and Fall of the Apple Industry.")

The Apple Show was discontinued and a Know-the-Valley Tour and a Harvest Festival held in the fall were substituted. The Valley produced an excellent cantaloupe called Hearts of Gold. The Chamber used this item for a Valley promotion. Each year the Valley hosted the Spokane City Chamber at a cantaloupe feed. Needless to say, the feed became very popular and was well attended. The Chamber also saw that the Valley was well represented at the Spokane Interstate Fair which was held each fall at the Fairgrounds in Spokane.

J. Fink Giboney was president through 1932 and 1933. Mr. Giboney was from Vera community and

was followed by John M. Booth, who was the principal of Central Valley High School. William J. Green, the County Agriculture Extension Agent in Spokane County for many years, was next in 1935. He was followed by Dr. W.E. Bayne of Millwood in 1936.

George W. Pierce, who was in the fruit business at Opportunity for many years, served in 1937. Ray B. McCabe of Vera, an accountant for Spokane County, was next in 1938 and 1939. Thomas H. Bienz, a Dishman druggist, was president during 1940. Bienz had served for some time in the State Legislature. Together with several others, including Ray Toole of Orchard Avenue, Bienz had much to do with legislature which made possible the Valley Fire Protection District. This was voted upon and approved by the people in 1940. (See "Early Fire Protection.")

These were the years of a national Depression which began in 1931 and lasted until World War II. The Chamber helped in every way that it could, including using Chamber funds to cash warrants for the teachers. In 1937 the Chamber became involved in a project that was to have a far-reaching effect on future Chamber history.

At this time there was wide-spread unemployment; business property, homes and farm lands were lost to mortgages and taxes. The federal government started what was to be known as the W.P.A. This made it possible for a city, a community, or public-owned organization to obtain funds, privately or through government grant, to finance public works such as streets, playgrounds, and water systems. The Federal Government would pay the unemployed men wages to work upon such projects.

Somehow the Chamber obtained title to about 150 acres of land near the center of the Valley. This land had gone back to the county for unpaid taxes. It was a part of a development called Pinecroft which had failed in the Depression. It consisted of some high cliffs and other land which was for the most part covered with boulders and not too suitable for farming. Due to its central location in the Valley, the Chamber felt that it could be developed into an All-Valley park and recreation center. It would also make work available to many needy families. The Chamber applied for help on the project and in early 1938, the Valley project became a

W.P.A. project and state and federal funds were appropriated for it. (See "Jackson and the Pinecroft Development," Volume I.)

Plans were made to eventually build an auditorium, a gymnasium, six tennis courts, a 60' x 135' pool and a golf course. Nothing permanent came from it, but much dirt and rock was moved around and the community benefited from the wages paid the unemployed people. The war years came and the project was discontinued.

In 1925, the Valley Woman's Club tried to have streets in the Valley named and numbered. In 1929 the Chamber appointed a committee to work on the project. Some work was done on this. People tried to cooperate, and the Opportunity Township started to put up signs on the corners.

In 1939 the county took a hand and changed the numbering and also the names of the streets to conform with an extension of Spokane city streets and numbers. Eventually everyone complied with the new system and by 1943, street signs were up over most of the Valley.

THE YEARS OF CHANGE

World War II was getting closer to America and to the Spokane Valley. The old days of the Valley were going and would never return. About 1941, a worried government decided to use the Valley location for an aluminum rolling mill, and a short time later, for the development of a large Naval Supply Depot.

Overnight, it seemed, all unemployment was gone. New people flocked to the area, prices advanced and material became scarce. People began to fix up their barns, chicken houses, basements, and attics to rent to the newcomers. All available land was used to produce food but soon the labor force was mostly the old, the women, and the young people. The armed forces or war industries took almost everyone else.

Gene Kenney was Chamber president in 1941.

Gene had a large apple operation at Otis Orchards. David Meigs held the job through the years 1942-1943. Meigs was manager of a large company handling cedar poles—logging, treating and delivering their product for utility poles and for piling.

Sig Hansen was elected for the years 1944-1945. Hansen was principal of Central Valley High School. Ray Kelley had been secretary much of the time since he was president in 1928. He resigned once more and Irving Smith took over until he was called to the service. In 1942 Kelley was called upon again.

The Valley was changing and the calls upon it were terrific. No longer could a small volunteer, unpaid group of men handle the demands. A committee was appointed and a new constitution and by-laws were adopted. Some of the changes were:

1. Active memberships were solicited from any interested person in the Valley with dues at $5 per year.

2. A board of directors would consist of 16 members, 8 from the active community clubs and 8 from active members.

3. Nominations were to be made in November with elections in December. A president would be elected and four directors from each classification voted for each year, after the first year.

4. Officers would be president, vice president and treasurer—these last to be selected by the board. A secretary-manager was to be hired. This last was the most important step taken.

5. There would be eight standing committees.

*   *   *   *   *

Facts from a bulletin, printed by the Valley Chamber of Commerce in 1945, are reprinted at the end of this history to provide an overall picture of Valley growth by the end of World War II. With the end of World War II, Volume II of this Spokane Valley history ends.

Home Life, Community Life

"May I remark here that the primary reason for the laxity in right living today, as I see it, is due largely to the fact that we are fast losing the American home. The automobile and the moving picture are rapidly taking the place of the evenings spent at the fireside with father and mother. Removal from parental restraint is a bad thing for the average boy or girl."

[*The Wide Northwest* by Leon L. West, Shaw and Borden Printers, Spokane, Washington, 1927]

Opportunity, Washington

COPYRIGHT
PHOTO BY

AERIAL VIEW OF THE SPOKANE VALLEY, 1933
The view is west towards Spokane. The cluster of buildings at right center is the
Opportunity commercial area. Sprague Avenue bisects the photo, with Dishman just
off the photo at the upper left, and the continuing road to Coeur d'Alene at right.
Photo by Leo, courtesy of Joan Schwisow

Home Life, Community Life

Chronological History

1920
Walking along the Appleway was considered dangerous. The County Commissioners granted permits for cement sidewalks in **Opportunity Center.**

1921
Forty new residences were built in the **Valley**. The estimated population was about 7000.

Spokane furrier, **Charles Bergman,** had an elegant stucco house built on the **Appleway** just off **Bowdish Road** with pools, fountains, and a sunken garden. He was French, his wife was Austrian.

A two-story brick and concrete building was erected in **Millwood** to be used for a **Masonic Temple**. It was built over the old **Wylie Hotel** site and housed the **Spokane Valley State Bank** which was first located in the **Byram Building** behind the **Byram Store** northwest of **Argonne Road** and the **RailRoad Tracks.**

Half of the **Opportunity Business District** burned. Only a bucket brigade was available to fight the fire. (See "A Place Called Opportunity," Volume I.)

1922
To replace the buildings that burned, **C.E. Johnson** erected a brick building in the **Opportunity Block** with 100-foot frontage on the **Appleway** and 60-foot depth.

Estimated **Valley** population: 10,000, $250 an acre for irrigated land.

Trentwood Community Club began erection of a **Community Hall** 42x90 feet.

1924
435 feet above the Valley floor, work started on the **Riblet Mansion**, named **Eagle's Nest.** It was a fourteen-room view home. (See article, "Eagle's Nest.")

The **Millwood Building Company** purchased the property at what is now N. 3223 **Argonne** and had a new bank building constructed there for $1000.

1925
Local papers reported that 100 new homes had been built in the **Valley** and there was an increasing trend for city workers to reside in the **Valley.**

1925

Dishman Commercial and Community Clubs were organized.

The Brown Block in Millwood was completed.

1926

The business center at Corbin Addition to Greenacres was developing. Vera Community Club was organized.

A Community Chest was organized to finance Valley activities.

The Opportunity Athletic Club was reorganized, Arthur R. Walker, president.

1927

October 15: At the Millwood Confectionery Store, the issue of Millwood incorporation passed 76-5. Millwood had 437 residents, a well established school, and 300-400 employees at the Paper Mill which had a payroll of $500,000. It was organized as a fourth class city. (See "The Town of Millwood," Volume I.)

The Opportunity State Bank was robbed of $1000 at 2 p.m. A robber with a pistol backed L.E. Cooke, cashier, and C.A. Schumann, his assistant, into a vault.

Spokane Valley Farms Company platted a new addition north of Greenacres across the river.

New Otis Orchards Community Clubhouse was built.

In the Valley, there were 21 4-H Clubs with 350 members, 14 CampFire Groups with 200 members, and 8 Boy Scout Troops with 200 members. A Boys And Girls Week Federation was formed. The Spokane Valley Scout Council was formed with M.B. Ford, executive director.

Orchard Park men formed an Athletic Club.

1928

A Community Hall was built at Greenacres.

Vera Power And Water installed water meters to measure usage.

1929

A.D. Griffin took over the nucleus of what became Kokomo from his brother-in-law.

A committee made up of the presidents of all the Community Clubs was appointed by the Chamber Of Commerce to number businesses and residences.

April: Domestic water rates in the Vera District were $1.50 per month minimum for 2,000 cu. ft. and 10¢ for each 133 cu. ft. over 2,000.

A new Byram Building was constructed in Millwood and along with the post office, ice cream parlor, hardware store and meat market became known as the Byram Block.

1930

Valley population: 11,163.

Population by township was as follows: **Opportunity,** 5280; **Greenacres,** 1255; **Mica,** 259; **Newman,** 795; **East Spokane,** 1529; **Millwood,** 493; **Chester,** 401. There were 1031 farms listed in the census. **Spokane Bridge** and **Saltese** were precincts, not townships.

Channon Price landscaped his home on the **Appleway** near **Walnut** by adding a cement curb edging the driveway and the sunken gardens. There were pillars at the entrance, a hedge in front and a brick fountain and bird bath.

Valley Kiwanis was organized with **John Booth,** president.

A new irrigation canal branching off at **East Farms** ended water troubles at **Otis Orchards.**

1931

The **Otis Orchards Community Clubhouse (Frank Shinn,** president) was destroyed by fire.

1932

The **Valley** reluctantly followed **Spokane** in adopting **Daylight Saving Time.**

Valley Boy Scouts, sponsored by the **Kiwanis Club,** dedicated a new 24-capacity Scout cabin at **Camp Sekani.**

Tri-Community Grange was organized.

1934

Plans were drawn for a new $25,000 **Dishman Community Clubhouse** to be built on the north side of the **Appleway** overlooking the **Subway.**

March: **Greenacres Community Club,** organized in 1907, voted to buy the old **Greenacres Hall** on **Center** and remodel it for a community clubhouse.

1935

Greenacres Grange organized with 109 members, one of the largest beginning memberships in the state.

Mica built a new **Grange Hall. Trentwood** had a **Grange.**

Dishman Commcercial Club bought the **Mandalay Restaurant** for a clubhouse. The **Community Clubhouse** was built.

1936

The first **Spokane Valley Directory** was issued by the *Spokane Valley Herald.*

Vera installed a domestic water system.

Otis Orchard's wooden irrigation flumes were replaced by concrete.

1937

The first **Millwood Fire Department** was located at the **Paper Mill** and remained there until the Town Hall was built in the '50s. Even the fire trucks were kept there. The Mill whistle blew to call the volunteer fire fighters to their stations.

Work began on the **Pinecroft Community Recreation Center.** (See Volume I, "Jackson and the Pinecroft Development.")

A new **Opportunity Community Club** was organized.

The first **Spokane Valley Fair** was held with six **Granges** and 28 **4-H Clubs** participating.

1939

A county fire truck was stationed at **Dishman.**

1940

An **All-Valley Band** was formed.

Census: 14,868 people in the **Valley.**

March: Valley residents voted for **Fire Commissioners** and a levy for the district of 2 mills.

1941

The **Spokane Weather Bureau** was moved from the Empire State building in Spokane to **Felts Field.** (See article, "Felts Field," Volume I.)

1942

Roof of **Dishman Community Clubhouse** collapsed under a heavy accumulation of snow.

1943

Pleasant Prairie Cemetery was incorporated. It began in pioneer days when a child was buried on the **Charles Frederick Farm.** Other burials followed until **Frederick** laid out 4 acres as the **Pleasant Prairie Cemetery**.

1944

February 18: **Vera Power And Light** began to buy its power from **Bonneville.** Rates dropped.

Rathdrum Prairie Irrigation project saw 3500 acres of land irrigated at **Post Falls**.

Our Home in Opportunity, 1924

[From an informal autobiography by Dr. Frederick L. Coddington (used with permission).]

We moved to Opportunity in 1924—my mother Mabel, my father William, my brothers Robert and John, and I, Fred. Robert was about twelve years old at the time, I was about ten, and John was six.

The house we moved into on Bowdish Road had belonged to Dr. Hines, a dentist. He had his dental office in the north end of the house at the end of a long hallway that opened off the living-room and kitchen.

It was a one story, sprawling building with a large, rambling, full basement.

The living-room in what had been the living quarters had a large fireplace but no mantle. The walls were plastered but there was no trim around the doors and windows. The flooring was badly worn near the front door. The cement porch outside was bordered by concrete railings topped with flower boxes, also cement. There were no steps coming up from the front lawn, just a slope of clay dirt which also formed the porch floor. Dirt tracked into the house badly.

Opening off the living-room through a wide arch was a roughed-in dining-room. The floor was rough diagonal planking. The walls were lathed but not plastered, and the ceiling was open rafters. Catto, our cat, often jumped from rafter to rafter above the table while we were eating. Some laths had broken off the wall between the archway and kitchen door. We, as well as Catto, could climb up into the attic there on the cross braces.

The kitchen had been plastered and floored but had no cupboards. The small sink was quite dingy, with open plumbing under it. A bare-looking breakfast nook had south windows looking into a screened-in back porch. The porch was of filled-in dirt with cement steps leading down to the back yard.

Below these rooms were several basement rooms with cement walls but dirt floors. One had a coal chute going into one half and a wooden partition down the middle. A window opened out of the other side where firewood, mostly match-blocks, were stored. [See "Yardley, Parkwater," Volume I.] Beneath the living-room was a large space, partially walled off and partially floored with cement. There was a drain in the floor near the north wall. Hot and cold water pipes led to a common faucet where laundry tubs had been. A chimney flue in the foundation below the fireplace was available for a central furnace.

Although there was much finishing to be done, the house had been solidly built. The rafters in our basement ceiling were 2 x 12's, placed about 12 inches apart. We were told that the architect had designed sawmills.

There was no indoor bathroom at first, so Robert installed an inverted lawn sprinkler in the rafters above the floor drain. He connected a section of garden hose with the mixing faucet.

It provided a delightful shower. Soon the neighborhood boys were coming to our basement every Saturday afternoon for weekly baths. They had only tubs for bathing in their own homes.

Our wood and coal range warmed up the kitchen on cold mornings. If we needed more heat, we opened the oven door. During the cold winter months, we put up a coal stove in the living-room. After our indoor bathroom was finished, we had a portable kerosene stove to warm it for bathing.

NEIGHBORS

Our neighbors on the south were the Allers. Their parents' names were the same as our parents' names—William and Mabel.

Herbert Aller, about Robert's age, had two sisters, one older and one younger. Herbert was a little taller than Robert. When they first met, he looked Robert over and said,

"I believe I could lick you!"

Robert did not challenge that statement and they became fast friends.

Our neighbors on the north were Mr. and Mrs. Zebedee Hirsch. They were both nearly 90 years old. Mr. Hirsch was thin and tottery and walked with a cane. He spent most of his day sitting on his back porch steps, drumming on the step with his right fingers and smoking a clay pipe with his left.

Mrs. Hirsch was portly but more active. She often came out of her back door to scold him about his smoking. Whenever I came to visit him, he always told me, "Boy, my wife is crazy. She says smoking will shorten my life. Why, smoking saved my life! I was a drummer in the Civil War. At the battle of Gettysburg, I was climbing over a stone wall. A rifle ball hit me in the right rear pocket and shattered my pipe. I wasn't even scratched!"

Our lot occupied a full acre of ground. It had been part of a huge red delicious apple orchard before subdivision. There were still 17 large apple trees left, but some were dying.

Our newspaper box was mounted on the telephone pole at the edge of our front lawn. Our mail box was in a cluster of boxes at the nearest street corner, Shelley and Bowdish, one eighth mile north of us.

Behind our house was a chicken house and a small privy, a garden that extended to the back of the lot, and a large irrigation ditch that brought water to our neighbors on the north. There was also a large irrigation ditch on our south boundary, bridged with heavy boards.

A 20-foot flower garden and strawberry patch lay between our driveway and the Allers' property. A well-worn path soon ran from our back door to theirs.

As soon as summer vacation started, Dad hired Frank and Byron Broom, along with carpenters, plumbers and plasterers, to finish our house.

After the bathroom was completed, we dug a new hole for the privy. We moved it to the northwest corner of the garden to use when working out there. The old hole under the privy was almost full. We covered it with a little dirt and planted a hill of smooth-skinned gray squash. Brother Robert and I both joined the 4-H Club. In the fall, we took first and second ribbons for squash at the fair. Our two entries were so large we couldn't get both together in the wheel barrow. We didn't divulge the source of our success.

THE NEIGHBORHOOD

On the northeast corner of Bowdish and the Appleway, on the north side of the Interurban Railway tracks, was Aarlis' Snowwhite Grocery and Market where we bought household staples. Charley and his wife, Lorena, ran the grocery. Old Mr. Aarli, Charley's father, had the meat market. Charley delivered groceries in a small truck each evening after he closed the store.

Mr. Lenny, the school janitor, lived on the northwest corner.

The business district of Opportunity was on the Appleway one half mile east of this intersection. Groves Garage, Mars Store, the barbershop, pharmacy, bank and Myers' Dry Goods Store were brick buildings in the Opportunity block. Dr. Hopkins had his office above the pharmacy and the Odd Fellows Hall was over the bank. There was a tiny wooden shoe repair shop between the bank and Myers' store. There were several houses west between Groves Garage and the Baptist Church on the corner. Turner Lumber Company was across the street on the north side of the Appleway. The telephone exchange was behind the Baptist Church.

About two miles straight west of us were the Dishman Hills. We did a lot of hiking there. To get there we walked through the Spokane University Campus. [See "Spokane University," Volume I.] There was an old sand pit behind the girls' dormitory. It had been converted to a garbage dump. It contained bed springs, auto bodies, cracked engine blocks, and odds and ends of machinery. We brought home from the dump many useful items including electric motors and bicycle parts.

When we went to the Dishman Hills, Herb Aller brought along his BB gun to shoot rats that fed on freshly dumped garbage.

Across the Dishman-Chester Highway was a granite quarry and a sawmill. We were fascinated with the work going on in both institutions. We watched men drilling dynamite holes in the face of cliffs, but they wouldn't let us near the place when they were blasting.

There was an open air shop where a man worked on polished granite surfaces designing grave markers. He painted the surface with whitewash and used a pneumatic chisel to carve letters and designs.

The sawmill had a steam engine that turned a six-foot circular saw and a huge bandsaw. Men rode on a large carriage that carried big logs into the saws. Machinery turned the logs over easily and carried sawed timbers to drying stacks. In another area, dried boards were run through large planing machines and came out very smooth. The place was terribly noisy.

The hills rose steeply behind the Inland Empire Granite Company and the sawmill. There were delightful areas to explore. We usually planned to eat our lunch by Horse Soup Lake, a little pond in Dishman Hills that dried out in the summer. There was a natural fireplace in a cliff beside the pond. Sometimes we built a fire and roasted wieners. Once we followed the range of hills southeast beyond the town of Chester.

There was a brick factory there where we watched men mixing wet clay and shaping bricks. They cut a mound of wet clay with fine wires stretched on wooden frames. The wet bricks were spread out on boards in the sun to dry. Later they were stacked in the kilns where they would be fired with coke. The yellowish gray color turned to brick red after firing.

On ten acres at the crest of the hill between us and the town of Chester, sat the Borgheld Strom home, a large two-story structure badly in need of paint. Borgheld sold sand from a pit on her land that was mostly second growth pine trees. Our township kept the road graded in front of her house, but Bowdish was neglected beyond that corner. At the steep part of the hill, it twisted back and forth and was full of ruts. Many detours were carved by cars getting around the deep washes. In winter, snow was often deepest on the far side of Stroms' land. The neighborhood kids often took sleds there and even built a jump slide for sleds to go over.

CORBIN DITCH

We often rode our bicycles to the Corbin Ditch in Veradale for swimming. That was a gravity irrigation system, flowing down the Spokane Valley from Post Falls, Idaho. Coursing many miles in an open cemented ditch, the water became comfortably warmed by the sun.

Our favorite swimming hole was a widened, deepened part of the ditch on a hillside in Veradale. An eight foot gatehouse was built over the ditch, upstream from the widened area. The valve controls in the building released a stream of water one hundred feet below to a turbine. It turned a pump which forced part of the water back up and over the ditch. That water irrigated land above the ditch level.

We dived into the wider part of the ditch from a pipe or its high bank. We could dive from the roof of the gatehouse into water five feet deep upstream.

Occasionally we rode our bikes to the paper mill at Millwood or went fishing in Shelley's Lake.

All of the neighborhood kids played croquet in Allers' front yard. It was a delightful pastime in the cool of long summer evenings.

Memories of Opportunity

HERBERT ALLER: In 1921 my folks bought a one-acre tract at 521 S. Bowdish Road—all orchard. They started a house which we moved into when it was only partly finished. Even when finished, we used an outdoor privy for years.

My dad did electrical work for the Davenport Hotel and the Paper Mill. He made some of the original fixtures in the Davenport.

The Opportunity Grade School was the focus of activities from the classroom to Scouts, sports, and community events. I have good memories of the fine teachers and their dedication to our education. I was swatted with the deadly wooden paddle only once and never forgot it.

Summers were filled with swimming in the Spokane River, the Corbin irrigation ditch, and at Liberty, Hauser, and Newman lakes. And working for 10¢ an hour pulling weeds, hoeing and cultivating, picking strawberries, thinning apples, and picking pickling cucumbers. Wages finally went up to 15¢ an hour.

It seemed that everyone had truck gardens,

SWIMMING IN THE CORBIN DITCH, 1940
The "ditch" brought water from the Spokane River to irrigate the area north of the river. Much of the "ditch" was a three-by-five foot wooden aquaduct that crossed the Valley on frame trusses, dipping beneath roads in square concrete ducts. (Left to right) Sally (Sampson) Fox, Mary Lou Sampson (Rice), Mavis Smith (Baum), Betty (Sampson) Strong.
Courtesy of Sarah Fox.

chickens, and maybe a pig or two. Milk was 10¢ a quart and delivered by Russel's Dairy [northeast corner of Bowdish and Valleyway, fenced]. Bread was 10¢ a loaf and other groceries equally low and delivered by Aarli's Grocery if desired.

The telephone building was not quite across from the Christian Church behind the Baptist Church on the east side of Robie Street between First Avenue and the Appleway. The telephone operators sat in long rows on their high chairs at the switch boards and were a fascinating sight for some of us who dared sneak into their work place to watch them.

High School time finally came and some of us were off to Lewis and Clark, transported in our dads' Model T's or Model A's. Opportunity didn't have a high school. We could choose a Valley high school or one in town. The Valley was a wonderful place for a kid in those days!

OPPORTUNITY BANK ROBBED

Spokane Daily Chronicle, November 28, 1927

A lone bandit walked into the Opportunity State Bank at 2 o'clock today, covered L.E. Cooke, cashier, and C.A. Schumann, his assistant, with pistol, and robbed the till of about $1000 after backing the two employees into the bank vault and closing the door.

The vault door failed to catch and when the front door of the bank slammed after the bandit had taken all the money in sight, Cooke and Schumann gave chase. They commandeered the car of Schoonover and came close enough to the bandit's car to get his license number.

The robber's car was too fast for the pursuing automobile and after a chase of about three miles, the following car was distanced. Schumann and Cooke say that the license number is that of a local owner and that they believe the robbery to be the work of a single bandit.

A Walk Through the Town of Dishman, 1930

[From "Growth in Dishman in Three Years Is Remarkable," *Spokane Valley Herald*, September 11, 1930.]

PERMANENT TYPE OF BUSINESS BLOCKS GUARANTY OF FUTURE

During the past four years probably no business center in the Valley has seen so many important changes, nor so much building of a permanent type of business blocks as Dishman.

Where the Brownson Motor Company now has its large garage and salesroom, the J.F. Brod home stood, a comfortable tree-shaded yard surrounding it. Across the road to the east a vacant lot invited small boys to play. Beyond a frame store building was the home of C.P. Price, owner of the Price Box and Lumber company, whose mill is west of the Brownson Garage.

Several more small dwellings filled the block on the south side of the street.

On summer days the box factory hummed pleasantly, occasional customers drifted into Art Dick's Barber Shop, wandered down the street to the post office, and stopped at the drug store for soda pop or an earful from Tom Bienz's new radio. About five o'clock in the afternoon, shoppers in search of something quick for supper hustled into Reinemer's Store, and homecoming husbands stopped at Lynn Brownson's Garage for a nice fresh drink of gas for the old Lizzy.

A nice, quiet little country town, Dishman was.

Then things began to happen. Years of faithful energetic work began to bring results to several Dishman firms.

DRUG STORE GROWS

In the other half of Reinemer's building, Mr. and Mrs. Thomas Bienz had been hard at work building up a flourishing drug store.

Their coming to Dishman was in July 1922, after Mrs. Bienz had taught for a year in the school, her husband being with a drug company in the city. Choosing this as a good location, they opened their store in the Dishman Building, being there but a short time when the fire burned them out.

They leased half of the new building put up by Mr. Reinemer and operated their store in it for five and a half years. Then, since both firms needed more room, Mr. and Mrs. Bienz bought the corner across the road and erected a fine modern building of two stories, having their own attractive apartment over their store.

They moved into the new location in March, 1928, where they are still in business.

In addition to the store building, Mr. and Mrs. Bienz have bought and remodeled the frame building which formerly occupied the site. This building is now the home of Burgan's, No.16, where Lynn Addington is now the hustling manager, and Frank's Market, run in connection.

ALONG THE STREET

Walk east on the Appleway and into other changes.

Channon Price's old home is gone, as well as all the other houses in the block. In their place is a solid row of business institutions. The W.R. Collier Barber Shop has been here for a few months. Next is one of the most recent additions, Doc's Snappy Service Station, where Harold Dockendorf deals out gas, accessories, and tires. The station is new, but Doc is an old timer here—seven years—and is well known.

The cars blocking the next driveway are those of the thirsty populace seeking a drink of Regina Root Beer at W.H. Robertson's stand. Robertson also operates the Liberty Service Station just across the road.

Farther on up the street are a number of fruit and vegetable stands where Valley products are on sale from early spring until mid-winter. Several of these dealers have been permanently located at Dishman for several years, among them Joe Falco.

Next comes the attractive Mandalay Inn, opened in June by Lew Hartig and Lon Kennedy, where the socially inclined may enjoy meals and dancing under pleasant surroundings.

And then, to show that Dishman is strictly up-to-date in amusement as well as business, here is the new Spokane Valley Miniature Golf course owned by D.C. Holmes and Sam Christian.

Across the road is the Valley Fuel Company whose proprietor, E.G. Pangborn, has been a resident for a number of years.

Going back toward the viaduct, we pass more fruit stands, where city people's cars are so thick on Saturdays and Sundays that a poor Valley resident can scarcely get through to his own fireside.

A newly shingled green painted building catches our eye, proclaiming the home of the Darby Fuel Company, one of the recent additions to Dishman. Next to it is the second-hand store just opened by Mr. Haynie. Presently we come to a neat little building with a striped pole out in front. Yes, it is the barber shop of Art Dick. The old frame shop where Art held forth for three years was burned last spring, a year after he had outgrown it. Art had promised his patrons he would build a new shop if business for three years warranted it, and the shop, as we see, is there.

Two barber chairs and every modern sartorial device make it a popular place. An added attraction is the beauty shop run in connection.

West of Reinemer's Store is the Spokane Hardware, which came into Dishman last spring; C.C. Mecum's Clothing Store opened at the same time although Mr. Mecum was not a newcomer having been in Dishman for several years; the remodeled post office, where mail and postal receipts are advancing steadily year by year; Gould's Cafe; the real estate office of Johnson and Johnson; and the Appleway Chevrolet Company. Here, in the location formerly occupied by Brownson's, John Pring, another energetic young man , is developing a good business.

Mr. Pring, while he is a comparatively new arrival in Dishman, having been in business only a year and a half, has made an excellent beginning. He reports sales for the first eight months of 1930 of 168 cars, a total of $84,327 worth of business.

Mr. Pring has entered the civic life of the community with enthusiasm and has made many friends.

Across the street from his garage is one of the real pioneer institutions of Dishman, the Price Lumber and Box Company.

But Dishman doesn't stop here. The viaduct divides it, but quite a group of business buildings are located on the other side, among them the Boyd Conlee Company's Grain and Feed Store, the office and lumber yard of the Standard Lumber Company, managed by Lawrence Nicholson, and the C.F. Schimmels Garage.

The Stockton Tourist Camp is a busy place in summer.

Another point of interest is the Dishman Hall, owned by A.T. Dishman, where the big free dance will be given Friday night. The picture show, put on by J.G. Heatherly, will be in the open air stadium, also owned by Mr. Dishman.

Another little business in which Mr. Dishman is interested is the pottery, run by Mr. Gorsek. Another real estate office, that of Tinsley and Tinsley, is also located in this district.

So that is Dishman today. Tomorrow, it will probably have something new to talk about, for it is a growing community.

Gold Discovery in the Dishman Hills

What excitement! Eleven samples of "gold ore" taken from the "ledge" of the Dishman Hills in early 1924, "warranted development of the property," according to assay reports in newspapers at the time.

Residents of Dishman with an inclination toward mining immediately attempted to secure options on the land adjoining the gold finds.

However those with real mining expertise said that although they agreed that surface indications seemed favorable, the possibility of a strike of any magnitude was remote. They reminded the populace that all of the land then under scrutiny had been patented thirty or forty years ago as mining claims and that the traces found had developed into nothing more exciting. They pointed out places that showed evidence of early prospecting both on the side of the Dishman Hills where the recent discoveries were made and on the other side near Moran Prairie.

The experienced miners said the present discoveries were what they called "a show of colors" and probably would result in nothing more.

The experts proved to be correct. Off and on in the early part of the century there were flurries of excitement such as that in 1924, but to date—nothing to warrant a gold rush.

Greenacres—1921, 1938

Before irrigation the population of what later became Greenacres was less than twenty with five make-shift buildings (some people spoke of them as "shacks") scattered among the bunch grass.

After irrigation the development of orchards in that district was very rapid. By 1910 a business district had taken shape with a lumber yard and a cannery said to have been built by Fred Myers in 1907.

At first the irrigation water came from Liberty Lake. About 1920 a large well was put down to supplement the lake supply and was used until 1923 when Greenacres was able to get water from a new South Branch of the Spokane River Canal.

At that time Corbin Addition to Greenacres was platted. It was different from the early settlements in that area: practically none of the acreage was planted to orchards for commercial use. There were family orchards, truck gardens, berry, poultry and dairy farms, and alfalfa fields.

By 1921 Greenacres had a brick school, two churches, electric, domestic water, telephones, a cannery, a commercial club, an amateur athletic club and had voted favorably for a $17,000 gym and auditorium for the school. The residents, however, were still mainly farmers.

The oldest known store in Greenacres was built by Harry Adams in 1903. Later there is record of a general merchandise store owned by George Wheeler and Sons which is said also to have had a service station. Still later the first post office was established on the premises of J.A. Moore who stocked hardware and farm implements, tires and auto accessories. Moore was the postmaster. A few doors down from the post office at this time was a general store and confectionery owned by L.C. Dougherty. Greenacres then was a township with a population of about 2000.

Memories of Greenacres

SARA (SALLY) SAMPSON FOX: My mother and father, Irene and Ewing Sampson, and their four daughters moved to Greenacres in the spring of 1938.

The effects of the Depression were still being felt in Greenacres and it seemed that most of the people, like us, were poor. Mom and Dad rented a 5-acre farm (the Lehman Place) that had many chicken houses and outbuildings including a root cellar for potatoes, apples, root crops and home-canned items. There was also a brooderhouse for baby chicks on the property and an outhouse, our "bathroom."

We had only cold water so Mother kept a large copper boiler of water heating on the back of the wood stove at all times.

The house was located on Beach Street (now Boone) between Flora and Long roads across the road from the electric train tracks. On school days two of my sisters and I walked part of the way to the elementary school at Mission and Barker roads on the tracks. It was fun seeing who could walk the farthest without falling off the rails and putting our ear to the rail to hear the vibrations after a train passed by.

The Greenacres Elementary School was a nice two-story brick building with wide front steps on the outside that went to the second floor. I remember also the balcony that went around the upper level of the gymnasium. From that balcony we could get to an addition that housed the library. The exciting thing about the library was the stack of cards that we "looked at by the hour" through a stereoscope.

My older sister attended Central Valley High School, located where Greenacres Junior High is today.

Times were hard. My father worked on WPA projects and irrigated land east of Greenacres for Jacklin Seed Company, twelve hours a day for $1 a day. He walked the two miles to and from work.

On our five acres we raised vegetables, berries, apples and other fruits. We also raised chickens, had a cow and a work horse.

My sisters and I spent our summer mornings

picking fruits and vegetables for other farmers so we could earn some money. Then we would go home and help harvest our own crops and do our chores. We helped Mother with canning. She always canned 100 quarts of everything on the farm. We helped my father with weeding and irrigating. We all worked very hard.

Although we had little money, our farm always provided us and our frequent company with plenty to eat. Mother was an excellent cook and cooked many big company-type meals.

Because we lived by the railroad tracks, many bums stopped at our place and asked for something to eat. My mother always cooked something for them and let them sit on the back porch to eat. We were not afraid of them.

The old Greenacres shopping center included McDowell's Grocery, the train depot, the community hall, a garage, and the electric building which powered the electric train. Dances, attended by both parents and children, were held regularly in the community hall. Clyde and Slim furnished the music.

At Christmas time we went to the variety store on the Appleway in the newer part of Greenacres called Corbin Place. We children each had 50¢ to spend and with that much money we were able to buy presents for the whole family.

Also on the Appleway was a big cold storage plant that sold crates and boxes for produce. The owners allowed people to take their produce there to sell. To add to our income my mother peddled eggs all around the area. Telephones were scarce. We didn't have one.

BERNICE SMITH: Frank and I and our four children moved to Greenacres September 17, 1937. We purchased five acres and a six-room, three-bedroom home with a bathroom on Mission Road just west of the Greenacres Grade School for $2500. Our payments were $20 a month.

An area from the railroad to Mission from Center Street (now Greenacres Road) to Barker Road was town-like with houses on lots. From the Appleway down Center to Mission, one block east to Barker and north on Barker to Trent was paved. Most of Greenacres was divided into three, five and ten-acre tracts for large farms.

Mr. Anderson was the agent at the railroad depot. I remember the large water tank next to the community hall and the potlucks and local entertainment at the hall. Also a hardware store, an IGA owned by Ed Anderson, a barber shop, a post office, drug store, cleaners, beauty shop and Beck's garage in the Corbin shopping area on the Appleway.

Dr. Epton who had moved from Spokane to Opportunity was the local doctor. He made house calls—$2 for the first visit, $1 after that.

Many pickers were hired by the owners of the raspberry and strawberry fields in Greenacres although my children picked too, early in the morning, to earn extra money. Indians from the Spokane Reservation camped near the big patches and picked in June and July. Wages for pickers were 25¢ for a 24 hallock (pint) crate of strawberries and 35¢ for a 24 hallock crate of raspberries.

The Valley was known for its Hearts of Gold cantaloupes. The warm water in the irrigation ditches and the long warm growing season of those days that warmed the rocks and soil produced melons of unsurpassed quality. A large irrigation canal with a network of tiled side ditches went down Barker Road. A ditch walker turned the water on at each farm at scheduled times.

In the old Greenacres area Olaf Nilson owned an 80-foot deep well that served domestic water to homes and the school and Methodist Church from 1918.

The Appleway Bank in the Corbin Shopping Center failed in the '30s, adding to the poverty of the community.

The auto interurban bus service to Greenacres was very important. All the furniture and clothing stores were in Spokane and few people could afford to buy a car. The buses came every twenty minutes during the early morning and evening hours and every hour the rest of the day. A ride into town cost 20¢.

THE GREENACRES DEPOT, C. 1930
The powerplant is to the left of the station.
Courtesy, Ted Holloway

Millwood,
The Valley's Only Incorporated Town

[For the early history of Millwood and the Paper Mill, see "The Town of Millwood" and "Inland Empire Paper Mill," Volume I.]

In the 1980s, a group of old-timers met and to the best of their memory, made the following map of Millwood as they remembered it in the 1920s. Those who contributed are H.G. Peterson, George Leitner, Adolph Larson, W.T. Schnell, Clinton Lavender, Dean Banta, Charles Siegenthaler, Mae Siegenthaler, Otto Ramelo, Paul Stafford, and Morris Heitstuman. The group contacted all the local newspapers and the museum in search of a picture, but none could be found.

The businesses listed below can be identified on the map (following page) by the number that appears before their names on the following list :
1. Inland Empire Paper Mill
2. Butler's Garage
3. Brown Block: Tiffin's Drug-Pharmacy, Medical Offices (Tiffins lived upstairs.)
4. Millwood Hotel
5. Masonic Temple: Spokane Valley State Bank, Millwood Mercantile, Lodge and Community Area (2nd floor)
6. Hardware Store
7. H.G. (Pete) and Freda Peterson's (Millwood)

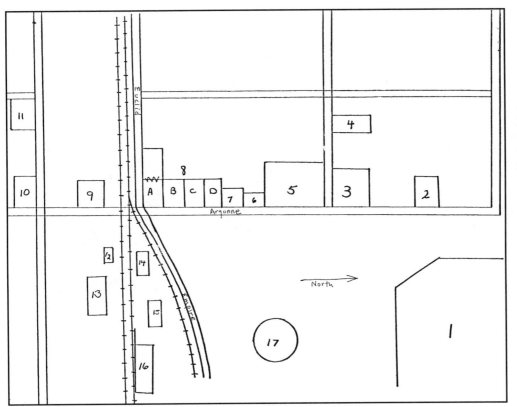

MILLWOOD IN THE '20s
Please see previous page
and below for number
identification.

Meat Market. Sawdust on the floor, a cat to catch the mice, meat smoker part of the building in the basement and still there at N. 3213 Argonne.

8. Byram Block:
      A. Post Office, Confectionary, Gas and Oil
          General Merchandise
      B. M&L Dry Goods   Electric Store
      C. Barber Shop   Grocery
      D. Jewelry Shop   Lunch Counter
9. Restaurant, then Hinkley's Grocery Store
10. Murphy's Boarding House
11. Grocery, Sampson's then Stough's
12. Depot-Electric and GN Freight
13. Lumber Yard (Kroetch)
14. SI RR Depot
15. SI Section House
16. Spokane Valley Growers Union Packing Plant
17. Bandstand

The group gave the following interesting details about the Byram Block in the '20s as they remembered it:

A.H. Byram and his wife, Myra, operated the post office, confectionary, and gas and oil on the south end of the Byram Block. They had two sons, Arnold L. who was born in the building and Andrew.

The Spokane Valley State Bank was established in 1920. The first location was in back of the post office section of the Byram Building until January 5, 1922, when it moved into the north end of the Masonic Temple on Argonne, just north of Trent Road. R.K. Wheeler was the bank manager and Elsie Carstens was teller. One window of the post office had a gold leaf sign, Spokane Valley State Bank.

The Meat Market was operated by Hallet and Younce until 1925, when H.G. Peterson took over. When the old building was torn down and a new one built, Peterson built his own building just north of the Byram Building.

The grocery store was run by Dude Sampson. After the mercantile moved into the Masonic Temple Building, Henry Schreader moved into and lived in the old store part for a short time.

The barber shop on the north end of the Byram Building was operated by Jim Jummer and later by

Mohr. Dude Sampson did some barbering at one time.

On the far right was the old foundation of Wiley's Hotel burned out September 25, 1912. The Masonic Temple was built on that property.

The town bum was an old Airdale dog that belonged to the Lyonaises, who ran the old White Hotel, later the site of the drug store.

Henry Peacock, who started losing his eyesight early, was often seen reading the town bulletin board on a power pole in front of the Byram Building.

An almost daily scene was someone leading a cow to or from the Carstens Dairy. Hans Carstens had one of the few bulls around and owned much property where Argonne Village is today.

In back of the Byram Building was an old apple orchard, later the site of the post office building built by Clarence Harsch, the Presbyterian Church, and homes.

The shoe repair shop was first operated by a family who were Seventh Day Adventists (name unknown). Later Peter Van Steenbergen operated it until the building was torn down. Then he built a brick building.

Walt Le Fevre lived in a basement apartment in the building when he was first married. Jack Sinclair and his son Virgil also lived there for a short time.

AUTHOR UNKNOWN (from the Millwood Archives): The Industrial Development Company, subsidiary land holding company of the Paper Mill, was concerned with the selling of tracts and lots from the Trent Bridge to Orchard Avenue. Neely and Young became selling agents for part of this land (eastern part of Millwood) after becoming associated with the company. Spokane Valley Irrigation District #10 were successors to the Industrial Development Company. Irrigation and power were provided as attractions for the potential settlers, and with the division into tracts and lots, population began to increase.

In 1921 a Masonic Temple was built on the Wiley Hotel site. It was a two-story brick and concrete structure built by Myers and Telander. In 1925 the brick and tile Brown building was completed on the site of the Millwood Hotel, which was moved just west of the new building. The first Byram building was erected on the corner of Euclid and Argonne in 1912 and later replaced by the Byram Block about 1926.

In the span of years, 1911-1925, other businesses were built and this commercial district became typical of the period.

JEANNE BANTA BATSON (mayor of Millwood, elected 1989): I was born in 1922 in a four-bedroom brick house on Dale Road in Millwood. I was the youngest of four children, all of whom went to West Valley High School. 1995-96 will be the first year that there has not been a Banta or Batson at West Valley High School.

All of my memories of growing up in Millwood are happy ones. We all knew each other and never worried about locking our doors. My dad, Horace Banta, was manager of the Sulphite Department of the Paper Mill so he always had a job, even during the Depression. My mother, Mary, made all our clothes so we were always well dressed. I only went to three schools in my whole life: Millwood Grade School, Dishman Grade School (in the fifth grade when Millwood had no fifth grade for one year) and West Valley High school. I never went to college and here I am, the mayor!

I started West Valley in 1935 and graduated in 1939. I remember the roller skating parties especially. After school a bus would take us to Patterson's Roller Rink north of town between Hawthorne and Hastings roads on Division. It was at a roller skating party that I had my first date with my future husband, Harry Batson (who was a Millwood councilman for twenty years.)

We roller skated on the side walks too, and ice skated between Donkey Island and the shore of the Spokane River. There was a classmate who also skated there. We called him "Pickle" because his parents owned a cucumber field in Pasadena. Pickle built a stove on the island and fired it up whenever we needed to warm our feet or hands.

One of my roller skating companions and best friends was Jean Buckland Green. Her father was Chester Buckland, manager of the Paper Mill and an early mayor.

We were really proud of our high school. Every spring we had clean-up day. All the kids went outside, raked the lawn and picked up paper and trash. There was no problem with discipline. Oh, the boys used to get a whack with the paddle, but no hard feelings. We respected the teachers' decisions and did as we were told. No back talk.

During lunch hour we danced in the gym. We had no juke box so sometimes kids who could play the piano were called upon to play. I was one of those.

Very few kids had cars. I walked to school no matter what the weather except once in a while when Dad let me take his great big old Buick to school.

The Paper Mill had two departments: the sulphite plant (where my dad was superintendent) and the paper mill. The paper mill rolled the paper. The sulphite plant included the log pond and the smelly wood chip cooking operation. My dad noticed that whenever a team and wagon from the Sulphite Mill leaked sulphite on the ground, the ground got hard. Sulphite was then used in the Valley to "hard top" the roads. I loved horses and would jump on the sulphite wagon and ride around with the employee spreading the smelly stuff.

Where our town park is now was then the town dump. A band played in the park each Sunday and there was a pool and fountain there. (See Volume I for photo of the Paper Mill Park.)

Historic Buildings

[Courtesy of Jeanne Batson]

During the '20s and '30s several homes and buildings were built in Millwood that later were included in the block named to the Register of Historic Places. Addresses and first known owners are listed below:

ADDRESS	EARLY OWNER, DATE BUILT
E. 9016 Frederick	Hans Carstens, dairyman (rented it out)1936
E. 9002 Frederick	William J. Moore 1938
E. 8944 Frederick	Charles Herrman 1928
E. 8936 Frederick	Frank Coleman 1922.
E. 8704 Dalton	W. H. Schleef 1938 (3rd mayor of Millwood)
N. 3320 Argonne	Inland Paper Company Building 1911
E. 8703 Frederick	(No record) 1938
E. 8710 Liberty	Joe Wyerski 1927
E. 8703 Liberty	Victor Maurer 1938
E. 8717 Liberty	Dr. Lyle Bailey. Built for him by masons and stone cutters who had bills with him 1935.
N. 3315 Dale	William Brazeau (first mayor) 1925
S. 3318 Dale	Horace Banta (Superintendent Sulphite Mill) 1921
N. 3312 Dale	Luther Williams (Pastor, Millwood Presbyterian Church) 1921.
N. 3306 Dale	Francis Stevens 1926
N. 3330 Argonne	George Brown, Hobart Brown, pharmacist Millwood Drug Store 1929
E. 8804 Dalton	W. C. Farnsworth 1936
N. 3221 Dale	Maude Posey 1918
N. 3203 Dale	Henry Martin 1936
E. 8902 Dalton	Millwood Community Presbyterian Church 1923
E. 8903 Dalton	J. H. Butler 1923
N. 3318 Marguerite	Waldo Rosebush (Superintendent Paper Mill) 1921
E. 8820 Liberty	Chester Buckland (2nd mayor of Millwood) 1924
E. 3302 Marguerite	Harry Salmons (date unknown)
E. 8903 Liberty	Harry Salmons (probably oldest house in Millwood). Salmons homesteaded the property from Argonne to Vista and Liberty to the river.
N. 3315 Hutchinson	Clarence Borden 1928
N. 3307 Hutchinson	Clarence Borden 1929
N. 3223 Argonne	Millwood Building Company (leased the building) 1924
N. 3205, 09, 11 Argonne	Byram Building 1929

Otis Orchards, Mica

HAROLD RINEAR (born in 1901) April, 1988: I am writing about the Otis Orchards Clubhouse and also the school that was nearby. I graduated from that school in 1923 with Ed Karrer, the man who has the Ed Karrer Gunnery near Millwood today. A graduating class of two.

There were many events held at the Clubhouse in the '20s and '30s. The commercial club met there and the Apple Harvest Festival was held there. Big dinners were held there with as many as 300 attending. My wife, Ethel McLachlan, Jane Clift, Mrs. Terry Grant, and Georgia Pringle were the principle cooks for those occasions. My wife and Jane Clift are the only survivors of the group.

Chamber of Commerce dinners were also held there and they also attracted huge crowds.

Ethel McLachlan and I were married November 16, 1925. Her folks lived on Corrigan Road at the time and we settled on the north adjoining place and are still there.

My Grandpa Rinear homesteaded the present townsite of Mica about 1880 and sold it about 1902. He started the store and post office there. The original building is still there although it has been added on to. My uncle Ezra Rinear homesteaded and started the California Ranch, but did not live there many years. As of June 1987 the original buildings were still there. The Carter place on Idaho Road belonged to a cousin of Abraham Lincoln who told my father that he and Lincoln played soldier many times using corn stalk guns. He got too old to farm his homestead and sold my father 80 acres. We kept it about 15 years and then sold it to A. A. Emerson who put the first buildings on the place. There is no trace of them now.

Mica, Harrington Addition, Trent School

CARLTON GOUDGE (Redwood City, California, 1988): In 1936 following my June graduation from West Valley High School, I was hired as office assistant (40 cents an hour) at the Mica Brickworks. Mother Nature certainly endowed the Mica-Clayton-Vera-Troy (Idaho) areas with fine clays—each distinctive mineral makeups. Gladding McBean & Co. and Washington Brick and Lime Co. depended upon these Washington resources and the nearby Idaho deposit of Troy Fire Brick Co.

FDR's WPA Program in the Depression generated numerous sewer projects in the Pacific Northwest that resulted in a rapidly burgeoning market for vitrified clay sewer pipe. The old Mica sewer pipe plant (adjacent to the old brick plant) found itself deluged with orders. At the same time, the brick side enjoyed increased business, particularly in 1936. These two factors generated the need for a No. 2 office man—the job that started me on my career with Gladding McBean and then later merged Interface.

I continued on with them for 45 years less the four years, '38-'42, at the U of Washington (Ceramic Engineering) when I was a part-time employee, and 3½ years in the Navy, '42-'46.

One of the highlights of my career was the construction of the new (current) brick plant at Mica in 1957. This occurred within my administration as V.P.-Gen. Mgr., Pacific Mica Brick Northwest Division, 1956-1967.

In 1959 we acquired the assets of Washington Brick and Lime Co., including plants at Dishman and Clayton. Due to high production costs and the rapidly shrinking clay pipe market, these plants were later razed. This left the Mica Plant alone in the Eastern Washington area.

Many Freeman people worked at the Mica Brick Works during my time there. I vividly recall several days when the Chicago Milwaukee "crack" passenger train got stuck in a Freeman snowdrift. Freeman households took in the passengers. Somehow during that snow the Dishman-Mica Road was kept open allowing us to get to work.

A few notes from other Valley pages of history—

Claire, my wife, who worked at the Naval Supply Depot during WWII is of the pioneer Harrington family. She was born and raised on land in Dishman labeled by County records as Harrington Addition. Her father deeded part of his land to Washington Brick and Lime in return for stock. The Dishman sewer pipe and brick plant was constructed upon that land.

I was raised in what was the first Trent School. My father purchased it in the twenties for $150 and had Beardmore Transfer (for another $150) move it a mile on Trent Highway to his 10 acre plot on University Road. He traded three acres to an unemployed, depression-hit carpenter who converted the school into a home. And now look at Trent No. 3!

Organizations Galore

Just as the irrigation districts of the Valley found that it was to their best interests to work as a unit called the Chamber of Commerce, so also did residents with similar interests or beliefs or purposes find it expedient and pleasant to associate in groups that became organizations. Probably churches and schools are the best known examples of such early organizing.

There were many others.

Early in Valley history, men formed lodges and fraternal groups. At Opportunity in 1910, Wilford Chapter of the Independent Order of Odd Fellows met for the single purpose of lending a helping hand to those residents in need. (See article, "A Place Called Opportunity," Vol. 1.) That group was so prestigious that it built its own hall in the Opportunity block. The Odd Fellows Hall became a gathering place for other groups in search of a meeting place.

Some pioneer men found the tenets of the Masons more to their liking and joined Orchard Lodge No. 200 F.A. & M. Beginning in 1910 with only 13 members from Dishman and Greenacres, by 1945, Orchard Lodge numbered 120 members.

Woman's Club

The lodges were strictly men's turf.

In December 1920, a group of women, feeling the need for social contact, organized the Spokane Valley Woman's Club. For women only, it became affiliated with the State Federation of Woman's Clubs with 58 charter members from the ten communities.

Founders were Mrs. Channon Price, Mrs. Flo Tobert Zuilke, Mrs. Rudy (Emma) Safranek, Mrs. Sam (Adeline) Pengelly and Mrs. Milton (Achsah) Rawlings, Sr.

Members were proud of the fact that at no time was their group exclusive or invitational. They kept its membership open to any woman who was a resident of the Valley. By offering a variety of selected programs that carried beyond local affairs into a wide range of thought and action, the women made friendships beyond the boundaries of their routine day-to-day experiences—so valuable during the sometimes lonely pioneer days. Sections of the club were the Garden Club, the Literary Group, and the Home Arts Department.

Kiwanis

Following the stock market crash of '29, the gloom of the Depression was widespread. Many residents were in financial need. The leaders of the Valley saw organization into a strictly-for-service group as a possible means of lending a helping hand. Aware of a group in Spokane called Kiwanis that seemed to have a similar purpose, on April 19, 1930, Valley leaders met with the Spokane Chapter at the Magnet Lunch in Opportunity (run by Tom Reedy) to organize a Valley chapter. John Booth, superintendent of Valley schools and principal of Central Valley High School, was chosen first president. All members agreed there was much to be done, but the club, like those it hoped to help, found the early thirties difficult.

Many of the members could not afford to devote the needed time nor funds to the club. A few of the more affluent members, namely Chan Price, Neil Baynes, Edgar Waybright, Bill Williams and probably a few others, paid dues in advance. This act

more than any other probably was responsible for holding the club together.

However, Kiwanis, in spite of its slow start, grew steadily and was able to accomplish many tasks that benefited the Valley. During the Depression years it sponsored an annual Christmas tree for underprivileged children. Its annual Growers' dinner was acclaimed as one of the cementing influences in farmer-urban relationships. Through the years rest rooms at Balfour and Vista Parks were built, homes for needy families were remodeled, and many improvements were made to Camp Easter Seal on Coeur d'Alene Lake. Through a scholarship program, the group has helped many young people complete their education.

Ladies Aid meeting at the Harry Nelson home on the Appleway, 1917,
where Makena's Restaurant is today.
Courtesy, Robert Nelson

Townsend Clubs

Also to combat the adverse conditions of the '30s, Townsend Club No. 1 was organized in the C.D. Holmes residence in Opportunity, January 1934, with a membership of approximately 50. Through years of many disappointments and changes, the group held steadfastly to the basic idea of "pensions and security for senior citizens" and felt that it was largely responsible for the abolition of the county poor farm and for the enactment of more decent state pension laws. It met in the Opportunity Town Hall.

Organizations Galore

Whatever a Valley resident's interest might be, in the '20s and '30s, there were always others who were willing to team up with him/her and organize a group or club. It was in this period that even Ku Klux Klan activities were documented. According to the *Valley Herald*, in 1924 that group held Valley initiations with fiery crosses.

Athletic Clubs were organized at Dishman (1920), Opportunity (1926), and Orchard Park (1927). In 1922 the Magnolia Chapter, Order of Eastern Star, was organized at Millwood. Commercial Clubs, with their own clubhouses, had large memberships at Dishman (1925) and Greenacres (1921). In 1935 the Dishman group bought the Mandalay Restaurant for its clubhouse and in 1933 the Greenacres group remodeled the old Growers' Hall for their meeting place.

Scouts and Granges

Children and young people were not to be left out. Both Boy Scouts and Girls Scouts had active troops. In 1918 the Rev. Paul E. Ratsch organized a Boy Scout Troop at Millwood. By 1945 more than 250 Boy Scouts over 12 years of age and 100 Cub Scouts, 9 to 13, met in various troops at Orchard Avenue, Otis Orchards, Foothills, Trentwood, Alcoa, Dishman, Opportunity, and Veradale. In 1927 the Spokane Valley Scout council was formed with A.B. Ford as leader.

The earliest records of Girl Scout meetings in the Valley are from a group that met in the Millwood School in 1935. There is also documentation in 1936 that Mrs. L.E. Paullin, Mrs. Frances Taylor and Mrs. Ruby Williams started Girl Scout Troop 13 that year at Orchard Avenue. By 1945 in Spokane and the Valley combined there were over 2000 girls and leaders enrolled with Valley communities accounting for about 350 of that number. The first Brownie Troop, Troop 33, was started in 1936, also by Mrs. Paullin.

Both Boy Scouts and Girls Scouts, especially in the early years, attributed much of their success to their affiliated mothers' organizations that stimulated interest and were a potent influence in providing leadership. Gunnar Berg, associated with the Rev. Ratsch in the Valley Boy Scout movement, was elected to serve on the national staff of the Boy Scouts' Headquarters in New York City.

High school girls who had grown up in the program organized themselves at West Valley High School into Senior Service Scouts and regularly gave time as hospital and occupational therapy aids at Sacred Heart Hospital and St. Luke's.

The annual fair at the Valley Fairgrounds gave young people (adults too) an opportunity to display animals they raised, food they prepared, handwork, and hobbies. Centering on these activities, Campfire groups, Granges and 4-H Clubs became popular. In 1927 there were 21 4-H Clubs in the Valley with 350 members and 14 Campfire groups with 200 members. In 1935 the Tri-community Grange was organized at Newman Lake with George H. Wendler, master; and in 1935, a new Grange Hall was built at Mica.

There were other organizations too, but all of these came into being before 1945, added much to community life, and survived for many years. Many still exist in 1994.

Valley Predecessor to Scouting

[From "Knighthood in Pioneer Days" by J. Howard Stegner, *Spokane Valley Herald*, December 16, 1954.]

Around the year 1900, about nine or ten years before the Boy Scout movement began, there was a national organization known as the Order of the American Boy. This was a sort of forerunner of scouting and also a character building organization.

I still have my button with the four M's on it. These stood for Muscle, Mind, Men of Morals. So you see, the objectives were about the same as in scouting. My brother Conrad organized several of these orders or companies. He organized the first one at Trent (now Irvin), the second one at the Foothills, the third one at Carnhope near the city limits, and the fourth one of Houston School students in Spokane.

Conrad was a natural leader of boys and soon became state commander of the American Boy movement. He was also captain of the order at Trent. This group was called the Ensign Monahan Company, honoring young Ensign Monahan who gave his life rather than leave a wounded comrade, Lieutenant Lansdale, in Samos. The monument at Monroe and Riverside is erected in his honor.

Our meetings were opened with the flag salute and conducted in much the same way a scout troop program is conducted. I believe we met about every two weeks in our old store building west of Trent School. (See Volume I, "The J.A. Stegner Store.") We had athletic contests; in the winter programs, debates with other orders or companies, boxing matches and something to eat, of course.

These companies of the American Boy did pretty well for a couple of years and finally died out.

About 1903 a lot of us boys would get together on a Saturday night and have a big feed. This went on for a while when Conrad got the idea of getting up something original in the way of a young men's organization. This was called the KCG, the meaning of which we kept secret.

Many of the young ladies of the Valley were burning up with curiosity as to what KCG stood for. I am sitting here debating whether it's a good idea to let the cat out of the bag after more than 50 years. I may get demoted, but here goes. Probably very few knew I was "knighted" anyway.

The name of our organization was The Knights of the Crimson Garter. In spite of the fact that we wore a crimson garter on one arm, no one seemed to catch on. I do not remember the names of all the boys that belonged to this group, but there were three Stitzs, two Stegners, Ira Hunt, Bill Hoffman, and others.

We had quite an initiation as well as a ritual ending with the knighting ceremony. Each member was equipped with a wooden shield about 30 inches high and 29 inches wide. This had a K at the top and the CG in a horizontal line further down, all in large letters. The candidate chose a name that he wanted to be knighted under, and after he knelt, each member would lay his lance on the candidate's shoulder. The leader would say, "I dub thee knight, arise, Sir So and So."

In good weather, we had a place where we met in the Pinecroft rock, down near the old Mahoney Place. A couple of times we met on an island in the middle of the Spokane River, about 100 yards down stream from where Riblets tram cable now crosses.

JUNIOR BOY SCOUT FAIR, MILLWOOD, SEPTEMBER 15, 1927.
Blazing Arrow Patrol from Opportunity pioneering lean-tos. Left to right: Herbert Aller, Jack Finch,
Howard Harris, (unknown), Fred Coddington, Allan Houk, Bob Goodrich, Bryan Callicoat,
Bob Nelson, Bob Coddington.
Courtesy of Herbert Aller.

(See Eagle's Nest.) This was a large island in those days with a very large pine tree on it. We would ferry over there in our row boat, cook up a big meal and end up with a big campfire made of driftwood.

On May 29, 1903, the KCG established a camp on the flat where the paper mill has its logs piled now. On the extreme east end of this flat was a fine grove of pine trees. This time we stayed overnight and all day Decoration Day.

The boys had fiddles and a mandolin and we sure had a fine time. The instruments gathered enough dampness during the night that first one and then another would snap a string before we got next to what was doing it.

Now after telling this story, maybe some of you people will know who to say "Sir" to.

VALLEY HERALD, MARCH 12, 1902

J. Conrad Stegner, captain of the Ensign John R. Monahan Company, No. 2, division of Washington, Order of the American Boy, has received notice of his promotion to lieutenant colonel and is placed in command of all the companies of this organization in the state. The Order of the American Boy has several companies in this state, although this organization is better known in the eastern states.

Stegner is considered young to have such honors, being only 19 years of age.

National Guard In the '30s

In the '30s when money was scarce, many Valley high school boys joined the National Guard. Carleton Goudge, who grew up at Trent and played football for West Valley was a member. He recently told me this story about his experience in the Guard:

The boys had two reasons for joining the Guard. One was the 90¢ per drill night that they were paid for drilling once a week. The second was the excitement of sleeping in a Pullman berth once a year when they were transported to and from Fort Murray (Fort Lewis) for a two-week encampment. Not many of the boys could have hoped for such a treat otherwise.

I decided to join Company A, 161st Infantry in June 1934, the night of the embarkation. I was hustled into an army uniform with a hastily put together back pack on my back, handed a Springfield .06 rifle and joined the rear rank of the first squad of the first platoon. As usual, the boys off to camp were given a royal send-off, marching behind the town band playing "We Are the Sons of the Highway"—the march the band always played in parades on special occasions such as this and on Armistice Day and Memorial Day.

I could not keep step and fumbled with my Springfield .06 while the other boys smartly changed rifles from left to right shoulders and right to left shoulders as our platoon marched down Division, along First, back on Riverside, then Main and finally to Trent and the all-Pullman train at the Great Northern Station that took us for our exciting sleepover.

Two weeks later, after the encampment, I marched the same route to the Spokane Armory perfectly in step and tossing my rifle at exactly the right moments again to the strains of "We Are the Sons..."

In 1935 the pay went up to $1.00 for privates, $1.40 for corporals, and $1.80 for sergeants.

That year the Pacific Coast Longshoremen (with Harry Bridges in charge) went on strike just when the 161st Infantry was at the annual encampment. (Many of our boys from the Valley were in this group.)

Something happened we never dreamed of. Governor C.D. Martin called up the Guard to help control the strikers. For six weeks the Infantry slept, part of the time, in the horse barn section of the Tacoma National Guard Armory and the balance of the time in tents at Camp Murray commuting to Tacoma in Army trucks.

A confrontation with rock and vegetable throwing strikers took place above the Eleventh Street bridge in Tacoma. Bayonets were fixed, and Springfield .06s were cocked to shoot above the head. That ended the strike and ended an experience that the Valley boys never forgot. It was a rude awakening to be involved in a serious strike. They learned the hard way that the National Guard had a real mission.

Those from West Valley that I remember who were in Company A when I was were Gene Carstens of Carstens Dairy in Millwood, Malcolm Sykes, Harold Peebles, Walt Knowles, Bud Messenger, Bob Philley, Bill Aris, Charles Bailey, and Dick Peebles.

I stayed in the Guard until 1939. Company A was called out again about a year or more before Pearl Harbor. A close buddy, Babe Schille, whom I had enlisted in the guard was involved in that. He was a star in all sports at West Valley, a leader. Later he was commissioned in the field in New Guinea and married an Army nurse there. In January 1942, I joined the Navy.

Clubs and Lodges

Community clubs were the hubs of community social and political life in the period from 1921-1945. According to a Spokane Valley Directory for 1941-1942 loaned to me by Stanley and Bernice Fahlgren, these clubs and their officers were active during that year:

COMMUNITY CLUBS	PRESIDENT
Dishman Commercial and Community Club	George Pierce Norman Tat, secy
University Place Community Club	W. W Tracy Mrs. R. Thompson, secy
Opportunity Community Club	Vincent Moore Mrs. E. Foedish, secy
Vera Community Club	Thomas Giboney T. C. Brenchley, secy
Greenacres Community Club	Sig Hansen Mrs. Lulu Ball, secy
Millwood Commercial Club	W. L. Clearwaters Ned Finch, secy
Orchard Avenue Community Club	R. L. Meader Mrs. L.C. Reeves, secy
Otis Orchards Community Club	Bill Coon Frank Shinn, secy

According to the 1941-1942 Spokane Valley Directory loaned by Bernice and Stan Fahlgren, these were the active men's and women's groups at that time.

LODGES	LEADER
Independent Order of Odd Fellows	Tom Smith, noble grand
Ramona Rebekah	E. Cundill, noble grand
Orchard Lodge No. 200 Masons	A. Black, worshipful master
Victory Chapter, Order Eastern Star	Inez Bailey, worthy matron
Concordia Lodge No.249 Masons	A. C. Collin, worshipful master
Magnolia Chapter Order Eastern Star	Pearl Tirk, worshipful master
Order of Amaranth	Alma Ness, royal matron
Royal Neighbors	Lillie Deal, oracle
Daughters of America	Helen Mahan, councilor
Veterans of Foreign Wars Post No. 7435	J.L. Barnes, commander
Ladies Auxiliary to V. F. W. Post 1435	Beatrice Payne, president
Valley Assembly Rainbow Girls	Rita Squire, worthy advisor

WOMEN'S CLUBS	PRESIDENT
Spokane Valley Woman's Club	Mrs. Neil Stewart
Greenacres Woman's Club	Mrs. C.T. Hobart
Otis Orchards Ladies Club	Mrs. Ethel Rinear
La Gaiete Club	Mrs. Wm. Green
Ladies of Kiwanis	Mrs. Harry Kelly
Dishman Ladies' Auxiliary	Mrs. Gerry Johnson
Orchard Avenue Woman's Club	Mrs. Dorothea Collier

GRANGES	
Valley View Grange	L.A. Pringle, master
Greenacres Grange	J. MacDonald, master
Trentwood Grange	Don Krueger, master
Tri-comunity Grange	G. Morrison, master
East Spokane Grange	Harvey Cobban, master
Opportunity Grange	Bert Porter, master

Eagle's Nest

Looking north between Pines and Argonne, you can't miss the imposing home perched high on a bluff overlooking the Spokane River. Three stories, with stucco exterior and a red-tiled gable roof, it has no parallel in the Valley.

Most Valley homes of historic interest are remembered because of their pioneer structure and birth, or because they were constructed by hand of native Valley stone. "Eagle's Nest on Tramway Hill," Fruit Hill Road, is one of a kind.

It was built in 1925 by Royal C. Riblet, holder of some 30 patents that never sparked much interest and an inventor of such curiosities as the square-wheeled tractor for use on Washington hills and an automobile turn indicator using a metaphor-like signal.

Today the property is owned by David and Harold Mielke, owners of Arbor Crest Winery, and maintained by them as a showplace for the Arbor Crest product. (1994)

The Mielkes attempt to maintain the 83-acre estate much as it was when Riblet constructed it. Now and then it is open to public tours.

The home, 24' by 58', is not of mansion proportions, but its three stories and its setting on the brow of a sheer cliff give that effect. Riblet took great pride in the home, but he said in an early interview that he did not set out to design anything spectacular. It was his object that the house be unusual only in the sense that it would contain the latest available in inventiveness. "A common sense home," is how he is said to have described Eagle's Nest.

Riblet's pride in the house was ever evident. He claimed to have opened the grounds to around ten thousand visitors in 1926 and averaged seven thousand visitors during the next eight years. Royal and his seventh wife Mildred were eventually forced to erect a sign reading, "Friends Welcome Anytime, Others Welcome by Appointment."

Because the house is constructed on solid rock and the lower floor is an above-ground basement, the home is considered to be the first daylight basement structure built in the Valley.

An oak stairway leads from the lower level to the main floor living-room, the largest room in the house. Magnesite was liberally used in the kitchen to line the built-in cabinets and for the floor. Riblet himself designed the china cupboard built into the dining-room wall with its frameless stained glass doors on rollers, an unheard of luxury in the Valley in the '20s.

From the many windows and generous porches on the estate, visitors can enjoy a variety of scenic views—mountains in all directions, the Spokane River curling below and a panoramic view of Valley and city and the fields of Idaho.

On the grounds are interesting buildings of native basalt (lava rock): a three-room gatehouse, a workshop containing drawings and models of Riblet's inventions, and a round gazebo with a brass roof.

The lily pond and swimming pool are surrounded by native stonewalls that also separate gardens and line walkways.

From the front porch, the visitor can follow in imagination the descent through rock crevasses over the Spokane River below of the once famous 1600-foot cable that allowed access to the estate by tramway at the rate of 800 feet per minute.

Valley folk are inclined to say that Royal Riblet invented the cable tramway. It was actually his brother Byron who put together the famous Riblet

Tramway Company; and it was also Byron who improved the tramway. Neither Riblet invented it. It was also Byron who drew Royal to the Pacific Northwest.

According to Riblet historian William Barr, writing in the *Pacific Northwesterner*, Vol. 31, No. 4, 1987, Byron made his way west working for the Northern Pacific Railway Company as a surveyor. He found his way to Spokane and "became Chief Engineer for the young Washington Water Power Company, supervising the layout of electrical railways and equipment and constructing a dam, pumping station and distribution system in the city. He constructed his first tramway in 1897 while employed by the Noble Five Mining Company near Sandon, British Columbia.

"Other mining companies in British Columbia were soon asking Riblet to build tramways for them, so he opened a factory in Nelson, B.C., with the help of his brothers. Walter was installed as office manager and salesman and Royal was put to work in the blacksmith shop that fabricated tramway parts."

A falling out occurred between the brothers and Royal attempted a competing company, Airline Tramway Co. Due largely to the Depression, it failed.

Riblet's life at Eagle's Nest was not all idyllic. He failed to take into consideration possible pollution from a nearby cement plant. The International Portland Cement Company, Ltd., had constructed a plant at Irvin across the Spokane River south of Plante's Ferry Park, close to the intersection of Trent and Pines, in 1910. At that time there were few homes in the area and when production began in 1913, the output was small. Riblet underestimated it at about 200 barrels while the true output at the time is estimated to have been from 589 to 811 barrels. Production gradually increased to 215,000 barrels in 1931. The Riblet property began to experience a covering of a fine white dust.

In 1939 the Riblets complained by letter to the cement company that the situation was "unbearable" but no satisfaction was received except the installation at the plant of what the Riblets considered inadequate dust control equipment.

In the forties, the response was that cement was necessary to the war effort and a law suit would be unpatriotic.

By 1951 when Riblet began his series of lawsuits, production had increased to 666,110 barrels. Riblet claimed the cement plant was a polluter and filed his first lawsuit May 1950. The disposition of Riblet's fifth lawsuit was still pending when he died May 11, 1960. He received from the litigation only small cash settlements through the years. The house high on the bluff is now listed on the National Register of Historic Places. Too late for the Riblets to enjoy, the air cleared and pollution ceased in the early 1970s when the cement plant ceased operation. It was subsequently used only as a storage warehouse.

Government and State/National Events that Helped Shape the Valley

"It is almost a truism in the field of political science that the individuals chosen by the free people of a democracy to govern them are a near-perfect reflection of the citizens who exercise their right of the ballot in making that choice. Indifference on the part of the voters almost invariably results in the election of poorly qualified officials—often actually dishonest ones—and professional competence in political office-holders is never the result of accident. A voting public which demands good government has always been able ultimately to get it, so long as it voiced its demands in terms of carefully marked ballots.

"It is equally true (though less often pointed out) that the statutes such a free people enact to govern themselves at any particular stage of their political history are also an accurate reflection, both of the problems of the times and of the political philosophy and experience brought to bear on their solution."

[From *The Book of the Counties*, p.3, 1953, A Publication of the Washington State Associations of County Commissioners and County Engineers in Cooperation with the State College of Washington.]

HARVESTING ON THE ARTHUR D. JONES RANCH
The work on farms such as this was eased when the REA brought electricity to rural areas.
Photo by Leo

Government and State/National Events that Helped Shape the Valley

CHRONOLOGICAL HISTORY

1921
The **Valley Chamber Of Commerce** was organized with **Terry Grant**, first president.

There was agitation in the legislatures of **Idaho** and **Washington** for the creation of a new state to be called **Lincoln.** It was to include **Eastern Washington** and **Northern Idaho**.

1922
Charles H. Leavy of **Vera** was elected prosecuting attorney of **Spokane County**.

1924
The **Ku Klux Klan** held an initiation with fiery crosses.

Native North Americans were granted **U.S.** citizenship.

1926
J.B. Felts of Opportunity was elected county commissioner.

A Community Chest was organized to finance Valley activities. Residents were agitating for zoning ordinances.

1927
To build community spirit, **Ray P. Kelley,** president of the **Chamber of Commerce**, offered a cup to the community with the most worthwhile achievements.

October 15: Citizens of **Millwood** voted to incorporate. (See "The Town of Millwood," Volume I.)

1928
W.A. Brazeau was elected first mayor of **Millwood.**

Valley citizens were to serve as auxiliary police answerable to the sheriff's office. They were named Minute Men by **Deputy James Cannon.**

1929
October 24-29: The stock market crashed and the Valley found itself in a deep Depression.

1930
The **Chamber** appointed a committee to work on the naming and numbering of Valley streets. **Opportunity Township** began putting up signs on street corners.

1931

The **Chamber** sponsored a **Homes Beautiful Contest** under the auspices of **A.C. Rickel.**

1932

Land tax assessments were reduced 15% to help the Valley economy. Schools had financial problems because of decreased tax revenue.

Ed Peirce of **Opportunity** was elected to the State Senate.

The Valley reluctantly followed Spokane in adopting Daylight Saving Time.

1933

Roosevelt was inaugurated the 32nd president of the United States. It was said that more legislation was passed (mostly to combat the Depression) in 99 days than had been passed in that length of time by any previous Congress. The beginning of the "New Deal."

A State Emergency Relief Act was passed to help combat the effects of the Great Depression.

March 6: President Franklin D. Roosevelt authorized a nationwide bank moratorium. All Valley banks were closed.

The state legislature permitted betting on horses.

County Commissioner J.B. Felts of **Opportunity** was appointed a member of a new Legislative Matters Commission to study the budget and prepare proposals for **Governor Martin.**

December 5: The Twenty-first Amendment to the Constitution was passed. It repealed the Eighteenth Amendment (Prohibition) that had been passed January 22, 1919. However **Spokane County** remained dry by action of city and county authorities pending action of the state legislature.

December 25: The **Spokane River** reached a 40-year high.

1934

August 12 (*Spokane Valley Herald*): When Mrs. Franklin D. Roosevelt left Spokane last Saturday night, she took with her a basket of gladioli with the greetings of the **Spokane Valley Woman's Club. Mrs A.C. Rickel, Mrs. A.E. Holt** and **Mrs. Harry Nelson** presented the flowers which were grown in the gardens of **Mr. Nelson** and **John Wilkins** of **Otis Orchard.**

1935

August 14: President Roosevelt signed the Social Security Act into law. It was amended numerous times thereafter.

Sales tax became effective all over the state. Stores sold tokens worth $1/5$ cent with which to pay tax.

A Spokane County Planning Commission was approved by the **County Commissioners.**

1935   **State Senator Ed Peirce** of **Opportunity** was made president pro tem of the Senate when the Legislature opened in biennial session in Olympia.

1936   President Roosevelt was reelected with a majority of over ten million votes. He was inaugurated January 20, 1937.

Political offices were held by **A.E. Holt,** State Senator; **Charles H. Leavy,** elected to Congress; **Jack Sullivan,** County Commissioner.

Property taxes for **Peters Hardware,** including inventory and equipment, were $3.36 for state, county, city and township.

A prowl car, operated by a Deputy, was placed in the Valley.

1937   First Aid Emergency Stations were established at **Greenacres** and **Otis Orchards**.

April 8: Spokane Valley businessmen with almost one voice approved the suggestion that the Spokane Valley be incorporated as a municipality. It did not happen.

1938   **WPA** projects improved local irrigation systems by replacing deteriorating high flumes with underground concrete pipes. A new concrete-lined canal brought water from the **Spokane River**.

1939   January: Both **Edgecliff** and **Opportunity Townships** voted for the return of road maintenance to the townships from the county and for a two-mill levy to be used for fire protection, dust or snow removal.

Part of the town of **Spirit Lake, Idaho**, was destroyed by a forest fire that started near **Mt. Spokane**.

The Legislature authorized the creation of tax supported fire districts in the state. The **Chamber** immediately organized a campaign to vote such a district embracing the entire Valley.

April: **County Commissioners** were urged by the **Chamber** to see that work continued on **Pinecroft Recreational Center**. (See "Jackson and the Pinecroft Development," Vol. I.) "$31,000 invested would be lost if the project were dropped."

September 1: Germany invaded Poland. World War II began.

1940   August 27: United States draft law was enacted.

Fire Protection District #1 was formed.

November 5: Roosevelt was elected to an unprecedented Third Term.

1941

December 7: The Japanese attacked Pearl Harbor.

U.S. Government built **Trentwood Aluminum Rolling Mill** in the Valley.

1942

May 15: **U.S. Government** awarded a $10 million contract for the building of a **Naval Supply Depot** at **Trentwood** in the Valley.

Spokane County Library was started with the appointment of a five member board. In the early days there was a volunteer lending library in the **Opportunity Town Hall**.

Daylight Saving Time began as "War Time" when President Roosevelt ordered that clocks be set ahead to save energy.

Terry T. Grant became president of the County Bar Association.

1943

Street signs were up over most of the Valley.

1944

November 7: Roosevelt was elected to a fourth term. He had brought together the enemies of the Axis powers into an alliance known as The United Nations.

1945

April 12: President Roosevelt died in Warm Springs, GA., at age 63. Harry S Truman succeeded him. Valley business houses closed during the hour of his last rights.

May 8: V-E (Victory in Europe) Day proclaimed.

August 6, 9: U.S. bombs fell on Hiroshima and Nagasaki respectively, ending World War II. The surrender of the Japanese was signed September 2 on the battleship *Missouri* in Tokyo Harbor.

September 2: V-J (Victory in Japan) Day proclaimed.

Early Government: Townships

In 1873, with only about one hundred people in the whole of what now constitutes Spokane County, there was no need for a multiplicity of government laws and regulations. Spokane County government, except for regulations dealing with roads, had little impact on the average citizen; and Territorial government was remote.

As more people arrived, more government regulations became necessary to provide a pattern of laws for the protection of everyone's life and property and to provide community services which individuals could not provide for themselves.

But a pattern of laws was not enough. There had to be organizations of officials to enforce the laws. In the early Valley, these officials were provided by townships, Spokane County, Washington State and either the Territorial or Federal Government (depending on the year).

The two organizations closest to the people in the Spokane Valley were townships and Spokane County. Let us look at the manner in which these two governmental units functioned in early history.

The present Spokane County was organized out of part of Stevens County on October 30, 1879. The only objection to the bill that was drawn up to organize the county was presented by the Hon. Francis Cook, a member of the Legislature from Pierce County and editor of the *Spokan Times*. He objected to the bill on the grounds an "E" had been added to Spokan.

The bill passed over Cook's objection and Spokan Falls became temporarily the location of the county seat. Also over Cook's constant objections, by 1881-82 the "E" was widely added to Spokane. (See "Land Rights" [footnote], Volume I.)

A land survey found that in 1900 there were forty-eight full townships and two fractions of townships in the County area of about seventeen hundred square miles. At that time a township was a unit of territory in a U. S. land survey, generally six miles square containing 36-mile-square sections, and had no governmental functions.

In 1909, the State Legislature provided that, by petitioning that body, townships could be organized with governmental functions. Men of Oppor-

tunity and Veradale took up the challenge and worked to make governmental townships possible in the Valley. Early news items in the *Valley Herald* indicate that Opportunity, Vera, and Newman townships were very active, with Opportunity the only first class township in the state. It even built its own township hall which still exists. (See "A Place Called Opportunity," Volume I.)

The township was derived from the New England Town Meeting and was a sounding board for residents to voice their concerns. In the Valley, monthly township meetings were held, administered by the Board of Supervisors and its chairman. The board was often spoken of as the Township Committee.

In the 1950s when the Opportunity Township Hall was refurbished, Frank E. Williams (who came to the Valley in 1894 and had lived here constantly since 1903) was chairman (or supervisor) of the Township Board. Other members were C.J. Newer and Otto Gaskell. A.B. Houk was clerk and Sidney M. Smith was treasurer. Jim Dowling was caretaker of the township hall.

Through the years, interest in Valley townships declined and in 1972, they were abolished.

Early county officials were an auditor, treasurer, sheriff (to act as ex-officio assessor), probate judge, superintendent of common schools, coroner and three county commissioners.

These officials governed all of the people in the Valley until Millwood became incorporated. Then that town elected its own officials, but even Millwood was provided some services by the county, such as roads, public health, elections, civil defense and law enforcement.

The three Spokane County Commissioners were (and still are) the Valley resident's closest representatives to local government. In 1993 a ballot measure gave the people of Spokane County the opportunity to increase the number of county commissioners to five. The measure was defeated.

County officials received (and still receive) most of their powers from the state. According to the Washington State Association of County Commissioners in their publication, *County Government in*

Washington State, 1953, "As early as 1863, when Washington was still a territory, the legislature passed a law which said that counties . . . shall have no other powers, except such as are or may be given them by law."

County laws are usually general in nature. For example, in the field of roads, the Legislature says that counties must construct and maintain all public roads which are not city streets or state highways. However, the Legislature does not attempt to tell a county when or where the roads must be built and what the surface must be.

Similarly the Legislature did not and does not say that a county must have one or more fire districts within its borders. The state leaves fire protection to the discretion of the people living in an area. In 1939, F.R. Salter of the Valley Chamber of Commerce petitioned the State to enable the Valley to establish Fire Protection District No. 1. (See "Early Fire Protection.") Once established, the operation and financing of the fire district became the responsibility of the electorate in the District.

Not all state laws giving counties a particular responsibility in some program are forever. As the needs of people change, the law also must be changed. Aid to the needy and sick is a good example. In pioneer days, "neighbor took care of neighbor." When the need was larger than neighbors could provide, poor farms for the helplessly poor and pest houses for those with communicable diseases were established by the county.

However, with the Depression of the 1930s, the burden of caring for the needy became too great to be sustained even by the counties and the state gave added aid through the issuing of bonds to finance works programs. With intervention by the state came increased county uniformity in state welfare programs.

The division of Washington into counties began before Washington was even a territory, in the days when the Northwest was still under British rule. Then the counties were large and there were not very many of them.

SPOKANE VALLEY FIRE DEPARTMENT, APRIL 7, 1946
The station on Park Road displays full equipment and personnel.
Courtesy of Jack Cunningham

Early Fire Protection

Early in the century Valley businesses were usually housed in wooden buildings—banks being the major exception.

Fires were frequent. When a fire broke out, the entire community was alerted by the telephone party-line operator or by the ringing of the school or church bell or both. A volunteer fire-fighting bucket brigade hurried to the scene of the fire and tried to save the burning building. Those heroic efforts usually were met with failure.

The devastating Spokane City fire of 1889 is a good example of the havoc wrought by a fire that ate through the wooden buildings of a business district as though they were tinder.

"At the time of that great fire," Esther Johnson of Freeman said, "my mother and father, Hans Johnson and Mary Stenzel Johnson, were standing on a hill near Freeman working side by side cutting wood when they saw a tower of smoke rising above the trees in the vicinity of Spokane twenty miles away."

Carl Goffinet (now deceased), told me a few years ago, of the 1921 fire that burned most of the wooden buildings in the Knight Block in Opportunity. (See "A Place Called Opportunity," Volume I.)

"Water was handed by bucket brigade from an irrigation ditch that ran behind the buildings," Carl said.

Channon Price, in his unpublished memoirs, noted that "[Dishman] fires were a heavy money loss and had a discouraging effect on the community. Why there were so many fires was anybody's guess," he said. Those he remembered were the burning of the A.T. Dishman buildings and the Dishman Trading Company, the Opportunity Box Factory, the A.R. Moore building, the Dishman Community Club, small buildings owned by F.R. Salter, the John F. Irby Apple Drying Plant at Willow and Sprague, the Merrick Davis Tire Store, the Safeway Store, the new Dishman Trading Center and a three-story brick building near Park Road being used by the Morrison Brothers Seed Company.

The Valley desperately needed organized manpower and equipment to fight the fire crisis.

In the thirties, adequate fire protection for the Valley became a priority project for the Chamber of Commerce and Thomas Bienz, president. The Chamber worked long and hard, lobbying the state legislature to enable a fire protection district in the Valley.

"At that time the only fire protection in the whole of Spokane County consisted of one truck stationed in Dishman just west of the viaduct on the south side of the Appleway," said Duane Marlow, now of Coeur d'Alene but a retired Valley fire fighter and battalion chief. "A.T. Dishman and John Pring built the building that housed the truck and rented it to the county. A red light hung in the street outside the building. The light was activated by pushing a button inside the building to stop the traffic so the truck could get out onto the four-lane roadway."

Finally, in 1939 the Legislature authorized the creation of tax-supported fire protection districts statewide. F.R. Salter, whose Dishman buildings had been damaged by fire, was quick to accept the challenge of circulating a petition in the Valley to form Spokane County Fire Protection District No.1.

Events moved rapidly. In March 1940, Fire Commissioners were approved by ballot and a two-mill fire protection levy passed, 1684-237. In September, James A. Bittle was hired as the first District No. 1 fire chief. In December, three Ford Mercury Seagrave fire trucks were leased from Howard-Cooper Corporation for five years with option to purchase at the end of the lease. Spokane County Fire Protection was in business!

Greenacres was chosen as the site of the first district fire station. A building constructed by Jacob Beck and Sons and located between Smith's Grocery and Beck's Garage was leased to the district by the Beck's—Jacob, Harry and Mildred—for $20 a month.

"The office was little more than a desk and a chair," said Duane Marlow, "and the bedroom consisted of one bunk bed. The garage was just large enough for that first Seagrave fire truck."

According to the district log, when the first fire truck went to Greenacres, there was great jubilation. It was met by the high school band and an outpouring of "Hurrahs" from the townsfolk.

Duane was hired by the Fire Protection District in 1941. He recalls that the trucks of that era were manned by two men even if it meant double shifting. However, earlier, during, and after the war, there were years when a truck was manned by only one man—when manpower was a problem. It was said that if a man walked by the station then, he was hired.

"Adequate water for the pumps was a major problem. There were about thirty-three water districts in the Valley at that time," said Duane. "To get enough water to fight a fire in Dishman, for instance, it was necessary to turn a valve at Park and Sprague and bring in extra water from Edgecliff. In Otis Orchards there was no source of water except irrigation ditches. That meant we largely relied on the water tanks on the truck. I can remember many times pumping water from irrigation ditches to fight a fire.

"When the Fire Protection District first started, fire fighters worked shifts of 48 hours on and 24 hours off, with three men rotating at a station. Wages were $50 a month, raised to $75 by 1941, and $140 in 1946."

A second station was opened at N. 2906 Park Road in the Orchard Avenue District in a building owned by the district. It was dedicated June 13, 1941.

In November 1941, Spokane County moved its fire department out of Dishman to the north side of Spokane. Fire Protection District No.1 took over the old Dishman location and put its third station in operation there.

In July 1943, the Fire District fought its first major fire. A high wind destroyed three businesses (Joe Falco's Fruit Stand, the Dishman Community Club, and the B & B Doughnut Shop) and five frame buildings in Dishman. The loss was approximately $20,000 and left eight adults and fifteen children homeless.

A second major fire, again in Dishman, caused a $1,000,000 loss in October of the same year. The Morrison Brothers Seed Co. warehouse containing 6,000,000 pounds of peas smoldered for several days. The town of Dishman was plunged into darkness and went without water for hours when its electric pumping system shut off while major power wires burned.

The District bought its first resuscitator December 1943. Water was still a problem, so the resuscitator was kept at the Greenacres Station, the location nearest the lakes and the largest irrigation ditches.

Demands for fire protection increased with the advent of World War II and the coming of war plants such as Alcoa and the Naval Supply Depot. In March 1944, the District received two 500-gallon-a-minute trailer pumper units leased from the Office of Civilian Defense and manned by Civilian Defense auxiliary firemen.

The department's fourth station began service at Otis Orchards in January 1945.

In October of that year the apple warehouse of John L. Gillespie and son, Paul, burned for a loss of $100,000, including 20,000 boxes of apples.

The old Greenacres station was moved out of Beck's garage into a new building on the north side of the Appleway and east side of Greenacres Road in October 1946, at a cost of $8981. Duane Marlow (who was sleeping in the station at the time), remembers that two young men coming home from the State Line wrecked the original station when they lost control of their car and hit the southeast corner of it.

"Both were killed," Duane said. "Firemen temporarily patched the station until the new station, now known as Station No. 3, could be built at the above Appleway location.

The next station built was No. 5 at Sullivan and Broadway in December 1954. This became headquarters until what is now known as No. 1 was built at a cost of $19,071 at Sprague and Balfour. In April 1957, a 40-foot high drill tower was built by a crew of firefighters at Station No. 5.

An entirely new training tower with a modern repair shop next to it was opened in August 1993, at N. 2411 Pioneer Lane.

Station No. 6, located on Sprague at the Freeway overpass, opened February 1961. After that, not until 1994 was there a new station. That year there were two.

Because a study showed that response time was too slow, in that year a ten-year plan was put forth. The first phase was the opening of the two new stations: one at Marietta and Sullivan to better serve the Spokane Industrial Park; the other at 12th and Evergreen. In the second phase Station No.8 would be built near Mission and Molter in 1996 to better serve the Liberty Lake area.

Retirement Plans, Hospitalization and Social Security Benefits Come of Age

As the years from 1921 through 1945 unfolded, government—local, state, and federal—and industry became more and more involved in aspects of Valley residents' lives.

On August 14, 1935, President Franklin Roosevelt signed into law the original Social Security Act. It initiated one of the most comprehensive programs for social welfare undertaken up to that time by direct legislation. It established a federal old age insurance system and made provision for federal cooperation with the states in unemployment insurance systems and in programs for giving financial aid to the aged, the blind, and dependent children. The measure also extended to the states federal aid for health and welfare services and for vocational rehabilitation.

[From *Alcotrend*, Vol.3 No.14, August 22, 1945, published by the Aluminum Co. of America, Trentwood Works, Spokane, Washington:]

ALOCA RETIREMENT PLAN AND SOCIAL SECURITY ATTRACTIVE

Coincident with the announcement of the company financed retirement plan for Alcoa employees, the following Old Age and Surivors Insurance program seems worthy of study. The Alcoa plan is designed to supplement payments all employees of Alcoa will be eligible to receive under the social security program.

The following material was furnished by the Social Security Board.

Every employee of an organization such as Trentwood Works Aluminum Co. of America, must have a social security card. Keep your card safe. It represents your insurance policy with the United States Government. It is the key to the benefits you are earning under the Federal Old Age and Survivors Insurance Program.

A one per cent deduction is made each pay day from your wages. This is matched by a one per cent contribution made by your employer. We submit a record of your wages every three months to the Government so that full credit under the Security Act is assured you.

The benefit payments you are entitled to are of two kinds: (1) the retirement insurance benefit paid you when you retire from work at age 65 or later; (2) survivors' benefits paid to your survivors when you die. The amount paid for each type of benefit depends upon the length of time deductions have been made from your wages and the total amount of such wages—in other words, upon how long you have worked and how much money you have been making.

[From the same publication, this announcement concerning Hospitalization:]

The Spokane Medical Service Bureau will offer starting October 1, 1945, a paid-in-advance hospitalization plan for families of the Trentwood Rolling Mill folks. It will be available through a monthly payroll deduction as will the present Medical Bureau service. Authorization cards covering the plan, which all persons who wish to take advantage of the plan must file with the Paymaster, will be available through the attendants in the first Aid Stations. Those attendants can provide information on the plan and will assist in filling out the application form.

Briefly, the plan is as follows: Hospitalization for spouse will cost 90 cents per month. Hospitalization for all children in the family age 18 and under is 75 cents per month—it makes no difference whether there are ten children in the family or only one, the cost is the same.

The worker may subscribe to either the hospitalization plan only for 90 cents per month, or he may take the full Medical Service Bureau coverage of doctor, hospital and medicine for $2.00 per month, or he may not subscribe to either—in any case he can still subscribe to the hospitalization plan for any or all of his or her family.

The Rural Electrification Administration Lights Up Rural Areas

By 1921 most of the land advertised for sale by Valley developers was irrigated and supplied with domestic water and power, making it possible for Valley residents living along the main roads or in established communities to have running water and electricity. No cooking on wood stoves for them. No trimming kerosene lamp wicks. No pumping water or carrying it from the river. No outhouses. None of that sort of drudgery for the residents of most Valley developments. They were served by Vera Light and Power, Modern Electric Water Company or Washington Water Power. They had washing machines, refrigerators, and electric stoves.

What about farm folks living in outlying areas— the Saltese, Mica, nearby Freeman, Pleasant Prairie, the Mt. Spokane Foothills?

Many were still pumping water, milking cows, feeding large flocks of poultry, herding livestock, cleaning barns and chicken houses, smoking their meat, and separating and cooling their cream—all by hand. But when they visited their citified friends and neighbors, they learned how much the quality of life on the farm could be improved if they had electricity, and they wanted it!

The more inventive tried gasoline pressured lanterns, gasoline-powered generator plants (that produced only flickering lights), windmills for pumping water, and cisterns for water storage.

The movement for rural power that had begun as a whimper in the '20s, increased to a clamor in the '30s. Community leaders held group meetings and took their problems to Washington Water Power. Little was accomplished. Washington Water Power replied that farm houses were too distant from each other. To string wire and plant poles across great spaces of unoccupied land was too expensive a proposition. (Aaron C. Jones, *Inland, the First Forty Years*; p. 21.)

Some of the farmers banded together and tried investor-owned co-ops, supplying their own poles and wire. This effort too had little success.

Meanwhile, far away from the Valley an incident occurred which was destined to help all of rural America. In 1924 Roosevelt, a victim of polio, visited Warm Springs, Ga., to swim in the therapeutic waters there. It is said that when he received an 18¢ per kilowatt hour bill for the electric light in his little cottage, four times the rate he paid in Hyde Park, NY, he was astonished and brought face to face with the problem of rural electrification. In 1932 when he became president, he made it known that his goal was cheap power for every house within reach of a power line.

Local residents with the same purpose wrote to leaders in Washington, D.C., and met in organized groups and worked for rural power through their granges.

On May 20, 1936, the Rural Electrification Act was passed and quickly was followed by the Rural Electrification Administration. This legislation established a federally funded program for the electrification of rural establishments not connected to central service electricity and promoted the farmer co-operative as the preferred instrument of electrification.

The stir to action in Spokane County was immediate. In our area John Service of Mica took the lead to get something done about rural electrification. But it was a struggle to get the outlying Valley areas the dependable type of electric service that was known in town.

"Many a farm wife literally pushed her tired husband out of the house to attend the community meetings, and some wives attended themselves. Many women helped sign up [prospective] members and shared in the record keeping chores. It was not uncommon to hear a preacher include a request for electric service in his prayers on Sunday morning. The interest, as well as the need, existed wherever one looked.

"Eventually that great 'cooperative' combined effort paid off. Inland Empire Rural Electrification, Inc. was established. . . A loan request to REA was approved, providing for $455,000 to build approximately 463 miles of line to serve 1,530 members. . .It was Christmas Eve, 1939, when the lights first went on at the Guy Lindsey farm in the Saltese. No youngster with a bright and shining new toy was ever more intrigued or delighted than the Lindseys and their neighbors.

"'Everybody turned on every light they had that night,' said Mr. Lindsey. 'The whole neighborhood was lit up like a Christmas tree.'" (Jones, *Inland, the First Forty Years*, p. 27.)

"'There really wasn't a celebration though. Everybody was too busy driving around looking at all the electric lights,' Lindsey said. 'We had been driving all these places for years, and we'd see just one little coal oil lamp burning in one window some place. It was kind of odd, seeing some of those old places all lit up.'

"...While the Lindseys and other joyful Inland members had something extra to celebrate for Christmas in 1939, there were thousands of other Eastern Washington families still in the dark. The co-op was in its infant stages. While several hundred miles of line had been built, thousands more miles remained to be built."

Lines were extended to Mica in 1938 and in 1940 connected for electricity to the big ski lodge operated by the Parks Commission on the east side of Mt. Spokane. Power was extended to the top of Mt. Spokane in 1954.

During the 1930s while Inland was building lines to rural people, the federal government was building two great power generating projects on the Columbia River: the Bonneville and Grand Coulee Dams. In 1942 when Bonneville's transmission lines from Grand Coulee to Spokane were completed, Bonneville contracted to supply all of Inland's power requirements.

Memories of the Early Years

In *Memories of Yesterday and Today, Freeman, Washington,* by Roberta Goldsmith, early residents of the Freeman farm country (just south of the Valley) described their living conditions and their utility problems before the coming of water mains and power lines, before the advent of the REA (Rural Electrification Administration):

ROBERTA GOLDSMITH: When the rain barrel was frozen solid and a huge icycle dangled like a sword from the rain spout, it was time to head for the pond to put up ice. The ice plow was a heavily-weighted, horse-drawn tool with a row of sharp teeth that cut a furrow 6" deep; then a marker scratched a line where the next furrow was to be cut. After the pond was all marked in one direction, the tool was turned and it was marked in crosswise direction forming checkerboard squares. They would be broken apart with an iron bar and snagged with ice tongs and pulled upon the bank where they were loaded onto bobsleds. When they arrived at the farmers' ice houses, the ice would be layered between saw dust and about three to six inches on top. This would keep well into the summer and everyone really looked forward to making home-made ice cream. After the ice was washed, it was used for making cold drinks too. These pleasures made the men forget about all the hard work it had been to put up the ice and how cold and wet they had gotten.

When the Freeman School was built in about 1910, it was completely a wood structure with windows on both sides and a small entrance way at each end called a "cloak room." The building was heated with a jacketed coal stove and was lighted by hanging gasoline lamps or lanterns. The drinking water was in a jug in the cloak room and disposable cups were used. As there was no bathroom, the only accommodations were the boys' and girls' "two holer." Electricity finally came about 1936 and this eliminated the gas lights and made it possible to get water into the building so drinking fountains were added and bathrooms were installed.

PAULINE MACKIE: We had no electricity or bathroom in the '20s. There was a root cellar and that was the only place to keep perishables. We were finally able to buy an ice chest. I took my washing to my mother's until we could afford a gas-driven washing machine.

W. J. BOY, a Freeman pioneer, was killed instantly and his son, Gale, was badly injured when a carbide house lighting plant that they were repairing "blew up." There was a big tank in the ground, and machinery and a bell container above it. Mr. Boy had just said he could hear the machine working and they would have plenty of light, when there was a terrible explosion and the whole top blew off. The explosion hurled a 100-pound container into the air. It struck Mr. Boy in the head, crushing his skull and killing him instantly. Gale was struck and fell into the pit. But for the heroic work of Mr. Nessly who was watching and who ran to the blazing pit and rescued Gale, the youth would have been cremated in a few seconds.

GROVER SIEGEL had his own electricity shortly after he came to Freeman in 1921, a 32-volt generator and batteries, so he was the first to have electricity and one of the first to have indoor plumbing. A few years later the people formed a group and bought electricity from the railroad. It had a depot and two station houses at Freeman.

Grandma's Washday Receet

Years ago a Freeman grandmother gave a new bride the following "Receet" for washing clothes. It appears below just as it was written. It might be well to copy this and hang it above the automatic electric washer and read it when things look bleak. (Courtesy of Roberta Goldsmith from her book, *Memories of Today and Yesterday, Freeman, Washington.*)

1. Bilt fire in backyard to heet kittle of rain water
2. Set tubs so smoke won't blow in eyes as wind is pert
3. Shave one hole cake lie soap in bilin water
4. Sort things, make three piles, 1 pile white, 1 pile cullord, 1 pile work britches and rags

5. Stir flour in cold water to smooth, then thin down with bilin water
6. Rub dirty spots on board, scrub hard, then bile. Rub cullord, don't bile. just rench in starch
7. Take white things out of kittle with broomstick handle, then rench, blew and starch
8. Spread tee towels on grass
9. Hang old rags on fence
10. Pore rench water in flour bed
11. Scrub porch with soapy water
12. Turn tubs upside down
13. Go put on clean dress, smooth hair with side combs, brew cup of tee, set and rest and rock a spell and count blessings.

Farming and Irrigation

"While economic storms are hitting the east coast and farmers are hard hit in other sections [of the country], the Valley goes calmly on its way without suffering. Our section is called not only the most prosperous in the state but probably the most prosperous in the entire Northwest. Built squarely on Mother Earth, there is no suffering in Spokane's Garden Spot."

[Editorial, *Spokane Valley Herald*, December 12, 1920]

SORTING AND PACKING CREWS AT THE GILLESPIE APPLE PACKING HOUSE, VERADALE, 1941.
Courtesy of Orville Kinkade.

Farming and Irrigation

CHRONOLOGICAL HISTORY

1920

March 20: **Spokane Valley Grower's Union** announced a very successful apple season: 193,374 boxes handled at 10¢ a box; 222,846 field boxes of apples hauled to packing houses at a cost of 2¢ a box.

May 28: The **Independent Fruit and Storage Company** began to erect a new building on the north side of the railway line, 250 yards east of the depot in **Opportunity.**

June 18: Orchardists held a meeting to determine how to fight the Leaf Roller (pest).

Telephone lines were installed for **Saltese** farmers. There were 12 subscribers.

1920-30s

The **Otis Orchards Fruit Growers Association** operated a boarding house on **Gilbert Road** near the packing plant. It was a two-story gray frame building erected in the early 1900s.

1921

The **Spokane Valley Irrigation District** watered an area of approximately 5000 acres of which approximately 900 acres were north of the river. Water was supplied by the **Corbin Ditch** to irrigate **Millwood, Pinecroft, Fruitland, Santa Rosa Park, Grandview,** and **Irvin.** The main canal crossed the river at **Spokane Bridge** and went down the Valley along the foothills. Water from the river was turned into a 42-inch main running from **Hayden Lake** to **Post Falls.** Four small irrigation districts totaling 7000 acres pumped water from **Hayden Lake.** At **Twin Lakes** a dam and regulating gates stored water for 2200 acres at **Greenacres. Newman Lake** supplied water for 2400 acres of the **Otis Orchards District** and 600 acres along the river. 4000 acres, including **Pasadena Park, Trentwood, West Farms** and a part of **Otis Orchards** were irrigated from the river at **Post Falls** and west to **Pasadena Park**

The **Growers Union** decided to build new apple packing houses at **Dishman** and **Vera.**

Apple Blossom Days Festival was held at **Otis Orchards** with free refreshments to the first 5000 in attendance. Over 1000 apple pies were consumed.

September 5-10: **Interstate Fair.** A novel exhibit was from the silver fox farms of the Inland Empire. The **U.S. Silver Fox Farms** on the **Appleway** had the largest exhibit.

1921–22 Harold Anderson moved his **Early Dawn Dairy** to ten acres of Valley land. It later became part of the 80-acre **Early Dawn** property at **S. 2409 Evergreen Road.**

1922 A second **Apple Blossom Festival** was held at **Otis Orchards.**

60 **Post Falls** irrigation tract growers formed the **Panhandle Growers Union.** 700 acres of apples were under union control.

Fruit stands became common along the highways offering a new outlet for homegrown fruit and vegetables.

The population of the Valley was estimated at 10,000. Land values for irrigated land had risen to $250 an acre. Production of fruit, truck vegetables, poultry and dairy products totaled $3,000,000.

1923 **D.C. Corbin** enlarged his gravity irrigation system begun in 1916 to form the **Spokane Valley Irrigation District #10.** He irrigated 5200 acres in the Valley from the south branch of the **Spokane River Canal** and sold tracts varying in size from a half to twenty acres. South of and adjoining **Greenacres,** he platted **Corbin's Addition** to **Greenacres** on a thousand acres, reserving 50 acres on the north side of the **Appleway** (which cut the area in half) for a business district.

1924 **East Farms** formed a new irrigation district.

The **Chastek Brothers** started the **Hercules Fur Farm** on **Trent Highway**, two miles east of Spokane.

A model poultry farm was established on the **John F. Davis** tract in **Opportunity.**

Fred Schrap, Greenacres, was the first grower to use paper cones to protect plants from frost.

1925 Apple orchards began to decline. About 90,000 neglected or unprofitable apple trees were removed. Small truck farms became a common sight. More early potatoes were grown. Bee keeping became a new industry. Cantaloupes, especially the Heart of Gold, asparagus and tomatoes were favorite crops. The Spokane apple show was discontinued. A "Know the Valley" tour and a Harvest Festival were substituted.

A weather station was established at **East Farms** and at **Dishman** to issue warnings of crop damage during the growing season.

1926 First All-Valley Junior Fair was held at **Dishman.**

E.H. Stanton Apple Warehouse in **Opportunity** burned.

200,000 apple trees were pulled out leaving 370,000, a census showed.

6 co-ops united to form the **Growers Federation.**

1927   **McDowell Warehouse** at **Otis Orchards** burned and with it 30,000 new apple boxes.

1929   **Cecil Whipple's** father (also named **Cecil**) bought five acres of land at the **SW** corner of **Pines** and **Main** for a truck farm. In the 1940s, small parcels were sold off.

Farmers believed chicken thieves were favored by an ordinance that required the muzzling or tying up of watch dogs.

Reconstruction Finance Corporation made a refinancing loan of $555,000 to **Spokane Valley Irrigation Districts.** In 1935 another loan was allowed to the **Trentwood Irrigation District.**

1930   **Sam** and **Angie Larango** operated **Berland's Cold Storage Receiving Station** in **Veradale.** They bought 2000 flats of raspberries a day and shipped to points all over the Midwest.

Rice's Meat Packing Plant at **Conklin** and **Fourth** was a Valley landmark. It was run by **Charlie** and his two sons, **Greg** and **Ralph.** Their Meat Market in the **Opportunity Block** was "the best place to buy steaks," say many old-timers.

John Gillespie built a packing house at **Vera.**

John Van Hees "who knew tulips and chocolate (not fruit)" came from Amsterdam with wife, Irmgard, and began fruit farming. They kept the farm going through the difficult '30s and the freeze of '37.

E.H. Stanton built a warehouse and apple packing plant at **Veradale.**

1931   March: The **Otis Orchards Cooperative Association** purchased a spray manufacturing plant west of the **Fruit Growers Association Warehouse** at **Kenney** and **Gilbert Roads**, built by the **Valley Growers Union** of **Opportunity.** Lime and sulphur was used to control pests.

1932   Annual **Yard** and **Garden Show.**

1933   **Valley Irrigation District** #15 was organized with a three member board.

1934   July: "At least 300 workers a day for the next six weeks are needed to save the food produced in the Spokane Valley. Approximately 500 youth are already registered but women workers who can act as supervisors are needed for the emergency." *Spokane Valley Herald.*

The government of France reduced to one-third the import duty on American apples and pears, an estimated benefit of about $2 million to the Pacific Northwest.

September 27: First killing frost 2½ weeks ahead of 51-year average date of October 13.

1934

First **Junior Livestock Show** at the Old Union Stockyards.

Trentwood Irrigation District was refinanced by a $35,000 check from the Reconstruction Finance Corporation.

1935

First Valley Fair.

1937

October: Members of the crews working on the **Barberry Eradication Program** covered all 236 properties from the Idaho Line to a point just west of **Pines Road**. The project netted a total of 2780 harmful barberry bushes which were destroyed.

The **Greenacres Cold Storage Plant** was built.

Valley strawberries of excellent quality began to appear in markets. Prices were disappointing at 10¢ a box for the finest or 3 boxes for 25¢.

1938

Spokane Cannery moved into a new plant adjacent to the **Milwaukee Railroad** east of **Sullivan** at **Vera. Harold Anderson** was plant manager with 50 Valley employees.

LaBarge began to manufacture berry boxes, crates, and hallocks at **Dishman**.

Spokane Valley Fair held in three buildings at **Dishman**.

1940

A four-day **County Fair,** successor to the **Spokane Valley Fair** was held at **Dishman.**

1942

Joe Falco's fruit stand in **Dishman** burned. The fire was fanned by high winds. (See article, "Fire Protection.")

1943

Ralph Lakin of the **Lakin Milling Company** was willing to pay 60 cents for clean, good white wheat at the **Opportunity Warehouse**.

1944

The **Central Valley Community Cannery** was operational.

At the **Fruit Growers** meeting in the **Opportunity Town Hall**, it was reported that raspberry hallocks were very scarce, almost impossible to obtain.

1945

Only 50,000 apple trees remained in the Valley.

[This period in Valley history saw the arrival of fox farms. Old-timers mention a large farm near what is now Park Place Retirement Center, another "out on Trent Road," and a 1925 clipping of unknown origin gives this information: "The U.S. Silver Fox Farm in the Valley was the largest circular type fur farm in the world. The business was believed to have been in its infancy although its inventory at the time was 500 foxes valued at $250,000 for breeding purposes. The previous year had seen 236 pups from 62 litters at the farm. The U.S.Silver Fox Farm was founded in 1920 when E.M. Robinson, president, brought the original stock from Prince Rupert Island and developed what was known as the Roosevelt strain."]

Farming and Related Subjects

[From the autobiography of Dr. Frederick Coddington]

About the first of June, we got a load of manure. We spread it over our entire garden and orchard area and then had it plowed under.

Fortunately, our plowman brought his team of horses and his equipment on a Saturday; we got to watch him. Wherever he couldn't plow close to trees, we spaded with shovels.

Soon we were helping Dad with the planting. We measured the rows, then stretched a manila rope across the garden to make the rows straight. Dr. Hines (former owner of our property) had left a one-wheeled hand cultivator and mechanical seed planter at the house. It worked well for corn and beans and peas.

Our garden flourished. We raised watermelons and cantaloupes. We had abundant tomatoes, beans, peas, cabbage, lettuce, spinach, rutabagas, turnips, onions, and potatoes. We also raised strawberries, gooseberries, raspberries, ground cherries, cucumbers, sweet corn, pumpkins, and several kinds of squash.

About every six to eight days in the summer, we got 22 hours of irrigation water. We had a ditcher attachment to bolt onto our hand cultivator. Dad could push it by himself to make fresh ditches before each irrigation.

Sometimes Robert pushed the ditch-maker. Then I often would attach a rope near the axle and help him pull it, like a horse. About two hours after irrigating, we would run the same pattern with the cultivator-weeder attachment. That left fewer weeds to be pulled.

Dad guided the water around our garden if our irrigation time came at night. Robert and I managed it only in the daytime.

Dad built shelves around the walls of the room south of our cellar stairs. There we stored hundreds of jars of fruit and vegetables that Mother canned. To get the heat out of our kitchen, she got a three-burner kerosene stove. She set it up on the screened-in back porch. We all had to pick and prepare food and help with the canning.

Every summer, a number of mothers volunteered to can vegetables for the school hot lunch program. The school furnished jars, lids, rubber seals, the home economics room, stove and kettles. Mother often helped one afternoon a week. Farmers brought in over-ripe tomatoes, string beans, carrots, dried beans, potatoes and sweet corn. During the school year a woman was hired for several hours a day. She prepared a kettle of soup for each classroom (a different kind each day) and cleaned up the dishes. Boys from each class were sent to the home economics room to get soup and utensils. Some of us took second servings to help empty the kettle. All who could afford it paid 25¢ a week for hot soup to go with our sandwiches. Any child who couldn't afford the quarter got the soup anyway. Boys packed the dishes and empty kettle back to the home-ec room. Fresh milk was 4¢ a bottle.

Farmers in the area needed more space for truck gardening. There were rumors that the marketing of apples had been badly mismanaged. Many of our neighbors were having apple trees pulled out of their orchards.

A man with a heavy team of horses brought in steel pulley blocks, steel cables and chains. With a chain, he fastened one block to the base of a tree. He attached the other around the bigger branches of the tree to be removed. With his team pulling on one end of the cable, tremendous force uprooted the tree. We burned our own apple wood in our stove, but it was difficult for farmers to dispose of

SPOKANE VALLEY GROWERS UNION, OPPORTUNITY, WASH.

the stumps and that year we accumulated in our backyard a big pile of them from neighboring farmers.

We began cutting the stumps down to a size that would fit in our fireplace. We bought a rusty two-man crosscut saw. Dad sharpened it and put a new hardwood handle on one end. Robert and I were able to cut big stumps with it. We bought a maul and a steel wedge to split them. It was a long hard job.

In winter weather we frequently burned up an entire stump overnight. It was often glowing the next morning, providing the most comfortable spot for dressing.

All leaves raked up in the fall went on our garden. Dr. Hines had left us a machine that chopped corn stalks into 2 inch lengths for cattle fodder. We processed corn stalks, weeds and small brushwood through it and scattered the pieces. All potato and fruit peelings, bones, cabbage leaves, and coffee grounds were piled on a compost heap. Every spring we scattered compost before plowing.

The fall of 1925 Dad bought an old second hand, two-vat cider mill and press. Some of the hardwood slats had to be replaced and one base plate was falling apart. We made a new one. Some bolts

needed tightening, but the oak framework and metal parts were good. We fixed it up and it functioned well.

Previously we had gathered up our cull apples and hauled them to the cider mill at Dishman. There they processed cider for 25¢ a gallon. Now we could make our own cider and vinegar.

Each Saturday of autumn we gathered all fallen apples from the ground into our wheelbarrow. We scrubbed off spray residues and rinsed the apples with a garden hose. Then we ran them through the press.

I liked the cider best at about three weeks of aging. It was still sweet with lots of carbonic acid tang like champagne. By eight weeks it had too much kick and tasted sour. Dad put that in a vinegar barrel in the basement. We always furnished cider for fall parties, especially at Halloween.

INSIDE THE APPLE GROWERS ASSOCIATION BUILDING

At the far corner of the Opportunity Grade Schoolyard was a hole in the fence.

It let my friend Bob Sandberg and me slip into the backyard of the Spokane Valley Apple Growers Association packing house. There, trucks loaded

Spokane Valley Growers Union, Opportunity, Fall 1919,
Courtesy of Libby-Graf and Robert Nelson.

with apples backed up to a window with a conveyer belt protruding. The belt carried boxes to a room where the apples were dumped into a washing machine.

When a farmer finished unloading his apples and no one was looking we got busy. We climbed onto his truck and onto the moving conveyer belt. It carried us into the washing room. Other belts carried us from one floor to another. We got off whenever we spotted workmen ahead.

Bob's mother was employed at the Apple Growers Association every fall packing apples. We visited her on the top floor and watched other women culling, sorting and grading apples. The wormy and misshapen apples were shunted on belts to a huge bin outside. Trucks later hauled them away to the cider mill.

Bob's mother's job was to grab an apple with one hand and a waxed paper in the other. She brought the two together in a twisting motion that covered the apple. She placed it in its proper position in the apple box on the stand beside her. When the box was full, she turned to the empty box on the other side.

A man stamped the size and grade on one end of the full box. He also recorded it on a tally sheet with the identity of the packer. He loaded it on a conveyer belt that took it to a special machine. There another man placed a box top over the apples and stepped on a foot lever. Two steel arms pressed the lid down onto the box, pushing the packed apples tightly together. He nailed the lid to the box with four nails at each end. The box continued on another belt which took it to a storage room.

We got to see the entire process of preparing fruit for the market. Sometimes we rode belts into the freight cars outside on the railroad siding. We often got caught and kicked off the belts. They warned us that we could get badly hurt, but that didn't prevent us from trying it again the next afternoon.

Sometimes we visited the engine crew switching cars on the siding outside. They let us ride in the cab and ring the locomotive bell.

George W. Pierce: The Rise and Decline of the Valley Apple Industry

[In the following article from the *Spokane Valley Herald*, January 2, 1958, a staff writer paralleled the life of George W. Pierce and the rise and decline of the Valley apple industry.]

When housemovers picked up the green weather-beaten building at E. 9416 Sprague last week and set it on new foundations back on First Avenue, the event could be called the period that closed the final sentence of a Spokane Valley historical chapter.

The building housed a firm that closed its doors after more than 25 years of operation. For more than a quarter of a century Mr. and Mrs. George W. Pierce operated the Growers Supply Co., and filled the needs of fruit, vegetable, and berry growers in the Spokane Valley.

The closing of the Growers Supply Co. punctuated a transition period that saw the Spokane Valley grow from a desert wasteland to one of America's great fruit growing areas [thanks to the arrival of irrigation], and then saw the orchards give way to thousands of modern new homes as the move to the suburbs made the Valley a vast residential area.

HERE IN 1909

Coming to the Valley in 1909, George W. Pierce had a grandstand seat to watch the pageant of time unfold in the Valley.

As a lad of 18, Pierce left his native Virginia to seek his fortunes in the fabulous west. He first worked at a little hamlet called Peach in the Grand Coulee country. A small fruitgrowing area, Peach now rests on the bottom of Roosevelt Lake, another victim of progress and the passage of time.

When Pierce first came to the Valley, as he put it, "I did everything. Jobs were not easy to come by. Irrigation of the Valley was just developing and I did my share to bring water to thirsty acres by digging [irrigation] ditches."

In Opportunity only two small grocery stores and a blacksmith shop comprised the retail district.

PEAK IN 1922

By 1922 orchard growth was probably at its peak here with 12,000 acres being in cultivation in the Spokane area. To a viewer on the surrounding hills the Valley floor presented a lush carpet-like appearance, broken here and there by the orchardists' homes and packing plants.*

In 1911 fruit raisers in the Valley formed the Spokane Valley Growers Union to market their product and built a mammoth $78,000 packing plant which still stands, cold and idle, just off Sprague and Union.

Pierce worked for this firm for many years, in fact was the last employee on the payroll. He was warehouse superintendent from 1920 to 1930.

The Great Depression put the final closure on the Growers Union operation, and George Pierce was forced to find another means of livelihood. Since there was still a great deal of fruit and crop gardening in the Valley, a firm supplying boxes, crates and sundry equipment seemed like a good bet. Pierce began operating out of his home at E. 12006 Fourth, where he still lives, and in 1932 he opened for business where the present Valley Creamery plant now stands.

Later he moved his business across the street, where he operated to the end of 1957. In 1940 he formed a partnership with Fred Schrap of Greenacres, which lasted until 1943.

After the peak of production in 1923 and 1924, apples began declining in importance as a cash crop in the Valley. Many reasons have been advanced for this. Some experts claimed that the Valley was trying to market the wrong kind of apple to be able to compete with Yakima and Wenatchee. Be that as it may, truck gardens were becoming more important, and thousands of acres were being given to raising the famous Heart of Gold cantaloupe and to berry raising. Even dairying began to surpass apples as an agricultural crop.

---

* In Volume I, p.113, this sentence was erroneously attributed to George Pierce.

FREEZE WAS FINISH

However, Pierce feels there would still be enough apple raising to keep him in business but for the fact that an unseasonal cold snap in November 1955 killed off most of the remaining trees.

"I really would have liked to have stayed in business another five years," he said. However, his health began failing him a little, and that hastened the decision to retire.

The Pierces have never considered living anywhere but the Spokane Valley, feeling that this is one of the finest places for good living that can be found in the United States.

Anna Louise Tinkham and George Pierce were married in 1921. She was a Spokane girl and they met through mutual friends. Both enjoyed dancing and this mutual like ripened into a romance that has continued for 36 years. Mrs. Pierce has worked right alongside her husband since they opened for business, keeping the books for the firm. The Pierces are the parents of a son, Roy D., who teaches in Franklin High School in Portland.

During his nearly 50 years in the Spokane Valley Pierce has found time for a lot of civic activities. He has been a member of Wilford Lodge IOOF of Opportunity for 41 years; a member of the Opportunity Grange for 25 years; a charter member of VFW Post 1435; a member of American Legion Post 9 for 20 years; a charter member of the Kiwanis Club. He was president of the Valley Chamber of Commerce in 1937, and chairman of the All-Valley picnic in 1936. This event, by the way, used to be the BIG event of the year in the Spokane Valley; when all, and we mean all, residents took the day off to play and visit with each other at Liberty Lake.

Long before the expression became a national colloquialism, in the Spokane Valley they used to say, "Let George do it," and his friends said they could always depend it would be done.

In 1970 Channon Price at the request of Tom M. Smith wrote his version of the "Apple" story:

[Early in the century] everyone was thinking and talking apples and planting apple trees. Sprague Road became the Appleway; the intersection at Appleway and University was Apple Center. Later we had the Appleway State Bank, Appleway Mercantile, Appleway Fuel, and Appleway Chevrolet. We had apple blossom parades with a queen and everything. In the fall after harvest we had apple shows. Everyone dreamed of the day when their apple trees would be full grown and they could count so many apples on a tree that would fill so many boxes and sell for so many dollars. They wondered what they would do with so much money. Meanwhile they planted berries and vegetables between the rows to make a living.

The nightmare in the dream was that the soil of the Valley was not deep enough or rich enough to support a grown bearing apple tree. As the trees grew larger, the apples grew smaller.

Around the apple packing plant they used to joke about buying berry hallocks for the apples and putting Jonathan apples in strawberry crates.

Many of the varieties were good but not suitable for storage and shipment. The local market could not use all the apples. Those suitable for eastern shipment were often consigned to eastern commission firms, and all too often the grower would get back a freight bill instead of a check. The knockout blow came in the 1920s. The trees were in a weakened condition from lack of nourishment and the strain of producing crops of apples. They were so severely damaged by long extremes of cold weather that many of them had to be destroyed.

The Valley, however, was not left without hope. People had learned that living in the Valley was nice. The damaged orchards were replaced by paved streets and beautiful homes.

Note: When George Pierce worked as warehouse superintendent for the Growers Union, he worked with an old friend, Harry Nelson, secretary-treasurer of the Union and a founder of the *Valley Herald*. (See Volume I, "Harry E. Nelson, 'Mr. Spokane Valley.'")

The two men enjoyed working together, but parted company in 1929 when Nelson went to Wenatchee to enter the apple packing industry there; and shortly thereafter, Pierce began his Growers' Supply Company.

In 1933, Nelson joined the state agriculture department as horticultural inspector and stayed there until he retired in 1949. When Pierce heard of Nelson's retirement, he promptly took his old friend on as office manager for Growers' Supply Co.

When the two met then, it is said they spent an evening reminiscing. Nelson recalled a letter he had received from Pierce when Pierce was in England during World War I. Pierce recounted seeing apples on a fruit stand in London; and when the dealer told him they came from Washington, Pierce wanted a look at the box. Sure enough, there was the Spokane Valley Growers' Union label on the end of the box. Nelson said Pierce wrote that he hugged the box in his arms and danced about the fruit dealer's basement much to the dealer's amazement. Such was the affection of George Pierce for the Spokane Valley and Spokane Valley apples.

Truck Farming

[From the autobiography of Robert Sandberg. In 1990 Mr. Sandberg of Lafayette, California, and formerly of Opportunity, Washington, was honored as "Distinguished Centennial Alumnus" by the faculty of the Edward R. Murrow School of Communications, Washington State University. He retired as senior vice president of Kaiser Industries. In his autobiography he writes:]

My father was killed in a railroad accident at Albani Falls in March 1914. I was born in September that same year. It was a vastly different world than the one we live in today. My family and I have witnessed historic changes in every aspect of our economic, industrial, governmental, social, and moral life—a complete revolution in the standard of living.

In 1919 soon after my mother's [second] marriage to Carl William Polson, my parents decided to buy five acres adjoining their apple orchard on S. Bowdish in Opportunity. This meant we now lived on a ten-acre orchard that was going to provide our living. Apples were doing very well and new land was being developed throughout the Spokane Valley to take advantage of this growing market. The growers also promoted the development of a very large apple packing and shipping center on Sprague Avenue and only a block from the grade school on Bowdish. During harvest it was not at all unusual to see twenty or thirty boxcars on the siding of the Milwaukee Railroad waiting to be loaded.

The purchase of the additional five acres turned out to be a real back breaker for my family. They had mortgaged their original five acres and the house to buy the extra acreage for $4500. Irrigation water was costing $10 an acre and ditching, spraying, pruning and other necessary expenses cut deeply into the income.

The worst came in about 1925 when Washington State College introduced a new way to control the woolly aphid, a miserable pest for apple growers. They recommended a spray which included oil to "keep it on the trees." The spray, however, killed the trees. Only a few farmers who did not follow the recommendations were spared the loss.

For two or three years a major employment was in the removal of the trees. This was done with a team of horses and a pulley system aided by a little dynamite to remove stubborn roots. The bonfires were unforgettable. The workers saved the largest limbs and cut them to stove size with a large circle saw powered by a gas engine. But the brush was yards long and perhaps 20 feet high. There were some very exciting BIG fires to create a little excitement in the Valley.

The farmers who lost their orchards turned to row crops. We called it truck farming. They raised strawberries, raspberries, tomatoes, cantaloupe, beans, peas, watermelon, squash (of all kinds), and lots of cucumbers for pickles.

Dad tried to run our ten acres as a truck farm. He bought a cayuse (a wild horse captured on the plains and half broken.) He was a mean animal, and totally unpredictable. Pulling a harrow or a ditcher he might just suddenly take off across the fields raising havoc with the neat rows of vegetables. We had chickens. We had a cow. Mother canned up to 800 quarts of fruits and vegetables a year. Still we were not making ends meet. Finally, Dad began working for other farmers, notably Ed Peirce, who was fairly successful and had gotten into politics. He became a state senator and later, when I was in college, he wrote a fine letter to the college recommending me for a scholarship.

As the Depression approached, Dad went to work for A.B. Groves in Opportunity. (See "A Place Called Opportunity," Volume I.) The Groves dealership sold the Gray automobile. It was not a winner. I shall never forget how hard Dad worked. It was six days a week from six to six. His pay was $80 a month, reduced later during the Depression to $40 a month. I can vividly remember his coming home for supper ravenously hungry and covered with oil and grease which Mother scrubbed out the next day on a hand scrub board.

I might prolong this discussion to emphasize the hardships of the time. In retrospect I can sense the problems, but my memories are not negative. They are positive in every sense as recalled some 70 years later. It was a great place and a great time to be of grade-school age. The school was one-half mile

WORKERS AT THE EDWARD PEIRCE FRUIT COMPANY, OPPORTUNITY, OCTOBER, 1931.
Apple Packing Shed in background, then located across present Sprague from what is now the White Elephant.
Notice the native stone loading dock wall that ran the length of the building and the empty boxes coming down
the chute to be sent to the orchards. The Interurban ran on the south side of the building.
Courtesy of Garner Coon.

away from the house, an easy walk. I had neighbor kids my own age and we were all compatible. Fred Coddington was my best friend. His father worked in a bank. Fred became a thoracic surgeon. Herb Aller became regional supervisor of the Audit Division of the IRS. Jerry Sage became a colonel in the Army and is widely known for his several escapes from Nazi prisons during World War II. His story was the basis for the movie called "The Great Escape." Bob Coddington became regional power manager for the Bonneville Power Administration. Bob Janosky, whose father farmed 10 acres and raised cucumbers and made many barrels of dill pickles every year, drowned in Shelley Lake.

Besides school there was much to do for young boys. We could hike into the foothills a mile or so away. We built trails and camps in the orchards. We slept out in the orchards when we had the courage. In winter there was sledding in front of the house or on the many hills which could be discovered in the woods and orchards nearby.

And there was work to do. I think I mowed the lawn from the time I was six or seven. I threw loads of wood and coal into our basement. I helped Mother pick and can food, and I played or dug around the irrigation ditches when we "had water," which was once a week in the growing season. I don't remember ever being bored as a child.

Let's think about this last statement. We didn't have a radio until late in the 1920s. No TV, no VCR, no reliable automobile to take on long trips. I don't remember seeing any magazines. The daily news-

71

paper was my source of information and it was well read. I could barely wait for the Sunday paper which brought a full page of comic strips.

Why no boredom? Well, we had lots of visitors. Family and neighbors. We had Sunday School and church and Boy Scouts. We did a lot of singing. Mother taught many songs to me and we sang together. Her favorite was "The Little Red School House." I could probably sing most of it today. And we talked. We talked about everything, what each did that day, what was planned, what was happening, what neighbors were up to. There was always something to talk about.

Particularly my mother kept after me to read poems and to memorize many of them. She wanted me to do recitations, and I did. James Whitcomb Riley's "Knee Deep in June" was a favorite poem. I also remember Mother helping me with school-work—English. Dad helped with math.

These were good years. I remember being active and interested in many things. I remember the simplicity of life, which has a charm of its own. I worry today about the complexity of life and the wide variety of experiences we all have in the 1990s. There doesn't seem to be a goal worthwhile except, perhaps, to get more. There is little time for introspection, to think about life itself and the beauty of common things in nature. I fear for those who have too much and still want more. It would seem far better to have less of the material wonders of this age and more time and determination to enjoy the natural beauties around us which are rapidly moving out of our reach.

Knee-deep in June

Tell you what I like the best—
    'Long about knee-deep in June,
    'Bout the time strawberries melts
On the vine,—some afternoon
    Like to jes' git out and rest,
      And not work at nothin' else!

Orchard's where I'd rather be—
Needn't fence it in fer me!
    Jes' the whole sky over head,
And the whole airth underneath—
Sort o' so's a man kin breathe
    Like he ort, and kind o' has
Elbow-room to keerlessly
    Sprawl out len'thways on the grass
      Where the shadders thick and soft
    As the kivvers on the bed
      Mother fixes in the loft
Allus, when they's company!
Lay out there and try to see

Jes' how lazy you kin be!
    Tumble round and souse yer head
In the clover-bloom, er pull
      Yer straw hat acrost yer eyes
      And peek through it at the skies,
    Thinkin' of old chums 'at's dead,
      Maybe, smilin' back at you
In betwixt the beautiful
    Clouds o' gold and white and blue!—
Month a man kin railly love—
June, you know, I'm talkin' of!

James Whitcomb Riley (1849-1916)

From U-Pick Marketing to U-Serve Gas

Elberta Walker and her husband Roy didn't intend to be developers. All they wanted was a site for their gas stations. "But it was all acreage in those days," said Elberta.

She was born Elberta Bascetta in 1915, one of eight children—four boys and four girls. At the time her parents, Joe and Congetta Bascetta, lived in the 200 block on East Sprague and leased a hotel at Sprague and Pine. "Not Pines," said tiny, gray-haired, 80-year-young Elberta. "Pine. That's downtown, next to Division. There's an engineering office there now."

After a short stay in Yardley, when Elberta was six years old the family moved to 7802 E. Mission where they truck farmed 80 acres of Valley land. "We had a home-made crew," she said.

When their home burned "about 1931," they bought the Mamer home which had to be moved to make room for Felts Field expansion. "Beardmore movers moved it onto our acreage," Elberta said. "Today it is the home of the *Senior Times*. You know who Mamer was, don't you? An early Valley flier. He was killed in a plane crash."

As far as Elberta knows, "U-pick Produce" in the Valley was an invention of her family and a turning point in Valley marketing.

"It was a hot summer," she said. "The irrigation flumes were breaking down. The market was tough. Our strawberries were ripe and labor was hard to get. We ran an ad in the *Chronicle* saying we had all the strawberries anyone wanted if they were willing to pick them. We did it to survive.

"It was a success! That was the beginning in the Valley of U-pick marketing—and we were able to pay our taxes!

"In those days especially farmers saw little need for educating girls. Mom and Dad couldn't read or write. They depended on us kids, so I was determined to finish high school. I left home and did it! I graduated from the old West Valley High in 1934 by living with and working for Mrs. Ed (Gladys) Bergh in the 11000 block on Mission. After high

school I went on—to Kinman Business School in Spokane.

"My business life began just about the time business began to bloom in the Valley. I worked in the plumbing department of the old downtown Ward's Department Store where the City Hall is today. Then as an extra at the Dessert Hotel. Waitressing paid 25 cents an hour. Then at Povey's Diner (where the Two Swabbies used to be on Sprague); at a heating company for $14.86 a week.

"Then the war came and I worked in the Supply Department at Galena Air Depot and a strange coincidence occurred:

"In 1939 I had worked briefly as a bookkeeper for Western Tank and Equipment. There I met a man named Roy Walker. He was affiliated with Inland Empire Refineries and had Idaho Chief and Idaho Panhandle gas stations. He had been in World War I as an orderly to General Patton.

"He enlisted in World War II and soon was transferred—Guess where!—to Galena Air Depot. In 1943 we were married and an entirely new life began for me."

After the war the couple bought some property on Sprague Avenue from A.T.Dishman and built the house she lives in today with her two brothers. (Her husband passed away in 1982.) "It was '$50 down and $50 when I catch you,' A.T. said. He financed most of Dishman," Elberta added.

"There was no water, nothing but a tumbledown chicken house, cheat grass and a gravel road on our property. We bought cheap cadmium pipe from the city and had a water line put in. Then we built a concrete block building and sold hamburgers. To get a quota of ice cream we had to buy The Fountain, then in the Byram Block in Millwood.

"But Roy wanted to go back into the oil business. In those days everything was acreages. I got my real estate license and helped Roy find sites for his gas stations. We always had to get 20 or so acres. So we developed the land around the gas stations, usually commercial and mobile home parks. There was the

R and E Addition at Mead, the Elberta Addition at Lincoln and Division and many more. But the one Valley people probably remember best is the U-Serve station at 8006 E. Sprague. It was the first U-Serve station in the Valley.

"First it was U-pick strawberries," reminisced Elberta.

"Then U-serve gas; then all those developments! There aren't many places where that could have happened. My mother and father came through Ellis Island, you know. Some day I'll tell you how my brothers built the old Dishman Rollerdrome—with A.T. Dishman's help."

The Early Dawn Dairy property, 2614 S. Best Road, Veradale, was purchased by Harold G. Anderson in 1923. The cattle were sold in 1973 and shipped to California. The dairy business was sold in 1978 to Consolidated Dairies (Darigold). Left to right: bull pens, horse barns, milking barn, plant in center; milkers home and family home (right). Twenty-fourth Street in background; Best Road, right foreground.
Courtesy of Roy Nyholm.

The Long Trail to the Early Dawn Dairy

By World War II the Early Dawn Dairy, founded, owned, and operated by Harold G. Anderson, had become one of the largest distributors of dairy products in the Valley.

During the war years expansion continued and Harold Anderson's two sons, Wes and Hal, and a son-in-law, Roy Nyholm, were taken into the business. It became a multi-million dollar operation with butter and ice cream manufacturing plants and Ice Cream Parlor restaurants in Idaho, Washington, and Montana and with 225 employees serving 12,000 families plus many wholesale accounts in the area. In 1960 the Washington State Dairy Federation honored the Anderson-Nyholm family by naming them "Dairy Family of the Year" for the Spokane area.

Roy and Marie (Anderson) Nyholm talked to me about the early days of Early Dawn Dairy in the office of their new home at Evergreen Point built on what was, less than ten years ago, Early Dawn grazing land. Wes and Alice Anderson and their brother Hal also have their homes on the former pasture land. Behind Roy's desk hangs a large colored aerial view of the 80-acre dairy in 1960, before subdivision of the area. The dairy plant is in the foreground of the photograph surrounded by unspoiled, expansive pasture land, with the picturesque shadowy purple hills that are south of the Valley in the background. It is a breath-takingly beautiful view of the Valley in by-gone years.

"In a way," Marie said, "we owe all of this to our brother Hal (Harold Anderson, Jr.) who was injured at birth. City life presented coping problems for him. Dad wanted the wide open spaces and a different kind of educational experience for him. On the original 10 acres here in the Valley at 24th and Best, he found both: Hal loved the farm, the animals and especially his horse, Blaze; and Edna De Witz, teacher at the little Saltese school where Hal was first enrolled, was wonderful for him."

The story of Harold George Anderson begins in 1896 in Sweden where a young girl named Ida Anderson and a young boy named Peter Anderson met and were married. (Ida didn't even have to change her name.) On a trip to Oslo, Norway, to visit her mother, Ida gave birth prematurely to their second son, Harold George (who ever after claimed to be a Swede although he was born in Norway).

Harold weighed only 3½ pounds at birth and was so tiny that his parents were not able to dress him for a long, long time. They kept him in a shoe box swathed in cotton and his ten brothers and sisters often referred to him as "the shoe box baby."

Harold was about five years old when the family came to America by boat, steerage class. That meant doing their own cooking en route. With scores of other immigrants they were processed through Ellis Island and came on by train to Spokane. On the train across the continent, as on the boat, again each family cooked for themselves. Fathers got off the train at station stops and bought needed food.

In Spokane Peter Anderson had trouble finding work. He was a carpenter and worked only seasonally. Money was scarce. Ida helped supply the essentials by keeping chickens and a cow and selling any extra eggs and milk to neighbors. Young Harold helped by selling newspapers on the streets of Spokane and bringing the money home to the family each evening. Thus the family of eleven children survived the lean early years in Spokane.

Harold was overjoyed when the *Spokesman-Review* offered him a regular route although it was too spread out to cover on foot before school in the morning. So each morning at about three or four o'clock, he saddled the family horse and rode from the home on the river bank east of the Green Street Bridge to the Review building to pick up his papers. Then, still on horseback he delivered them, finishing just in time to arrive at school before the "late bell" rang.

Adding to the family income seemed more important to Harold and his family than attending school. After the eighth grade, he quit. At 15 years of age he became a bell hop at the Spokane Hotel. Later he liked to tell of the celebrities he showed to their rooms—such as Mary Gardan, the opera singer, and Teddy Roosevelt who gave him a silver dollar tip.

Harold had many other odd jobs, all adding to his knowledge of business practices that would help him later when he established his Early Dawn Dairy. He delivered groceries in a horse-drawn cart for Coleman's Grocery on Second street in Spokane. Next he delivered for the Sanitary Grocery but in an up-to-date delivery truck with canvas curtains that rolled up and down depending on the weather and had SANITARY GROCERY painted in big letters on each side.

The owner of the Sanitary Grocery was Angus MacDonald who lived across the street from the grocery store. Angus had six daughters, one of whom was Jessie. Using every excuse in the book to spend time across the street, Harold eventually married daughter Jessie who then worked as the Green Wood operator at the telephone company on the north side of town. Her older sister Georgie was her boss.

About two months before he and Jessie were married, for $1800, with his brother-in-law, Andrew Freeborg, and his uncle, Carl Anderson, Harold bought a one-third interest in the Liberty Dairy in Spokane. At Liberty he drove a morning and an afternoon route, earning $15 a week plus all the milk the household could drink.

The story is that Harold and Jessie were married on a Saturday night and that when the alarm clock went off at 3 a.m. Sunday morning, Harold was up and off delivering milk! Jessie's dream of a honeymoon was not realized until many years later.

Later Harold built a service station on Mission and Division, bought the Quality Grocery nearby and eventually he and his father-in-law, Angus McDonald, had the Merit Grocery on Nora and Division—all the while hoping to somehow get back into dairying.

In 1921 he was able to rent a little milkhouse that had once been a carriage house on Mission in the East 200 block. While making the place usable, he came across a barrel of bottle caps printed, "Early Dawn Dairy." *

Anxious to begin business, Harold used the bot-

tle caps and assumed the Early Dawn name for his business and carefully delivered to a neighbor's back porch his first order: two quarts of raw milk and a bottle of cream. (This was before pasteurization.)

Harold bought the milk for his dairy from farmers who kept their cows along the Little Spokane River. In 1924 the city passed an ordinance making it unlawful to bottle and sell milk not produced where it was bottled. What a dilemma! He must find dairy buildings with grazing land.

After hearing that the Coeur d'Alene Creamery was for sale, he and Jessie went to Idaho to check it out. On the way home he stopped to visit Fred Hewitt, a friend, who operated a dairy farm in the Valley. To his surprise, he found that Fred's dairy was for sale.

When he discovered that Jessie his wife, although a city girl, had fallen in love with the beautiful Valley landscape, he returned the next day and bought the buildings and ten acres of what later became the 80-acre Early Dawn Dairy. Thus ended a long trail that began in Norway, crossed the ocean, and meandered around for a spell in Spokane before it found its resting place in our Valley.

Harold began his dairy operation in the Valley with two employees, the Hewitt boy and Joe Phillips. These two milked 44 cows by hand. There was only one milk route and Harold delivered that, about 700 quarts of milk a day. The hand bottler bottled only four quarts at a time. The furnace was fired with match blocks, the statements were written out on the dining-room table, and the back porch of the house became the dairy office.

Almost immediately after taking over the dairy, Harold found himself in the midst of a milk war. Milk was selling at 10 and 11¢ a quart. To survive the competition, Early Dawn began to bottle Orphan Annie milk at 5¢ a quart. (Harold said "it was all the same milk!")

All of Harold's energy and any extra money went into the dairy, much to Jessie's chagrin. Although

---

* The milk caps had originally belonged to Donald K. McDonald. You may remember from Volume I that with R.A. Hutchinson and A.C. Jamison, he pioneered irrigation in what later became known as Opportunity and Veradale. Veradale was named for his daughter, Vera. McDonald remained in the Valley area for many years and then turned his attention to Wilson Creek. There he drained swampy land and

made it suitable for farming. He had two ranches at Wilson Creek—the one near town was the Early Dawn Dairy. The milk from the dairy was put on the train each morning and delivered to 220 E. Mission where it was bottled and delivered.

It was in this building that Harold Anderson later found the barrel of Early Dawn caps.

she fed all the hired hands and did the laundry for the dairy, she didn't have a refrigerator in the house. Food was kept outside in the big dairy walk-in refrigerator in the milk house. One day she put her foot down and said she had carried food back and forth to the ice box long enough. The next day a refrigerator was delivered.

1932-1941 were critical years in the history of Early Dawn. Harold and Jessie almost ruined their health working long hours to meet the demands of the business during the Depression. During the war milk was not rationed but cream was and it was next to impossible to get trucks or even tires for what trucks the dairy had. Harold bought small failing dairies just to get their trucks.

He formed the Spokane Valley Canning Company to help Spokane Valley farmers market their tomatoes and string beans.

This was Harold's normal workday schedule during those years: he got up at four in the morning to take his milk route, came home to cultivate and irrigate their large vegetable garden, and in the evening, he packed tomatoes and other vegetables to sell on the routes.

In 1949 Harold purchased a competing dairy and began to hire help. He also eased the work load by purchasing pasteurizing equipment and by taking his sons, Hal and Wes and Roy Nyholm (Marie's husband) into the business. Expansion began with the acquisition of a butter plant in Tekoa and continued with acquisition of plants in Coeur d'Alene and Sandpoint. Soon, Early Dawn served eastern Washington, northern Idaho, and western Montana. By 1980 the business was diversifying by operating Ice Cream Parlor restaurants.

In Jessie's eyes, one of the most memorable events in the family history came in 1953 when she and Harold finally got away for their long delayed honeymoon. The dairy gang saw them off on a trip to New York to see the World Series.

"Harold Anderson, his wife, Jessie, their family and their many loyal faithful employees were the elements on which Early Dawn was built," said Wes Andersom. "Jessie may have been a city girl, but she proved that she could 'be country.' She worked long hours cooking, washing, and ironing for the many hired farm hands who boarded with them in the early years. In later years, Harold Jr. worked in the plant. I was production manager; Roy Nyholm was sales manager; Alice, my wife, ran the print shop producing the forms and stationery, and Marie worked in the office and did payroll. The grandchildren, Lorilee and Linda Nyholm and Mark and Dale Anderson did various jobs at the dairy and in the Ice Cream Parlors during their high school and college years. Early Dawn was truly a family enterprise."

Canneries

Before the residential influx of the World War II years, the majority of Valley property owners had acreages planted in orchards and gardens. Much of the produce, in addition to being used to feed families, was marketed commercially either fresh from the farm or in a preserved state. Pickling and canning were popular methods of food preservation, both for home use and commercial disposition. Often farmers had contracts with canneries for the bulk of their harvest.

In 1938 Harold Anderson, founder of Early Dawn Dairy, operated a commercial cannery between Sullivan Road and Conklin, adjacent to the Milwaukee RR in Vera. Estella Hanson and her husband, Myrten, worked there during the war. At that time Reid Duncan was in charge of the cannery office; Jake Mattson, the warehouse; and Myrten, the cannery itself.

"The cannery was considered a war effort," said Estella. "All forms of tomatoes (from whole to ketchup), green beans, squash, and pork and beans were canned there for the Armed Forces. Dog food for Armours was another cannery product.

"Because help was so scarce during the war," continued Estella, "Myrt and others worked 16 to 20-hour work days. Cannery workers, especially men, were almost impossible to keep. Those with a 1-A draft classification soon became members of the Armed Forces. Others worked a few days, then would disappear for better paying jobs at Farragut, Fairchild or the Naval Supply Depot at Velox. Some even went to the Boeing plant in Seattle.

"Myrt often left for work at 6:30 in the morning before our children were awake. After cleaning the conveyor belts when the cannery shut down for the day, he wouldn't get home until 2 A.M. the next morning. He was seldom home for meals. We realized our children wouldn't know their father if the war lasted forever (and we thought it would.) So at many dinner times, I took one-year-old Lavonne and seven-year-old Del to the cannery. We either brought the meal from home or went to the restaurant where Myrt ate near the cannery so they could spend some time with their father.

"It was during the time of rationing and food stamps. Cans were a critical commodity. Each empty can shipped into the cannery had to be accounted for. Dented empties were sent back to be remelted, but dented full cans could be given to the crew. These went out of the cannery without food stamps as they could not be guaranteed not to 'puff' and explode within six months.

"After the belts were silent for the night, freight cars out had to be loaded and freight cars coming in with empty cans to be filled had to be checked in. This entailed a lot of record keeping. I often took inventory as the men loaded and unloaded.

"We were all surprised one day. Two well-dressed men who had come in on a freight train appeared and asked for work. Myrt hired them on the spot. However, they seemed all too willing to work long hours and do hard jobs and kept popping up at unusual places and times. We called them "Snoopy One" and "Snoopy Two" behind their backs. We suspected them of being government men checking on our use of rationing buttons and tickets. One day they appeared with their suitcases, asked for their checks, and left on a freight train. We found out later that we were right: they were government men making sure rationed goods were not being used for illegal purposes."

*   *   *

In 1944, Karl B. Emery, Smith-Hughes Agricultural Director at Central Valley High School, obtained a community cannery for the Valley. Residents could take their surplus produce there and can it using cannery facilities or have it canned there for them.

Emery's idea was not only that the cannery would help ease the war-time shortage of food by encouraging preservation, but would also be an inducement to town folk to "Come out to the Valley, buy the produce and CAN it while you are here."

Emery's plan worked. The Central Valley Community Cannery became a popular destination. Although it was not completed until the middle of July 1944, interest in it was so widespread that 40,175 cans of fruits, vegetables, and meats were poured through the equipment by 377 families from the Spokane Valley and the city of Spokane. Tourists from as far away as Syracuse, N.Y. and Sullivan, Ill., made use of the cannery to take back choice Spokane Valley produce to their home-town communities.

Immediately after the successful 1944 season, Emery made plans to improve the facilities for 1945. He increased the equipment so that 50 per cent more users could operate more efficiently at one time. He opened early enough in the season so

that early produce, such as asparagus and peas, could be processed.

The kitchens of Valley old-timers continued to steam with the good smells of home canning. But for "gardeners" who settled here from eastern cities and had no idea how abundantly a package of seed would produce in fertile Valley soil, the Community Cannery was a welcome answer to the question, "What do I do with all this squash or corn or spinach?"

The Interstate Fair

Valley people love a fair. Even in times of economic stress when Fair attendance lagged, and finally when there was no Interstate Fair at all, somehow Valley people were able to keep the idea going by organizing local fairs and festivals.

Are you old enough to remember the crowds at the All-Valley Junior Fair at Dishman in 1926? Or at the Junior Livestock Show (much like a fair) in 1936? Or at the Spokane Valley Fair held in three buildings at Dishman in 1940?

Fairs and Valley people have a long history of togetherness. The title, Spokane Interstate Fair, first was applied to a carnival-like event that was held in September 1901, at the present site of Playfair Race Track. A grandstand designed by Kirkland Cutter was built and, although remodeled, is today among the oldest and most noted racetrack grandstands in the United States.

For thirty years thereafter the fair was a recognized annual event heralded by Valley residents. In addition to encouraging the production of prize livestock and garden produce, it offered a variety of unique and special attractions. Valley old-timers

still talk of September 1927, when Charles Lindberg in the *Spirit of St Louis* made a guest appearance at the Fair.

A decline in attendance began in the late '20s and reached a low point when the Depression became full blown. The 1930 Fair season became the last for more than twenty years. The grounds and buildings were sold to the city of Spokane.

Ups and Downs

In October 1935, a corporation known as the Spokane Fair and Racing Association leased the fairgrounds from the Spokane Parks Department. The corporation spruced up the grounds and grandstand and operated a 16-day racing season and called the site Playfair Race Course.

At the same time interested businessmen were trying to revive the annual fair by promoting local regional fairs. During the '40s, a small Spokane Valley-County Fair located in the 8100 block of East Sprague Avenue in Dishman. In 1944 it moved to the Playfair site for a three-day run.

In 1945 a determined Fair Association began

work to revitalize the Spokane Interstate Fair and continued that effort for seven years. In 1952 the Association was successful in securing the present 97-acre site on the southeast corner of Broadway and Havana and reopened the Fair there in late August of that year. The public responded with its support and the search began for a manager.

THE MEENACH BROTHERS

Charles and Ray Meenach were born in Valleyford, just south of the Valley. Their father was an ardent fair fan and early instilled in his sons the excitement of bringing home a blue or purple ribbon.

Charles once said his first big thrill came at age 12 in 1922 in the show ring at the old Interstate Fair. He was showing his five-month old Chester White Junior Champion Gilt against his father's Junior Champion Yearling Sow for the grand champion—and he won the purple rosette!

As a 4-H member Charles continued his interest in animals and won a trip to the National 4-H Club Congress in Chicago and was a member of the demonstration team there that won the National 4-H demonstration championship that year.

At Washington State University he studied animal science and after graduation in 1931 worked for the Agricultural Extension Service for 23 years.

In 1955 when the Interstate Fair needed revitalizing, Charles Meenach was right for the job and was hired.

At that time the fairgrounds consisted of 97 acres, just as it does today. However the buildings were far fewer: a main exhibit building (still there but much improved), a quonset hut with a dirt floor, one livestock barn, and some stalls. There were no trees, no flowers, no walks, and no grass—the grounds were dirt and rocks.

Charlie (as he was called by his friends) insisted that the grounds be clean, attractive, and appealing to the public. With the help (and sweat) of devoted board members, numerous businesses, and individuals who donated their time, materials, money,

and the use of equipment, the Fair took on new life. It became the showplace of the Inland Empire and one year won an award as one of the best landscaped fairgrounds in the United states. Masses of brilliant petunias bordered the entrance road; and beds of State Fair zinnias, a rose garden, dahlia plantings, a sunken garden, shade trees, shrubs, and acres of green grass created a park-like effect.

The public responded. The Fair became a major Fall event in the Spokane Valley. In 1960 it got a big boost when state law demanded that the County assume ownership.

The story does not end when Charles retired after 21 years service in 1975.

Brother Ray had worked with Charles as assistant manager the previous year. He became the new manager November 20, 1975.

His background was similar to Charles's. He received a degree in animal husbandry from Washington State University and farmed 400 acres between Valleyford and Spokane on the Meadowbrook Farm. On his farm his specialties were grain, alfalfa, and hogs. He had been a swine exhibitor at the first Junior Livestock Show in 1935 and attended every show for its 52-year history.

Later he served as president of the Junior Livestock Show and served as a livestock judge throughout the Northwest, specializing in the swine division.

When Ray became fair manager, his son took over his farm.

During his years as fair manager a youth center and indoor arena were added. By 1984 more than 300,000 people attended the 10-day event.

Ray served as Interstate Fair Manager for ten years, until 1985. That year the Fair hit a slump with attendance dropping almost 100,000. With much work and added attractions, interest returned in 1987 with a record high attendance of 353,515. Since that time, constant refurbishing and rebuilding have continued to make the Fair a major herald of Fall in the Spokane Valley.

The Junior Livestock Show

In the early days most Valley families had a garden, some chickens, and livestock. Usually the children had much of the responsibility for taking care of the animals and many developed a special relationship with their charges. Out of this interest in breeding, raising, and nurturing poultry and livestock grew the Future Farmers of America and 4-H groups.

In 1936 five men connected with the Old Union Stockyards in Spokane contacted FFA instructors and 4-H Club leaders and invited their youthful charges to participate at the Old Union Stockyards in what they hoped and planned would be Spokane's first Junior Livestock Show.

The objective of the Show, according to the founders, "was to stimulate interest among young people in the breeding, rearing and improving of domestic livestock" by providing a source of livestock knowledge for youth, by teaching youth to win and lose gracefully, by giving youth an opportunity to meet the business people who were sponsoring the show, and to encourage them to be better citizens.

Extra bonuses for the entrants were the chance to gain marketing knowledge about livestock and the chance to learn about the necessity of keeping abreast of changing consumer demands—more lean meat, for example, and the practical kinds of livestock to produce.

Although there was little time to get their animals ready and very few youngsters owned or could acquire creditable animals, one hundred and thirty-nine boys and girls entered baby beefs, lambs, or pigs in that first show. In contrast to today's totals, this was a small number and the quality of the animals entered was far inferior, but it was a beginning that was followed by continuing momentum.

It rained in 1936 for that first Junior Livestock Show. Participants and livestock got wet in spite of borrowed and rented tarps. There were no sleeping quarters except a few tents and some cots borrowed from the Forest Service. Hot dog stands and home-packed lunches were the only sources of food on the grounds.

Yet none of this dampened the spirits of the participants or the founders. The show was small and founders felt certain there would not be creditable entrants enough to claim the prizes, but they offered $3150 in premiums to be divided among the Future Farmers and 4-H members regardless. The placing of the animals by the judges was on the 1,2,3 basis down to 15th place in the fat cattle division, to 5th in the hogs and 5th in the lambs. Premiums offered ranged from $10 for first place to $1 for bottom placings in the cattle and $5 to $1 in the hogs and lambs. Champions, grand champions, and reserve champions were selected from among the top-rated animals. Boys and girls whose entries failed to reach an upper bracket in the judging received no money but relied for profit upon prices received in the sales ring.

In 1946 Show Town was organized with a view toward setting a pattern of conduct, maintaining order among the exhibitors during the show, and governing exhibitors' activities. Before the opening of the Show, all exhibitors met and went through the democratic process of electing Show Town officers: a mayor, a police chief, secretary, historian, police officers, and council members.

In the early years one of the officers from the State Patrol, County Sheriff, and Spokane Police took turns acting as advisor to Show Town officers. In later years the State Patrol did it. Especially, Trooper John Mittman is remembered for the professional and kindly manner in which he guided the Show for many years.

Being a participant in the Show had its emotional moments and its ups and downs. Having an animal crowned Champion was an undisputed high. Sad moments came when animals were disqualified for not making the weight requirement. At first any animal, even though of low grade and quality, was permitted to go through the regular auction sale. As the numbers increased and boys and girls became more experienced in selecting and fitting animals properly, those below grade were sifted out.

Other low moments came on sale day when an

animal belonging to a child who had become attached to it was sold. Russ Gladhart, manager of the Show from 1940-1979, once said that he had "more than once seen boys and girls break down hanging onto the necks of steers they had raised from birth, just before the animals entered the sales ring." Parents, too, had high and low moments— when they either heartily agreed or disagreed with the decision of a judge or when they saw their youngsters high or low. But it was all part of competition and learning how to become a good winner or loser.

Frank Funkhouser, who it is said "was an attorney by profession but a stockman by sentiment," was one of the founding five and president of the Show that first year. He summed up the intent of the founders in his opening day speech when he admonished the crowd saying, "America's greatest resources are not its gold, silver, timber, wheat or apples, cattle, or pigs, but its YOUTH. A few years ago it was discovered that this country was spending 12 billion annually for crime. That is many times more than the total cost of all our educational institutions."

In the early years awards were presented at a banquet. Major Fred T. Crimmins, speaker at the eighth annual banquet of the Spokane Junior Livestock Show at the Davenport Hotel in 1944 said, "No doubt many of you young people wish you could get into some branch of the military service to help win this war. Let me tell you that in the work you are doing [learning to provide food for the country] you are rendering as worthy and worthwhile service to your country as though you were on the very battle front itself. The ribbons that you have won represent something fully as important as the ribbons and medals worn by the men of the Army and Navy."

After World War II, facilities were improved. In 1947 the first dormitory—a steel quonset type building—was built for boys only. Ready for the young stockmen, also, was a new mess hall in connection with the restaurant at the stockyards so all meals could be obtained without leaving the grounds. Another new building contained showers, wash basins, and lavatory facilities.

In 1949 two more boys' dormitories were added and in 1952 a girls' dormitory and a 120 x 100 foot quonset show pavilion.

In 1950 the high light of the show was a 15-minute visit to the Old Union Stockyards by President Harry S Truman. He presented the grand champion awards to the exhibitor of the prize 4-H club and Future Farmers of America livestock entries. At the same show an announcement was made of a $15,000 building to be built at the Old Union Stockyards the following year. In 1979-80 judging contests, such as fitting and showing, and carcass contests were greatly expanded and the Junior Livestock Show was moved to its present home, the Interstate Fairground.

The Beginning of the Old Union Stockyards

[Spokesman-Review, May 17, 1914}

Spokane is to have a new Livestock industry in the establishment of a stock market to be known as the Spokane Stock Yards company. It has been incorporated with a capital of $500,000 by the following, who have been elected officers and directors of the new corporation: Walter N. Roberts, president; Harry A. Flood, vice president; John H. Roberts, secretary; James C. Cuinningham, treasurer; D.M. Drumheller, Frank C. Robertson, R.J. Danson, R.L. Rutter, and E.S. Sweet.

Most of the officers and directors of the company are well known here, having resided in Spokane and the Inland Empire for the last 25 or 30 years, and nearly all of them have, during the time, been actively associated with the business interests of this city. In addition to these men, the company has among its stockholders some of the most representative stockmen in the northwest.

The company has purchased the entire business and holdings of the J.H. Roberts Bros. company, including the horse market, which was established in Spokane in 1902, together with the real estate holdings comprising some 21 acres of land located in the East Side Sundicate addition, and immediately adjoining the packing houses of the east.

The property has a frontage of 1100 on the Northern Pacific railway right of way.

OLD UNION STOCKYARDS, LOCATED AT FREYA AND TRENT IN THE '30s.
Courtesy of Jim Seabeck, president of Stockland Livestock Exchange.

Charlie Rice, Meat Packer

In looking through the archives, the references to Charlie Rice were usually in relation to his Veradale Packing Company. But when I talked to Valley people about Charlie Rice, the talk was always about "those thick steaks from Rice's Opportunity Meat Market."

Then there were the people out at the Stockyards. They knew another side of Charlie Rice; they knew *him*. Russ Gladhart of Junior Livestock fame knew him for 50 fifty years. In 1988 he wrote an open letter for the magazine the Chamber of Commerce published for the Junior Livestock Show. I have found no better picture of Charlie Rice. I quote it here:

"Charlie has supported and attended every Junior Livestock Show since it started. Throughout those [show] years, he would always ask for a sales list early, so he could go through it and pick out exhibitors he wanted to support, especially those who needed help. Many times during a sale, he would stop everything, call me over to where he was sitting and ask, 'Does this lad need help?'

"Charlie grew up in Washington in the Big Bend country of the Snake River," continued Gladhart. "He farmed, chased wild horses, herded cattle. He was known as a rough, crusty little bowlegged 'rangatang.' His nick name was Boots. He was so little; his boots were nearly as big as he was.

"He went from the Big Bend country to Montana to work on a cattle ranch, but soon got tired of working for someone else. He went to Big Timber, Montana, to learn the meat business. From there he moved to Grangeville, Idaho, and started a butcher shop—then one in Pullman, Washington.

"Bigger things beckoned Charlie, On January 1, 1930 he arrived in Spokane with a wife and two boys. He didn't have a job but soon went to work for the Spokane Union Stockyards. He either walked to work or caught a ride with Chuck Glover. Chuck had a commission company at the yards.

"Again, the urge to be his own boss charged Charlie's competitive spirit. In 1932, on a shoe-string and with help from a friendly banker, he opened the Opportunity Meat Market and built his own little packing house on the land that he had gone in debt to buy. He bought, killed, and processed everything by himself, with the exception of one or two extra people on killing day.

"His motto was always quality and sanitation. I have heard him say many times, 'cleanliness is next to godliness.' He lived up to that statement; his place was always above reproach.

"In 1948, he and his sons built a new plant at Veradale and later added to it."

(Concerning that plant, a December 29, 1954 *Valley Herald* article gives this information: "The Rice family, Charles M. and sons Ralph and Gregg, has purchased the 120-acre Shelley Place including lake, in Veradale. They plan to develop it into a grassland cattle ranch.")

Continued Gladhart, "I have traveled with Charlie. One time I went to Olympia to attend a Brand Dept. meeting. It had to do with what he called 'those dam two-bit tri-podders.' These were people killing and selling meat without a license. He picked me up in his big Cadillac. We had just got to the freeway, and he started to clean his pipe, then fill and light it. Both hands were every place but on the steering wheel. He also used them to talk. I couldn't stand it any longer, so I said, 'Charlie, you don't have time to drive—just pull over and I will either drive or get out.' He pulled over, without missing a word or a puff. And he chewed tobacco at the same time as he smoked.

"When we got to Olympia, I took him to a motel. The next morning I was walking along the street going to the meeting place. Suddenly I heard cars honking, brakes screeching, the sound of bumpers making contact. There was Charlie. He saw me and was going to give me a ride but he stopped without any warning to those behind him. I rushed into the car and said, 'Charlie! You are going to cause a terrible wreck!' His retort, 'These dam drivers in Olympia don't know anything. This is the second time I've been honked at and I don't like it. They stay too close behind. To h—l with them.' That is Charlie.

"You always knew how you stood with him—never any doubt—if someone needed to be told off, he got told. Charlie doesn't hold grudges. He's a shrewd judge of livestock, he could figure yield and carcass value in his head quicker than most can on a calculator. I've seen him make monkeys out of some smart young buyers. He was always for the boys and girls. He would often say, 'They need to be encouraged, how can I help?'

"Yet he firmly believed they should earn whatever they got. He always had high principles and lived by them. I could always go to Charlie and get a ham, bacon, or whatever, if it was for a worthy cause. He would say, 'Help yourself.'

"Charlie was a self-educated man. He quit school after the sixth grade. He was a good citizen. Last fall on election day, when I went to vote, there was Charlie [at 93]. He couldn't walk so they let him vote sitting in a chair. On his way out he remarked that it is a privilege and a duty to vote and he was going to do it until he was gone.

"Charlie gave a lot and took little. He believed in integrity, hard work, and results. The world would benefit from more people like Charlie Rice. Thank you, old friend, for all you have done for me and others."

The letter is signed "Respectfully, P.R. Gladhart, Veradale, WA."

CHURCHES

"During the war years, the [Opportunity Presbyterian] church suffered ravages that could be borne with courage and hope only by a congregation having an unfaltering faith in the justice of God. Attendance at church services suffered because of transportation difficulties and a flag bearing 113 blue service stars hung in the sanctuary. Before the end of the war, nine of the blue stars were replaced by gold to remember those who were killed in service.

"Two trees planted in front of the church are living memorials to these boys."

[*Opportunity Presbyterian Church History and Directory*, Patricia Smith Goetter, 1988]

GIRLS BASKETBALL TEAM AT SPOKANE JUNIOR COLLEGE (ONCE SPOKANE UNIVERSITY) 1934
Spokane University was started by the Christian Church as a Bible College.
1st Row: Peggy McKay, Virginia Patten, Eileen Nichols, Martha Fenstermacher; 2nd row: Mary Helen
McDonald, Brita Penilly, Helen Larned; 3rd Row: Delberta Ash, Mabel Cory; (standing) Katharine Stiles.
Photo by Leo, Courtesy of Katharine Krell.

Churches

CHRONOLOGICAL HISTORY

1920

An All-Valley Sunday School Rally took place at **Greenacres.** The *Valley Herald,* September 3, announced that the following Sunday Schools had registered: **Greenacres, Opportunity** and **University Place Chrisitian; Greenacres, Saltese, Dishman** and **Opportunity Methodist; Opportunity** and **Orchard Avenue Community Presbyterian; Vera, Newman Lake, Otis Orchards** and **Trent Congregational; Opportunity Baptist, East Greenacres** and **Parkwater Union Sunday Schools;** a delegation from **The Hutton Settlement** and a Sunday School that met in the **Millwood Grade School.**

December 20: **Vera Community Church** was completed at **Sprague** and **Progress** under the leadership of the **Rev. Jonathan Edwards.** (See article, "Veradale, Veradale United Church of Christ, Dr. Edwards," Volume I.)

Millwood Community Presbyterian Church was organized with 78 members. **Paul E. Ratsch** was pastor.

1922

The **Methodist Church** at **Bowdish** and **Sprague** built an addition for a Beginners' Department.

Parsonage added to **Greenacres Methodist** property.

1923

Redeemer Lutheran Church was organized and services were held in the homes of members. (See article, "Redeemer Lutheran Church.")

September 23: The cornerstone was laid for **Millwood Community Presbyterian Church** on land bought from the Paper Mill. The building was dedicated the following year. **L.N. Williams** was pastor. The west wing was added in 1927. In 1937 a Mueller pipe organ was purchased, new pews in 1941, new carpet in 1942, and a manse in 1943.

1925

A.C. Rickle was called to pastor the **Opportunity Baptist Church.** He was a Valley pioneer who came to the Valley in 1907. When he built his first home in **Opportunity,** it was among the first 50 houses in the entire **Opportunity-Dishman District.** A daughter, **Juanita (Rickel) Johnson,** a long-time **Central Valley** teacher, was born in the house in 1908.

1926   A **Newman Lake** congregation united with the **Otis Orchards Community Church.**

1927   January 23: First portion of the original **Redeemer Lutheran Church** on **Argonne Road** (a chapel) was dedicated. **H. Schlesselman** was the pastor. (See article, "Redeemer Lutheran Church.")

October 14: **Opportunity Baptist Church** was destroyed by fire and services were held for a time in the unoccupied **Christian Church** on **S. Robie**. At that time the name was changed to **Spokane Valley Baptist Church.**

The congregation of the **Opportunity Christian Church** united with the congregation of the **University Christian Church** and met in **Science Hall** at the college. It was called the **Spokane United Christian Church.**

1928   July 22: Just nine months and eight days after being completely destroyed by fire, services were held in a new **Spokane Valley Baptist Church at Opportunity.**

Limits of **St. Paschal's Parish** extended to include people living in the district south of **Trent** and east of **Park Road** to **Argonne Road**.

1929   A new brick **St. Joseph's Church** with stained glass windows and oak pews was built to replace the "little white church on Trent" built in 1892, destroyed by a careless camp fire a year earlier. Cost: $16,500.

1932   July: Tent meetings were held at the **Millwood Gospel Tabernacle** for two weeks.

Two-week summer school held at **St. Paschal's** for Catholic training.

1934   May 12 (*Spokane Valley Herald*): Many people of the **Upper Newman Lake** area met at the **Green Mountain School** Sunday afternoon to organize a Sunday School.

When **Spokane University** closed its doors, the **Opportunity Christian** congregation that had united with the University congregation returned to its former building on **S. Robie**.

1935   **Lester Burton** organized an adult choir at **Opportunity Presbyterian Church.**

November 17: (*Spokane Valley Herald*) "Evangelist **A.D. Bohn**, speaking Sunday at the **Opportunity Town Hall**, predicted that, in spite of world-wide efforts for disarmament and peace, the world is heading for the greatest war that has ever been fought."

1939   **Dishman** and **Opportunity Methodists**, merged in 1936, completed preliminary plans for a single building, and laid the cornerstone at the corner of **Main**

1939

and **Raymond. Day Imus** donated the land for the church and parsonage. (See article, "The United Methodist Church.")

In memory of **Dr.** and **Mrs Jonathan Edwards**, their children presented a bronze plaque to the **Vera Community Church. Dr. Edwards** served the church for eleven years until 1924 . (See article, Volume I, "Veradale, Veradale United Church of Christ, Dr. Edwards.")

1940

St. Mary's Catholic Church at **Veradale** was completely renovated and stained glass windows installed.

A nondenominational church was organized at **Chester** by the **Rev. R.H. Hesseltine**. In 1947 a building was dedicated on a lot donated by Karl Thompson. A Sunday School, organized by **Alex Simpson** had been carried on as far back as 1910.

Fall: **Elders Keith Olson** and **Victor Riches** of the **Church of Jesus Christ of Latter Day Saints (Mormon)** organized a home Sunday School at the home of **Hyrum Maughan** in **Greenacres**. Before 1940 Valley **Mormons** attended church in Spokane at a chapel located at Fifth and Howard.

1941

February 9: Adjoining the original chapel, **Redeemer Lutheran** dedicated a recently built House of Worship.

Grant Cole became the first full-time pastor at **Opportunity Christian**. The **Doliver** home adjoining the church property was purchased for a parsonage.

August 17: **Mormon** meetings were held at the **Dishman Theater** until February 1942 when the **Veterans of Foreign Wars** building at **Valleyway** and **Sycamore** in **Dishman** was used. There were 24 members. **Hyrum Maughan** was the first Presiding Elder and **Eldon Jones** was the first Sunday School Superintendent. **Laura Wagstaff** was the first Relief Society President.

At the annual meeting of the **Spokane Valley Baptist Church**, the **Davidheisers, Janoskys**, and **Rickels** burned the mortgage.

1942

Edgecliff Community Baptist Church opened.

1943

St Paschal's had a school, Sisters' convent, rectory, and temporary chapel in the school basement.

1944

January: The **Mormon Church** purchased the Veterans' Building for $1500. In 1945 the Primary was organized with **Erva Orme** as the first president. By 1946 the congregation had renovated the building and the membership was 255.

1945

Millwood Presbyterian Church announced that there were sixteen gold stars on its service flag honoring the boys who lost their lives in World War II.

Opportunity Methodist Church, corner Appleway and what is now Bowdish Road,
built in 1919 and painted with crankcase oil.
Courtesy of Patricia Smith Goetter.

Church Was a Big Part of Our Lives:

[From Dr. Coddington's informal autobiography.]

We attended the Opportunity Methodist Church, just three eighths of a mile from our house. It was on the southwest corner of Bowdish and the Appleway (later called Sprague). The church was rustic brown, wooden, one story. The sanctuary was a high beamed ceiling with steel wires stretched for sliding curtain room dividers. There was a hot air furnace under the middle aisle. A metal grating about four feet square in the floor sent up a blast of hot air. When girls stood over it, their dresses ballooned out like hoop skirts.

There was a raised platform for the pulpit and piano. At the back of the room, a low-roofed lean-to addition housed the raised choir loft. On each side of the choir, doors led down into small Sunday School rooms. Behind those rooms was a larger one for primary classes. It was heated by a wood and coal burning kitchen range. That room served well for pot luck dinners. The choir loft served for staging plays and Christmas pageants.

It was a struggling church and sometimes couldn't pay pastors all their salary. Gifts of food and firewood often compensated for scarce money. A lot of fine people worked hard to make the church succeed.

Clyde Mahan, a part-time carpenter who owned five acres facing Shelley Way, was my Sunday School teacher. His grammar and diction were often faulty, but he loved and believed his *Bible* and he was every bit as honest as Abraham Lincoln.

After his Model T Ford delivery truck was destroyed by a freight train at our grade crossing between Shelley and the Appleway, he bought himself a big flat bed truck with a Ruxtel axle that gave him a wide range of low gear. It could pull through irrigation ditches in a damp field with a heavy load of hay.

On Christmas Eve he heated a dozen large rocks in a bonfire. Piling them in the center of his truck bed, he surrounded them with deep fresh straw. He covered the straw with strips of canvas. The older kids from our church sat on the canvas with their feet to the rocks. They covered their legs with warm blankets. Mr. Mahan drove us into the yards of the ill and elderly to sing Christmas carols. We stayed warm even when it was snowing and windy.

Mahan's garage, chicken house, and cowshed burned to the ground one night. The truck and livestock were saved. Early one Saturday morning friends from all over the community gathered in the Mahan yard with picnic supplies and carpenter tools. Under Clyde's supervision, a two-story barn was built in one day.

Mother taught a Sunday School class of marriageable girls. When one of them became engaged, it was an excuse for a quilting bee. She would assemble her class at our house on a Friday night for a potluck dinner. After dinner the girls would retire into the living-room, leaving Robert and me to do the dishes. There they made the quilt according to Mother's directions. When the quilt was finished, it looked very pretty. The party was over and the lucky girl took her quilt home.

The Methodist Conference bought twenty acres on the shore of Lower Twin Lake, ID. The grounds were named Twinlow. At the first Epworth League Institute at Twinlow Park, we lived in tents and ate in a larger tent. Carpenters had set up two large rest rooms on the hill. Classes and services were held in the open. We had a delightful week of supervised games, swimming, and evening campfires. We did lots of singing accompanied by ukeleles, band instruments, and one battered piano. The following year a dining hall and kitchen were in operation and men were working on a small dormitory building.

My brother Robert graduated from high school in June 1929. He got a job with the Washington Water Power Company as a member of a crew surveying for a power line in Fourth-of-July Canyon near Worley, ID.

When Robert left for his surveying job, I took his place as janitor for our church. For five dollars a month I swept floors, dusted pews and woodwork, and in winter stoked the furnace and kitchen stove very early on Sunday mornings. In summer I kept the lawn watered and mowed.

From my salary I made my first pledge of 50¢ a month to the church.

The hymn, "The Little Brown Church in the Vale," always brings back good memories of that congregation.

The United Methodist Church

The United Methodist Church, in 1994 located at E. 10428 Main, is a combination of three pioneer Valley churches that had their beginnings as follows:

In 1906 an interdenominational group, including many Methodists, met for Sunday School and worship in the basement of the original Opportunity Grade School at the corner of the Appleway and Bowdish Road. A short time later the group moved to the Opportunity Town Hall.

Also in 1906, the construction of a Methodist Church building was started in Greenacres. Unfortunately this burned before services were held. A second church was built in 1908.

In 1910 a group of Dishman residents met for Sunday School and worship in the then new Dishman School.

On Wednesday evening, April 15, 1908, during the superintendency of Rev. U.F. Hawk, Methodists from the interdenominational Opportunity group determined to form their own church. They also determined to build a temporary building. Land was donated by Clyde Mahan on the southwest corner of the Appleway and Bowdish. During the cold and rainy fall of 1911, the Opportunity Methodist Church was completed at that location.

From the memories of the late Mrs. J.I. Collins, we learn that the building in 1924 was painted with a mixture of crankcase oil and brown pigment and that the "stained glass windows" were panels of colored paper cut out by the women of the church. Mrs. Collins also related that Oscar Reinemer hauled the lumber for the building from Hillyard with a team and sled. (See also "Church Was a Big Part of Our Lives" by Dr. Coddington.)

A Methodist Church was built by the Dishman group in 1914, and came under the charge of the same pastor as the Opportunity group, the Reverend M.R. Brown.

By the early thirties, both the Dishman and the Opportunity churches were inadequate. The two groups merged. Preliminary plans were laid for a single new building and in 1939 members broke ground, completed the basement, and laid the cornerstone for the new building at the corner of Main and Raymond, the site of the present day Memorial Chapel. The land was donated by Day Imus.

When spring arrived in 1940, the social hall and Sunday School rooms were completed and "moving day," April 14 , Palm Sunday, found both Dishman and Opportunity Methodists settling into the new building. By the fall of 1942, the sanctuary was complete and services were held there. Among the memorial gifts was an electric organ provided by the Greenacres Church. This proved to be a signal of things to come; for in 1970, a group from Greenacres joined the United Opportunity and Dishman Methodists, thus uniting three pioneer congregations.

Of interest to historians is the present-day lighted bell tower. The bell is from the old Dishman church that was built in 1914. When the new church was built in 1939, Clyde Mahan and John Coddington took the bell down and moved it to the new location.

The bell tower of that building was supported by walls of the building and the roof rafters. About 1960 the roof rafters were noted to have sagged and the tower tipped. Both bell and tower were taken down. The bell was stored in the basement for years.

In the late 1970s, memorial funds were solicited to house the historic bell in the present tower with its lighted cross. Knox Abbott spearheaded the fund-raising drive and Agnes Niles contributed substantially in memory of her late husband.

Redeemer Lutheran Church

[*Spokane Valley Today*, August, 1987]

The 1100 member congregation of Redeemer Lutheran Church, N. 404 Argonne Road, expects to occupy its new 10-acre site at Dishman-Mica and Shaeffer roads early this fall. The groundbreaking for the new church, which will cover about 22 acres of the site, was held June 8, 1986. The remaining ground will be used for parking, recreation, and future projects.

The new structure will feature a high school-size gym and an open-room teaching concept for the Sunday School with flexible dividers to accommodate various class sizes.

The Argonne Church home on Argonne Road is for sale.

Redeemer Lutheran has been an important part of Valley community life since the '20s. Shortly after irrigation set the Valley abloom, Reverend Vandre of Rockford canvassed the Valley for Lutheran prospects. By 1923 nine families were recruited (although only men could hold office) and an organizational meeting was held January 1924.

That fellowship of believers called themselves Our Redeemer of the Valley. The name Lutheran Church of Spokane Valley had been temporarily used.

It is interesting to note that the name has been changed many times. When the young congregation was incorporated June 12, 1926, the Articles of Incorporation stated that the non-profit corporation would be known as Redeemer Evangelical Lutheran Congregation of the Spokane Valley.

In 1976 the official name, stated in the Articles of Incorporation as amended by the congregation, read Redeemer Evangelical Lutheran Church of Spokane.

Adjoining the present sanctuary is a 24'x 48' assembly room (as it is now called) which was the first portion of the original structure. It was dedicated January 23, 1927. A $2500 loan used for the project and granted by the General Church Extension Board, was paid in 1939. The present House of Worship was begun in 1940, and dedicated February 9, 1941. When a Hammond organ was installed in 1946, a publication of that company described the church as follows:

"This harmoniously proportioned church was designed by the Reverend J.F. Merz himself (then pastor) without the assistance of an architect; and its furnishings, including the valuable mahogany altar, pulpit and lectern and hand wrought iron hanging lamps were designed by him and hand-made by church members. Over eight thousand hours of volunteer labor went into the building, members of the congregation manning the plows, slips and tumble bugs and doing construction work with advice and guidance from one hired carpenter. The women and young folks, too, took a hand.

"To look at this beautiful church of Gothic inspiration and modern, functional design, no one would guess that Pastor Merz, who made the first miniature model as well as planned the building in every stage and supervised construction, had not had one ounce of formal training along those lines. The congregation did not even allow themselves the 'luxury' of a paid contractor, and at all points limited hired help to a tiny minimum, with the happy result that the entire church plant is free from debt."

INTERESTING HISTORICAL FACTS

Along with his pastoral duties, Pastor Merz was also responsible for spraying the trees. At that time the property, like so much of the Valley, was orchard. In 1937 the fruit trees were removed to allow parking space.

In 1932 it was necessary for the congregation to post "No Hunting" signs.

During the pastorate of Reverend H.L. Schlesselman, German services were held at 10:00 a.m. every first and third Sunday of the month in 1927. In 1931, the early morning German services were again a part of the life of the church and continued through 1945.

In 1937, James Caro was given congregational authority to begin a Men's Club.

Until 1946 when the Hammond organ was purchased, Redeemer had a pump organ. The organ "pumper" was paid 35¢ a Sunday, 50¢ when there was a communion. The present Conn organ was presented as a gift to the congregation by Mr. and Mrs. William Tanke in 1966.

In the '40s when Valley growth spurted because of war related activity, Redeemer also grew. A janitor was hired for the first time in 1944 and was paid $120 a year. The first copy machine, a renovated mimeograph, was purchased in 1944. The following year the church council approved a filing cabinet for the Reverend Merz. A call was made for a volunteer secretary. That office was filled by Louise Peters.

From that time, Redeemer Lutheran Church continued to grow in numbers, additions to the plant, and in activity. In 1951, the Christian Day School program was added but was terminated some years later.

In 1959 Pastor Arthur Fergin and Carl Kappen, a member of Redeemer, realized their dream when the New Hope Training Center for the Handicapped held its first class in one of Redeemer's classrooms. This Center soon outgrew church space and moved to N. Willow Road, a church-owned residence at the time. New Hope Training Center is now located on church property at N. 421 Mullen Road.

Redeemer currently has two pastors using a team approach as they serve members. They are Reverend Philip Streufert, lead pastor, and Reverend Douglas Brauner, assistant pastor. It is their hope, and that of the congregation, that the new building will be a means of greater service, not only to their people, but to the entire community.

The new building is expected to cost between one and two million dollars.

Opportunity Presbyterian Church, southwest corner of Pines and Main, as it was from 1919 to 1949. Reverend John Clayton on steps. Note the apple orchard surrounding the church.
Courtesy of Robert Nelson.

Opportunity Presbyterian Church:

[Excerpts from *Opportunity Presbyterian Church 1913-1988,* by Patricia S. Goetter, 1988.]

Opportunity—the community—had been in existence only eight years when Opportunity—the church—was organized on March 2, 1913. It started life as the Neighborhood Presbyterian Church of Opportunity with a charter membership of 65. By 1917 it was referred to optimistically as the First Presbyterian Church of Opportunity, but before long had settled into the name which it bears today.

Sent into the field by the Presbyterian Home Missions Board, Dr. S.M. Ware organized the original church body, drawing upon a Sunday School which had been formed a few weeks earlier by the Sabbath School Missions of the local Presbytery.

The first church meeting was held in the newly constructed Opportunity Town Hall, a building still in existence on Sprague near Robie. Services continued to be held there until 1916, when the congregation voted to move west a couple of blocks to larger quarters in the Opportunity Grade School at Sprague (then Appleway) and Bowdish.

With no real home of its own, the church made do with what was available. Session meetings, informal and mobile, were often held in the lumber company office or, as recalled by Rev. Ray A. Weld, "in Mr. Hammond's store with the elders sitting on nail kegs to discuss the business of the church."

During the early years of the church, the salaries of the pastors were subsidized by the Home Missions Board. In turn, each pastor was expected to serve in a missionary capacity in both Opportunity and Yardley. To do so Pastor Weld, who had begun his pastorate at the church in 1917, "drove back and forth with a horse furnished me by Mr. Harry Nelson."

It was during his tenure that the congregation made its move to the schoolhouse to accommodate the growing membership. In answer to obvious need and concerted "prair," members laid building plans, paid their pledges in Liberty Bonds, and on November 23, 1919, dedicated their red brick, steepled sanctuary on the Pines Road knoll above the growing Opportunity community.

The notable day was announced by 300 printed handbills and was marked by music and thanksgiving. It must have been a bittersweet occasion for, as attested to by plaques affixed to the stained glass windows of that building, three young men of the congregation—Edwin Olsen, Tom Blezard and Ralph Kramer—had been killed in action in France in October of the previous year, one month before the Armistice at Compiegne.

Complicating every effort in that period was the worldwide flu epidemic of 1918-20 in which nearly 22 million people died. Despite the fact that "owing to the influenza epidemic and sickness generally," only half their scheduled meetings were held, the church's Women's Guild in 1919 raised $225, twice as much as the church's benevolence receipts of $117.

During Dr. J. Fraser Cocks' tenure as pastor, early in the 1920s, an unsuccessful attempt to establish a choir was made, and a consideration to build a manse got no further than that.

The matter of the church debt was of great concern at that time, so much so that officers decided to "invite" the Sabbath School and the flush Women's Guild to join the move to pay off creditors.

When the Rev. A.B. Blades assumed the Opportunity pastorate in 1924, there had been several short-term pastors. It appeared he would be another temporary shepherd: his term was set at six months. It lasted more than 10 years, and despite difficult economic times, it proved to be a period of increased vigor, independence and membership, with the congregation growing from 99 to 176 in the first two years.

At the time of Rev. Blades' arrival, the church was said to be in "distressing financial condition," and during much of his tenure the Great Depression challenged the survival of individuals and institutions in Opportunity as much as in the rest of the world. Both church and members lost money when the Opportunity and Dishman banks failed. But Pastor Blades who was described as being "a happy man—cheerful, hopeful and optimistic—" was the right man for the times.

Because attendance at movies was frowned upon then ("King of Kings" was the exception), Pastor Blades organized and directed the young people of the church in The Happy Hour Players, a dramatic club that entertained the community with productions at the grade school auditorium. Tickets went for 35¢ (adults), 20¢ (children), and 50¢ (reserved seats). Receipts were used to purchase hymn books which in 1950 were still in use in the Sunday School.

In a recent interview, Octavia Blades Edwards, youngest child of Pastor and Mrs. Blades, remembers Opportunity as a fine place in which to grow up, and "those dear people" who despite the times, gave the Blades family $200 and food for a vacation trip east in their stuffed-to-the-running boards Model A.

Hard times were not over when the Rev. Donald R. Caughey accepted the pastorate at OPC in 1935, following Pastor Blades' retirement; but receipts did increase during his time there. In an attempt to increase Sunday School numbers, he devised a plan wherewith prizes would be awarded for consistent attendance, but in his 1937 report noted that he, Mrs. Caughey and their two children were the only ones who had qualified. He added that he still hoped their select group would soon be joined by others, and he apparently had some success. By 1940, the Sunday School was prosperous enough to purchase chimes for the bell tower.

Overnight it seemed the Valley changed as world conflict reached even into the sanctuary of the parish church. The ambiance of war was ever present. Servicemen were entertained by church families, women knit for the Red Cross, the church voted to subscribe for $10,000 War Risk insurance on the building, and a red and white satin service flag set with 113 blue felt stars, hung in the sanctuary. Two of those represented Pastor Almond, who became a chaplain in the U.S. Army and Pastor Caughey, a chaplain in the U.S. Naval Air Corps.

Ultimately, nine of the blue stars were replaced with gold, representing the lives [lost] of Chester Bennett, Jerry Coble, Arnold Derifield, Ned Finch, Andrew Gnagey, Wesley Hagen, Raymond Keller, Leon Stuart, and Richard Titus. The accompanying Roll of Honor was marked with such notes as, "Died in a Japanese POW hospital," and "Killed in action over Kiel, Germany."

Two evergreen trees were planted in front of the church as living memorials.

A Church for Yardley

[From a true story by Lois Seehorn Larson, formerly of Yardley, now of Portland, Oregon.]

My family lived in Yardley in the '20s and '30s. It was about five miles east of Spokane near the Northern Pacific Railroad Division Yards. In the town were warehouses where produce and manufactured goods were stored while awaiting shipment by rail. My sister Erma and I liked to watch the freight cars switching back and forth making up trains on Yardley's numerous tracks. The roundhouse where mechanics repaired and checked the gigantic engines after each run was a busy place, too.

At one time entrepreneurs expected Yardley to become a Spokane satellite. Surveyors' markers still remained on lots they hoped to sell to trainmen, roundhouse mechanics, and office workers. Two rival boarding houses catered to trainmen between runs. The most popular of the two was operated by the Strong family.

We knew the Strongs. They lived in the back of the rooming house. All the family helped prepare and serve meals and helped keep the bedrooms clean.

One quiet summer night, the Strongs walked to our house to visit. Mrs. Strong and Mother were planning to start a Sunday School and church in Yardley. They had found an itinerant pastor who was able to arrange to preach once a month, so they wanted to start a campaign to raise money for materials and labor to build a one-room country church. They enlisted the help of as many Yardley men and women as possible. Potlatch Lumber Company donated some material and sold some to the group at cost. Railroad men donated money and labor. The women held a series of socials to raise money.

I can remember one strawberry ice cream social in particular. My father drove a wagon to the Stanton Meat Packing Plant for large slabs of ice. Then after Mother made the mixes, Father turned the crank on our ice cream machine and other borrowed machines. Some of the women made cookies and cake and stemmed strawberries. These tasty refreshments sold for 5¢ an item.

Soon the little church under the locust trees was in use. A pump organ was donated. This especially pleased Mother because she was to become the church organist. Everyone felt pride—Yardley had a church of its own!

Yardley also had a jitney service into Spokane and back twice a day. Erma and I were returning from Spokane one summer day in the open air vehicle. Ahead of us was a small truck kicking up clouds of dust. Through the dust we could see the driver of the truck smoking a cigarette and flicking ashes with one hand while he drove with the other. We wanted our driver to pass the truck but he couldn't because of the dust screen.

To our horror we saw the truck driver throw the burning stub of the cigarette into the dry grass along side the road. Immediately the grass flamed. But the truck driver continued on. The gentle wind fanned the flames and the fire spread rapidly—toward the new church that Yardley folks were so proud of.

My mother screamed, "Stop! Let us out. Fire! Fire!"

She jumped from the jitney, untied her long underskirt and ran toward the church, beating at flames as she went.

She screamed to me to run to the nearest neighbor's for help. I could see her, a frenzied robot, beating at the crackling flames now burning under the locust trees and licking the side of the building. Flaming dry leaves fell from the locust trees onto the roof. It burst into flame.

Neighbors came running with buckets, shovels, and gunnysacks. Someone shouted, "I have the key to the church!" But it was too late. The roof caved into the blazing interior. There was no way to save the precious church.

Exhausted, Mother had to be helped to a place where she could sit down. The church, songbooks, benches, and the treasured organ were destroyed in minutes. Nothing was left. She gave way to sobs and tears.

Weary and heart broken, we walked the mile to our house in the hot noon-day sun. Mother was in a daze.

I whispered to Erma, "How could God let our Sunday School burn?"

Spokane Valley Churches, 1941-1942

OPPORTUNITY
Spokane Valley Methodist, Rev. H.L. Slick
Spokane Valley Baptist, Rev. Luther
Plankenhorn
Spokane Valley Christian, Rev. Wm. Sutton
Spokane Valley Presbyterian, Rev. George
Almond

GREENACRES
Greenacres Methodist, Rev. O.S. Baker, supply
pastor.
Greenacres Christian, Rev. George B. Thomas

DELMONTE
St. Paschal's Catholic, Rev. Frederick Brohman

TRENT
St. Joseph's Catholic, Rev. M.P. Sheil

VERADALE
St. Mary's Catholic, Rev. M.P. Sheil
Vera Community Congregational, Rev. P. Wm.
Westwood
Seventh Day Adventist, Glenn Knudson

MILLWOOD
Millwood Community Presbyterian, Rev. L.N.
Williams
Christian and Missionary Alliance Tabernacle,
Rev. H. Larson

OTIS ORCHARDS
Eden Community Congregational

DISHMAN
Redeemer Lutheran, Rev. J.F. Merz
Church of Jesus Christ of Latter Day Saints

Schools

"When the question of the high school was first suggested, a good deal of bitter opposition was aroused. Many people felt that the education of children at public expense should end with the grammar grades. But just as 'a continual dripping of water wears away the stone,' so, in time, enough people came to our way of thinking to permit the organization of the [high] school.

"You will still find many who object strenuously to the so-called 'higher education' for the masses of the people."

[*The Wide Northwest,* by Leon L. West, Shaw and Borden Printers, Spokane, Washington, 1927]

A 1924/25 CLASS AT THE YOUNG SCHOOL, YARDLEY AND CATALDO.
Row 1: Paul Fumith, Jack Megary, Howard Larsen, Geoge Moline, Paul Rainey; Row 2: Margie McDougall,
———-, Esther Gumm, Filameda Carlos, Rose Williamson, Irene Howlet, Kathryn Beldon, Opal Box, Vernon
Harris; Row 3: Shirley Coleman, Beatrice Bryant, Alma Heinzerling, Miss Anna E. Heller, Mabel Jensen, Lucil
Baley, Virginia Harris; Last Row: Vivian Moline, Mary Zahniser, June Shaeffer, Alma———-, Audrey Larsen.
Courtesy of Mary and Martha Summerson.

Schools

CHRONOLOGICAL HISTORY

1919   The **Orchard Park District** became a second class district.

1920   The **Seventh Day Adventist** remodeled their school at **Otis Orchards.**

Millwood High School classes were held in the **Millwood Grade School** building. It had a Commercial Department headed by **Mrs. Raymond Kelley.**

1921   A conference was held to decide whether or not to annex **Orchard Park** to **Spokane. Spokane** rejected the offer, believing that the assessed value of **Orchard Park** land had not kept up with the financial liability of the enrollment.

Pleasant Prairie, Trent, and Orchard Park met to discuss the possibility of forming a union high school.

Consolidation of school districts was favored. **Moab, Canfield Gulch** and **Otis Orchards** united in 1922.

Lone Fir and **Saltese** formed a high school district.

The **Spokane Valley Woman's Club** approved plans for a **Union High School** with a community auditorium.

In **Otis Orchards** a low one-story high school was erected immediately west of the **Cobblestone School**. It had the largest gym in all the surrounding areas. Demolished June, 1970.

1922   **Opportunity** approved a $20,000 bond levy to be used for an addition to the school.

A high school addition to **Millwood Elementary** was built.

A.B. Ness, for whom a school was later named, became superintendent of **Orchard Avenue District**, succeeding **C.O. Gordon.**

1923   August 31: **Central Valley Union High School District #201** was formed from **Quinnemosa** #160, **Liberty Lake** #78, **Saltese** #39, **Lone Fir** #128, **Greenacres**

1923

#113, and **Vera** #40. The first high school in the district began in the **Vera Grade School** building with less than 100 pupils. It was first called **Appleway High School**. Students objected to the name and it was changed to **Central Valley High School**. Later **Mica, Chester,** and **Opportunity** joined the **Central Valley District**.

June 20: The completion of **Parkwater School** was authorized by the Millwood Board.

Moab School on **Starr Road** consolidated with the **Otis School.**

Brick school at **Greenacres** burned and another one erected immediately.

1924

Five rural school districts joined to form the **Post Falls District** and a $43,000 bond issue was voted to finance a new building for the union high school.

March 12: **Trent, Pleasant Prairie** and **Orchard Park School Districts** became Union High School District #202. The **Orchard Park** District comprised **Parkwater, Orchard Avenue, Dishman, Millwood** and **Pasadena Park Schools.** On August 1 construction of a high school building was begun on a 7 ¾ acre tract facing **Trent Road** near **Argonne** adjacent to the elementary school. Union high school cost: $95,000.

May 1: **Orchard Avenue** approved a $32,000 bond issue and contracted for two identical schools on July 1. Sites: 2⅔ acre immediately east of the **Orchard Avenue Community Hall** and 1⁹⁄₁₀ acre in **Pasadena Park** at intersection of **Argonne** and **Upriver Drive**. First four grades in each building. To relieve crowding in **Orchard Park, Parkwater,** and **Pasadena Park.**

West Valley School District #363 was formed.

1925

Otis Orchards purchased a dark gray Reo, its first school bus. Cost, $2738. Its capacity was 38 students and it served the **East Farms** to **Moab** route. **Henry Mints** was the first driver.

February: Students moved into the new **West Valley High School.** High school subjects had been first taught by the district in 1910 in the **Orchard Avenue** school building.

Post Falls had its first high school commencement with 11 graduates.

1926

The first night school was held at **Central Valley**.

New concrete and brick gym at **Spokane University**. Old wooden one burned in 1924.

June 19: Old one-room cobblestone schoolhouse at **Pasadena Park** sold at auction for $1,665. It was converted into a house.

1926

November 12: The **West Valley Board** authorized a kindergarten on a trial basis. **Mrs. Cora Berg** was the first teacher. It was popular from the beginning but had to be discontinued during the Depression.

1927

West Valley assumed the responsibility for the educational guidance of young patients at **Edgecliff Hospital**. (See article, "School at Edgecliff.")

CV voters approved a new high school building on 122 acres on the back part of the property on which the old building stood. There was 600' frontage on the **Appleway**. The site was donated by **Spokane Valley Farms Company**, owners of **Corbin Addition** to **Greenacres**. The new building opened in January 1928, with a library.

Otis Clubhouse, the site of graduation exercises, burned. From thenceforth, graduation was held in the high school gym. The first **Otis** graduation had been held in the Fruit Growers Warehouse.

1927-28

Departmentalization began for 7th and 8th grade students at **Millwood**. It was considered successful and continued until the 1936-37 school year.

1929

School safety patrols were organized at **Dishman, Millwood, Orchard Avenue** and **Parkwater**.

May 3: **La Verne Almon Barnes** of **Opportunity** was awarded the first Doctor of Philosophy Degree ever conferred at **Washington State College**.

Consolidation of all Valley school districts into one district was seriously considered in order to equalize the tax support for schools. One district had only $1,026.76 assessed valuation backing each child, while another had $8,047. The problem was not solved.

1930

For safety reasons, national specifications for school buses were written. All had to be chrome yellow to be easily recognized.

August 25: Classes were held in a new $25,000 cream stucco grade school that replaced the **Cobblestone School** at **Otis,** destroyed by fire the same year.

Spokane University Boy's Dorm burned.

A frame gym was built at Central Valley.

The first hot lunch program began at **Otis**.

Visual aids were introduced into Valley curricula.

1932

Summer school with two 6-week sessions was held at Central Valley.

The **Valley Chamber of Commerce** with **J. Frank Giboney** as president tried unsuccessfully to raise enough money to help the financially crippled **Spokane**

1932

University. The **University** closed and became **Valley Junior College**. In 1935 it became **Spokane Junior College** and moved into Spokane. (See article, "Spokane University," Vol. I.)

Parkwater Grade School closed and pupils were sent to **Orchard Avenue School**.

West Valley High School discontinued transporting pupils because of the Depression. However, $16,000 was voted in bonds for an addition to the high school.

Liberty Lake voted to keep its own school rather than transport its pupils to **Vera**.

1933

Idlewild, Green Mountain and **Newman Lake Schools** consolidated with **Otis Orchards**.

1934

Senior girls at **CV** formed a club to promote girls' athletics.

June 9 (*Spokane Valley Herald*): "14 students will receive graduation certificates at the first annual commencement of the Spokane Valley Junior College, Monday night."

1935

Thanks to the **WPA**, 40 men were employed to erect a 70x40-foot Industrial Arts Building at **Central Valley High School**. At **West Valley High School** 21 men were employed on a 50x32-foot locker room and shower for boys. An addition, 20x20 feet and two stories high to **Greenacres** school building was for fuel below and a library above. (See "WPA to the Rescue.")

1937

Central Valley was one of twelve schools granted a new agriculture department to deal primarily with animal production and farm management. Willard Kaiser, director.

1938

40 members of the **West Valley Band** got new orange and black military caps, orange and black capes and black sweaters and white pants. The band was busy rehearsing for the Armistice Day football game with **Central Valley**.

Kiwanis Club organized a safety patrol at **Otis Orchards**. A patrol was also organized at **Central Valley**.

Washington State passed a minimum wage law for teachers: $100 per month.

1939

Failure to pass a 5-mill levy for **Opportunity Grade School** resulted in a one-member reduction in faculty and the continued use of an inadequate heating plant. Lack of voting interest rather than opposition was given as the reason for the failed levy. 370 votes were required. Only 339 were cast, 300 of those were favorable.

Redford Hall at **Spokane U** became a home for the aged when the University defaulted on its mortgage payments.

1940   A four-room school was built at **Dishman** with a gym and locker rooms and other auxiliary facilities. Labor and some materials were furnished by the **WPA**.

August: 2-room **St Paschal's Parish School** was built at **Park** and **Marietta**. Two classrooms were added in 1942.

1941   A gymnasium to seat 900 spectators was built at **Opportunity Grade School**.

Central Valley High School's Douglas Field was the first high school field in the area lighted for night games. **Central Valley** Student Association furnished the labor.

1942   A kindergarten was started at **Orchard Park School** in **Millwood** and at **Veradale**.

1943   The **East Trent District** was divided in half. Residents west of **Flora Road** joined the **Trent School District** and residents east of **Flora Road** consolidated with **Otis Orchards**.

1944   July: Ground was broken for the new **Trent School** at **Trent** and **Pines Road** four classrooms, an office, library, and teachers' room. Cost: $39,000. In 1945 a cafeteria, gym, and four classrooms were added to the original building.

Trent voters purchased 72 acres of land southwest of the school building.

Washington State Patrol formed school safety patrols at schools.

1945   Kindergarten opened in **Opportunity Elementary**.

July 1: **Veradale, Greenacres, Saltese, Lone Fir, Liberty Lake** school districts consolidated with **Opportunity** to form **Central Valley Union HighSchool**.

AIR VIEW OF SPOKANE UNIVERSITY CAMPUS, EARLY '20s
Photo by Leo, Courtesy of Robert Sandberg.

School in Opportunity

[From the informal autobiography of Dr. Frederick Coddington.]

The Opportunity Public School was on the SE corner of Bowdish and the Appleway. It was a large brick building with a large auditorium on the second floor. Many plays, operettas, and community entertainments took place there. Courts of Honor for Boy Scouts from the entire Spokane Valley were held there.

In the basement was a gymnasium equipped for basketball. Troop One of the Scouts met weekly there. On the roof was a belfry with a large school bell. The bell rope came down beside the east stairway into the first floor hall. A wooden knob was mounted on the first floor hallway ceiling beside the stairway. We could take a half hitch in the bell rope around the knob. Sliding down the stair railing, we grabbed the bell rope and swung far into the hallway. The half hitch around the knob prevented our weight from ringing the bell. Good luck kept it from breaking off the knob.

Opportunity Township had no high school. The graduates from our grade school were welcomed into four neighboring high schools: Lewis and Clark and North Central in Spokane (used mainly by children whose fathers worked in Spokane), Central Valley High School just east of Veradale, and West Valley High School in Millwood, both closer than the Spokane schools. Later, John Rogers High School was added to the list of choices. Most of my classmates entered the Valley schools; but Virginia Aller and I went to Lewis and Clark. Our fathers worked in Spokane and transported us.

High school was a big change from grade school. There were usually only about twenty students in a class at Opportunity but there were nearly 200 in my freshman class at Lewis and Clark.

There were seven class periods in the school day at high school and a first and second lunch period. Eighth period was meted out as punishment for various infractions of school rules. My first semester consisted of English, Latin, algebra, general science, and physical education. In P.E. on Mondays we wore gym suits and took calisthenics or ran around an indoor track. On Wednesdays and Fridays, we had our choice of swimming or basketball. I always chose swimming unless I had an open wound. Squinty Hunter, the basketball coach, supervised gym activities. Pete Hupperton, the swimming coach, watched over our swimming. In the middle of the period, he lined us up beside the pool and took roll off a mimeographed list on a clipboard. Then he had us step one pace forward and inspected our ankles. If he found the slightest trace of dirt, that boy was sent to the shower and had to report back with clean ankles. Pete also was allowed to administer hacks to any boys caught running on the slippery, wet tile.

Miss Helen L. Dean taught Latin. One day after class, she called me to her desk. She wanted to know why I never smiled in her class. Frankly, I was frightened at the thought of making an error translating Caesar's *Gallic Wars*.

We had a large auditorium on the first floor, with the largest pipe organ in the city. We often had special convocations with entertainment or pep rallies and evening concerts and lectures in the auditorium. Rear Admiral Richard E. Byrd lectured there and showed some excellent movies after his first trip to the South Pole. Richard Halliburton talked to us about some of his world travels. John Finnegan, the Irish tenor, performed in concert in conjunction with Pietro Yon, a pipe organ virtuoso.

Dad worked at the Fidelity National Bank. He

didn't finish work until 5 p.m. I studied in the library until it closed at 4:30. Then Frank Miller (whose father worked at the telephone company) and I killed a half hour walking at least part way downtown and exploring the stores.

Every Thanksgiving Day our football team played North Central. We always got worked up in a fever of excitement before those games, so intense was the rivalry. Unfortunately, North Central usually beat our team, but we all had a lot of fun.

GETTING A COLLEGE EDUCATION DURING THE DEPRESSION

My graduation from Lewis and Clark High School in Spokane took place in January 1932. The Great Crash had occurred in the fall of 1929 and the Great Depression continued for about ten years thereafter. We had little money but always had plenty to eat from our garden.

In spite of the fact that jobs were scarce and money even scarcer, our class had a proper graduation. We rented caps and gowns and got out of school a week before the end of the semester.

Many of my classmates started college immediately, but I had no money. There were several interesting classes that I had not been able to fit into my previous high school schedules, so I got permission from Mr. Louis Livingston, the vice principal, to return to high school for a semester of post graduate study.

As soon as school was out the following spring, I began to job hunt. I became Ed St. John's hired man. He paid me a dollar a day for ten hours work picking tomatoes and cantaloupes.

My friend Bob Sandberg was one of my classmates who had started college (Spokane University) the January we graduated. He told me that the tuition at Spokane U was much less than at other schools. I looked at their curricula and found that I could get good chemistry courses and mathematics and that the school was accredited for transfer to the University of Washington. An added plus was that Spokane University was only three quarters of a mile from our house. (See "Spokane University," Volume I.)

I enrolled and Bob got credit on his fall tuition for attracting me into the school. My high school days were over!

I sold my motorcycle for eight dollars to apply on my tuition and walked the distance to and from the

U four times a day. I made some money by helping Clyde Mahan haul alfalfa hay for farmers. I had hay fever and my nose would be plugged all night from the dust of the hay. I hated to hear Clyde's voice on the phone offering me a job but I desperately needed the money.

In the spring of 1933, Clyde accidentally sawed off three fingers of his left hand. I rented his saw and hired Dorall Graham to help me cut wood after school and Saturdays. We made out pretty well.

OUT OF WORK!

To make my money situation worse, after seventeen years of service, that spring Dad lost his job at the Fidelity National Bank in Spokane. The Fidelity was purchased by the Old National Bank system. The Old National fired experienced family men and hired recent college graduates at much lower salaries. It was a cruel and discouraging blow to my father. No other jobs were available. He decided to try truck farming and rented the Hegberg land across the street from our house. He was able to borrow on his life insurance policies to get started. He bought a horse to pull the cultivator and ditcher and a Model T Ford that he made into a flat-bed truck. He bought two little pigs and we built a pen for them at the back of our lot. We fattened them on cull vegetables and fruits and field corn. Our vegetables were nice, but people were so short of money that we had to sell them at rock bottom prices.

Mother got a job as social worker for Spokane County Welfare Department. She drove all over the Valley visiting families of people who could not find work. She arranged food, clothing and welfare funds according to their needs. She also took a job as choir director for the Veradale Community Church. That job paid $25 a month for weekly rehearsals and Sunday morning direction.

By spring quarter I had run out of tuition money, but the school extended me credit. Although the faculty had foregone their salaries to keep the University open, Maude Sutton, the art teacher, put me to work spading her flower beds. That way I worked off my tuition by the end of the term. She credited me with fifty cents an hour and applied my credit to her back salary. No money changed hands.

I applied for jobs everywhere, but they were scarce. Finally, in desperation, I went to Sacred

Heart Hospital, explaining to the sisters that I had determined to study premedicine. They gave me a temporary job as relief orderly, replacing those on vacation. Part of the time I worked in surgery mopping the operating floors with soap and disinfectants after each operation. I was paid one dollar a day plus room and board for six days a week.

Later that summer Vernon Moss, Bob Goodrich, and I found jobs at Fairfield, Washington, helping with the seed pea harvest. Our boss, a young farmer named Rettkowski, had about a hundred acres of seed peas. We could sleep in the haymow on straw above the horses. I was to drive a team of black horses hitched to a hay wagon, and Mossy was to be my loader. Mossy rolled pea vines along one side of my wagon, pitched them into my wagon, and I placed them at the back of the wagon.

On Saturday evenings, we returned to Opportunity in Mossy's Model A Ford roadster.

By fall our two pigs weighed over one hundred pounds apiece. Dad hired a butcher to process them for us. That winter Dad rubbed smoke salt into ham and bacon slabs every other evening. Mother made head cheese and scrapple and country sausage. We surely ate like kings even though we didn't have much money.

The Spokane University was defunct that fall, but the teachers opened it as a junior college. It was still accredited with the University of Washington. Although I was the only student in Professor Ellis Harris's biology class, he met with me faithfully.

Mother developed a hobby of decorating wax candles. Hoping to earn some money, I peddled them for her in my spare time but was not very successful. Many housewives looked longingly at them, but didn't have money for frivolous things in those days. I did much better peddling fresh eggs. I also earned money sharpening students' ice skates. Sometimes I carried home three or four pairs at a time.

Early in 1934 J.W. Moss, office manager for Washington Water Power Company, found Dad a job collecting power and water bills. It didn't pay a fancy salary and the job was not always pleasant (calling on people who were in arrears), but Dad was glad to be employed again. Many of his contacts were in desperate straits.

When school was out in June 1934, I signed a note for seventy dollars back tuition. A railroad extra gang was raising and straightening the Milwaukee Railroad tracks through Opportunity. They were taking on extra hands if the applicant was twenty-one years of age. I applied for a job and told them I was twenty-one. They employed me promptly to dress track. I followed the tamper crew and shoveled dirt, filling in the space between the ties. It was hot, hard work. I quickly found that there is no shade on a railroad right of way. I earned two dollars a day, paying back ninety cents of it for room and board and health insurance.

Before the summer was over I did other jobs with the crew such as managing the tamper generator car.

When I first joined the extra gang we were encamped on a siding in Veradale. We slept in a box car with about 16 double deck bunks. We ate in another box car with a kitchen in one end and a long table. They fed us well, although there were always some who complained. Every evening after dinner I went for a swim in the Corbin Ditch with other workmen. When camp moved to Post Falls, we swam in the Spokane River, and when it moved to Spirit Lake, we swam in the lake.

I occupied an upper bunk in the corner of our bunk car. It had a good ventilating window and a good electric light above it. Often when I returned from my swim, I lay on my bunk and read until dark. On Friday nights I caught the evening freight train and rode back to Opportunity. Although the train stopped in Opportunity, the engineer slowed it down to two miles per hour at Bowdish Road so that I could jump safely off with my suitcase. This saved me walking an extra half mile.

At the end of August I made plans to go to Seattle. I was anxious to see if I could work my way through the University of Washington.

The timekeeper in our crew lived in Chester and rode the train to and from camp on a permanent pass. He said he could get me a round-trip railroad pass to Seattle. I applied for it and it came through.

The next move for the camp was to be Newport. I decided to quit before the camp moved. I got my final check, paid off my note at the Spokane Valley Junior College, and bought myself a second-hand steamer trunk for two dollars. That left me sixteen dollars for the Seattle junket, but I did have my pass. I would have to find part-time jobs quickly, but I was full of enthusiasm.

GREENACRES SCHOOL, 1926-27
Mr. William B. Schnebly is the teacher. The students marched in step in and out of the school to the beat of the teacher's clap, clap, clap in rhythm to a phonograph record.
Courtesy of Katharine Krell.

VERA SCHOOL AT SPRAGUE AND PROGRESS. (1905-1960).
Courtesy of Patricia Smith Goetter.

The Arrival of Union High School Districts

Shortly after the turn of the century, at various times and at various places in the Valley, high school courses were offered on a more or less demand basis. Usually a school room or a portion of a school room in an existing building was "the high school."

East and West Valley

As early as 1910 School District #143 (Orchard Park) tried a high school of sorts at its four-room Orchard Avenue elementary building. Only freshman classes in very basic subjects such as English, history, and math were offered. The average daily attendance was only four students, so the program was abandoned.

At Vera a high school attempt in 1912 also had a hard time for lack of enrollment. However when the Vera program was reorganized during the 1914-1915 school year, it was considered successful. Population was increasing and 31 students were enrolled.

In 1914, high school students from Orchard Avenue and Millwood were combined in one class at Millwood Grade School, making enough enrollment for Millwood to provide a reasonably consistent high school program. By the 1916-1917 school year, the program was so well established that the state accredited it—the first high school so recognized in the Valley.

During the 1917-1918 school year, Pasadena District was annexed to Millwood, increasing the number of students enrolled in the accredited program to exactly 100—actually too many students for the space available at the grade school.

What to do about the housing! Facilities were woefully inadequate.

There was no answer but to build an annex onto the Millwood Grade School expressly for the high school program. The voters authorized the additional space and that same year a new high school addition to Millwood Elementary was completed. For the first time students had manual training and domestic science quarters, a gym, showers, locker rooms, and a stage! During the latter part of December 1923, three districts—Trent (#118), Pleasant Prairie (#52), and Orchard Park (#143)—presented petitions to the County Superintendent to call an election to vote on the proposal to form a union high school district and to vote bonds for the erection of a separate high school building. The issues were brought to a vote and on May 1, 1924, the voters expressed their approval by more than a ninety per cent majority. As a result, West Valley High School was built in 1925.

There was such pride in the high school that when it was dedicated, the *Valley Herald*, February 21, 1925, gave the entire front page and many articles inside the paper to describing the ceremony, staff, school board personnel, curriculum, architecture, contractors, district growth, and future plans for students and building. The headlines read: *West Valley High School Dedicated to Service.* Each contractor, each source of the specialized materials used in the construction were detailed. The school board had secured the best of everything for the new building: tons of steel, one hundred ten thousand feet of construction lumber, rough lumber for the gymnasium running track, marble columns from Vermont to give distinction to the massive ten ton blocks of granite quarried on special order for the entrance arch, blue velour curtains for the commodious stage, two dumb waiters, and master stone cutters to carve over the entrance way this quotation from Alexander Pope: "Education forms the common mind; just as the twig is bent the tree's inclined."

Due to the population influx in the Valley after World War II, the building, by mid-century became overcrowded and inadequate. A new West Valley High School was opened at 301 Buckeye in 1958 and the old West Valley High School was converted to Argonne Junior High School.

Central Valley High School

In 1910 when the experimental high school program was tried at Orchard Park, Opportunity and Trent also tried a high school program and also without success. Greenacres, too, made an attempt at high school during the 1910-1911 school year but that also was discontinued after a very brief trial. From that time on, Greenacres remained a non-high school district until 1923.

In August of that year Central Valley Union High School District #201 was formed by a vote of the people of Quinnamosa District #160, Saltese District #39, Opportunity District #162, Vera District #40, Liberty Lake District #78, Greenacres District #113, and Lone Fir District #128.

The high school classes, with an enrollment of less than 100, were held in the Vera Grade School building until enrollment warranted the construction of a separate building in 1927-28. The building constructed was first known as the Appleway High School. This name was not agreeable to the students. They conducted a contest for renaming the school. The name chosen was Central Valley High School.

CV, as the school was called, was located on a 72-acre tract, facing the Appleway (site of the current Greenacres Junior High School.) Adjoining it on the north was a 5-acre play field.

The building had a frontage of 121 feet and a depth of 64 feet in the wings on each end. It was three stories high. There were ten classrooms, a principal's office, a superintendent's office, boys' and girls' showers, and fuel and boiler rooms. All corridors were eleven feet wide. The building was constructed at an approximate cost of $43,000. The campus contained 13 ½ acres with a front of 600 feet on the Appleway at Greenacres.

One hundred fifty pupils took residence in the new building with its completely equipped labs, and domestic science and manual training rooms.

The site was given without obligation by the Union Agency Company of Spokane, promoters of the Corbin Addition to Greenacres.

The building was completed and furnished four months after the ground was broken. With donations of material and labor plus the proceeds of many student fund-raising projects, shortly thereafter a large frame gymnasium was built adjoining the school.

By 1945 Opportunity furnished about two-fifths of the 368 students enrolled in the CV District. Central Valley at that time was also giving instruction to 550 adults in the various programs sponsored by the Smith-Hughes Agriculture and Home Economics Departments. In addition, on June 7, 1945, Mica District #25 also became part of the Central Valley Union High School District #201.

A major change in organization took place on July 1, 1945. All of the electors of the component parts of the Central Valley Union High School District #201 voted to form a single consolidated school district #356.

This was a significant step forward according to information supplied by then County Superintendent Van W. Emerson's Office. It set the stage for the subsequent development of the District. In July 1951 Central Valley District #356 became the second first class district in Spokane County. Spokane District #81 was the first.

Several additional steps were necessary before the Central Valley District #356 reached its present boundaries. On July 1, 1952, the Chester District #71 transferred to the Central Valley District. When the new Freeman District was organized in 1956, a major portion of the former Mica District #25 was transferred out of the Central Valley District. The final step in rounding out the district as it was in the 60s occurred July 1, 1962, when Spokane Bridge District #172 territory lying south of the Spokane River was transferred to District #356.

Pioneer School Recycled

[By Nan Waters, Central Valley teacher]

1958 was the year of the big post-war classroom bulge in junior high-age students. Valley school districts were scrambling for classroom space. Bowdish Junior High School, in the Central Valley District, was being built, but would not be ready for September occupancy.

In the emergency, to house seven seventh grade classes, the district (#356) elected to re-open for one year the old Vera High School on the corner of Progress and Sprague. The building actually had been condemned during the war years as unsafe. Parents were discouraged from watching basketball games because of the rickety condition of the gym balcony. The library consisted of a dictionary and one old set of encyclopedias in the central lobby.

Newly hired, I was assigned to Vera that year.

With all the extreme dedication of a new teacher, I was usually the first to enter the building Monday mornings except for Mr. Robideaux, the custodian. I often noticed an odor of sewer gas when I entered the building.

"Good grief!" I said one spring Monday morning to no one. "That odor is ba-a-ad today!"

I went to my room, opened all the windows, closed the door, and forgot about it.

At about 10:30 a.m., lavatory break-time, I lined my kids up and we descended to the basement where the lavatories were and where the trucked-in lunches were served.

A dear little girl sidled up to me, face twisted in nausea.

"Mrs. Waters! *What* are we having for lunch?" she whispered.

By lunchtime, thankfully, the odor seemed to have dissipated somewhat. What had it been? I decided to do some sleuthing.

I asked Dave Carlson, the teacher who had the room next to mine, what he knew about it.

He stammered around a bit and then told me that one of his students had contributed a calf heart for a dissection lesson the Thursday before. After the lesson, Dave placed the heart in one of the old-fashioned cupboards lining the room and forgot all about it until he was met by the smell on his arrival that morning.

He hurriedly placed the heart in one of the basement garbage cans. The kitchen lunch crew, who also met with *the smell* on their arrival, promptly disposed of the culprit.

The fire escapes at the old high school were rickety metal affairs. When we had drills, usually my class did not have to use them because we were lucky enough to occupy one of the four downstairs rooms. But one day we were watching a film upstairs when the alarm sounded. Jim Swarz bounced to the window, pushed it up and the students clambered out and down the fire escape to the yard. My duty was to climb out last, then close the window. That was before the days of slacks for lady teachers. I vividly remember the shrill whistles and "Yea, Mrs. Waters!" catcalls as I stood on the metal grill outside and struggled to lower the ancient warped sash in the considerable breeze.

The following year Bowdish was ready for occupancy and the venerable old structure stood vacant for several years.

Then one day I noticed the lot was empty.

I miss the square brick edifice with its pagoda-like four-cornered bell tower, although I shall never forget "Yea, Mrs. Waters!" or the decayed calf heart.

The rural flavor provided by such experiences has gone. The old Milwaukee train that daily thundered past behind the old Vera School and drowned out my "words of wisdom" no longer runs. A Valley arterial is being considered currently (1994) for part of that right-of-way. The only remaining school in the area that I know about of the Vera vintage is in the Deep Creek community, west of Airway Heights and it has not been a school for many years.

High School Football

[From the *West Valley News*, November 9, 1933.]

Eagles Ready to Stop Bears

Playing their last game of the season, the West Valley Eagles and the Central Valley Bears will tangle in the annual Armistice day game at Central Valley Saturday at 2 o'clock.

A thrilling, clean, hard-fought game is anticipated by local fans. Both teams are in good shape and are raring to go.

West Valley has for the past seven years overpowered the Bears, but a fairly even break is the hope this year. The weights are practically the same, and speed will be a major factor, both teams possessing it.

Central Valley hasn't lost a conference game this season, and rumors are going around that they won't. If the Bears win, they will tie Cheney for the county championship.

Seeing action for the last time in high school football, many boys from C.V. and W.V. will play as they have never played before.

Probable lineups:

W.V.	Positions	C.V.
Sohns	L.E.	Gillingham
Drotter	L.T.	Freiser
Yamamoto	L.G.	Cox
Mank	C.	Bead
Worthington	R.G.	Scharf
Nelson	R.T.	R. Schafer
Morisset	R.E.	Nystuen
Koeppel	Q.B.	Reese
Adley	R.H.	Murball
Chesebro	L.H.	Hurtig
Sturges	F.	Gaskell

Same Trophies Awarded for Armistice Day Game

As in the past, two trophies, the True and Brownson, will be awarded at the Armistice Day football game between Central Valley and West Valley Saturday afternoon.

The True Trophy, presented by the True Oil Company, is a sportsmanship award the purpose of which is to cement the friendly feeling existing between the two schools and to stimulate people's interest.

The advance ticket sale, spirit shown at the game, originality of stunts, and general sportsmanship are taken into consideration.

Central Valley has won the trophy in 1929, 1930, and 1932. West Valley won it in 1931.

The Brownson trophy, presented in 1930 by Lynn Brownson, is to stimulate even greater interest in the Armistice day game.

The plaque is to be in the possession for the following year of the school winning the game. West Valley has been the winner for the three years since it was first presented.

The True trophy is to become the permanent possession of the school that wins it three years in succession. The school that wins the Brownson trophy the greatest number of times out of ten years will become the owner.

WEST VALLEY FOOTBALL TEAM, 1935

(L to R) *Row 1:* Peter Goldberg, Harold Schimmels, Charles Bailey, Oliver Scharwat, Glen Mank, Carlton Goudge, John Wacholtz, Milton Rawlings; *Row 2:* Martin Koshman, Joe Hunt, Richard McLeod; *Row 3:* Coach Ward Mauer, Ray Parrott, Elmer Johnson, William Wilson, Thomas Williams, Stanley Martin, Albert Rawlings, Stanley Anderson, Clayton Smith, Francis Schille, Sam Manfred, Ben Wilson, Henry Hageman or Don Worthington?, Robert Grater, Asst. Coach Howard Damon.

Courtesy of Carlton Goudge; Names: Carlton Goudge and Harry Olson.

WPA to the Rescue

Money for Valley public schools normally comes largely from two main sources: the state, which apportions money according to the number of students per district, and the taxable wealth of a community, which is represented by the amount of money school districts are able to realize from levy assessments. (Levies must be approved by a vote of the people.)

Following the market crash of 1929 and the subsequent bank closures, both of these money sources deteriorated: school populations declined as residents moved away in search of jobs; and with the decline in population, also the taxable wealth of the Valley deteriorated.

The '30s became a difficult time for Valley schools. For the first time in the history of the West Valley District, during the 1929-1930 school year, a levy failed to pass. It was a levy that had been carefully calculated by the administration and school board, but taxpayers were fearful and the levy failed.

In his *History of Orchard Park Schools*, Arthur Ness describes the financial difficulties of the West Valley School District during the '30s and the ensuing war years.

"Times were hard, of course, as the delinquent school tax showed, but the economic crisis had not struck full force in the Valley at the time the board decided to ask for a special levy of three mills. At the end of the school year 1929-1930, the district had a net warrant indebtedness slightly under $25,000 and delinquent taxes amounting to $13,657.17. It was primarily to rectify this unsound financial condition that the directors requested the extra levy.

"But people had become extremely tax conscious by this time, and that was especially true of the large tax-payer. At the caucus held to explain the reasons for the levy, a compromise proposal was presented, namely that the request be reduced from three to two mills."

But even that small millage failed to carry.

By June 30, 1932, the financial condition of the West Valley School District was very unfavorable.

"Fewer children were being born. Many families had moved out of the district in search of employment, no new families moved in, and school enrollments fluctuated uncertainly."

Kindergartens were suspended in an effort to cut expenses.

By 1934 every individual item in the West Valley school budget had been cut to the bone. The following economies were in effect:

1. Teachers' salaries were reduced 20%.
2. As vacancies occurred, they were not filled.
3. Janitors' salaries were reduced 10-20%.
4. Kindergartens closed.
5. The Parkwater school was closed. (Parkwater had joined the city in 1929, but West Valley continued to use the building at a nominal rent.)
6. The cost of transportation was reduced.
7. Office help was cut.
8. Repair and replacement of text books were suspended.
9. Building repairs were postponed, except in emergencies.
10. The use of supplies of all sorts was restricted.
11. Manual training and art classes in the departmental grades at Millwood were suspended.

By resorting to those drastic economies, the per pupil cost was decreased from 42.8¢ per day to 27.3¢. But money problems continued.

Ness continues: "On March 26, 1934, all married teachers, with one or two exceptions, were refused contracts for the ensuing school year. The idea was to provide vacancies for young unmarried teachers who had great difficulty in finding positions. Only those teachers who would suffer a hardship by being dismissed were to be retained.

"This action of the board did not pass without tremendous repercussions. Good teachers are loved and admired by the children, and they are powerful influences in determining the attitude of the parents. Even mediocre and poor teachers have admirers and friends in the community. Now a considerable number of teachers were refused re-employment, and a number of the parents were much upset.

"However, the policy was not changed, and it remained in effect until our country entered the war, when a shortage of teachers made it imperative to again appeal to the married members of the profession for help."

WPA TO THE RESCUE

There was little opportunity during these crisis days to bring about plant improvements—until the resources of the WPA were tapped.

Again, I quote Mr. Ness: "The inadequacy of the playground area at the Dishman School had long been a vexing problem. In the spring of 1935, it came to our attention that a strip of land, located directly north of the building, was for sale at a reasonable price. On June 14, the board decided to purchase the tract and have it conditioned for playground purposes with WPA labor.

"At this point, it becomes my duty to say a good word for the Works Progress Administration in connection with numerous improvements effected in our building and ground facilities. In our district, the WPA did a lot of valuable work which otherwise would have been economically impossible. All of our playgrounds were re-conditioned and greatly improved by facilities such as tennis courts, handball courts, and baseball diamonds the WPA workers built. They moved hundreds of tons of dirt, hauled away rocks and obstacles, filled in depressions and leveled areas previously unsuited for play purposes, seeded them and put them in tiptop shape for use by the children. All this work was done with picks, shovels and wheelbarrows, and the men employed were thus able to provide the minimum essentials of food and clothing for themselves and their families. The work of maintenance and repair, for which practically no funds were provided during the '30s, was given a tremendous impetus through WPA efforts.

"Our desks and other equipment had received little attention for several years and were in a sad state of repair. The WPA men moved in, and for months worked on desks, tables and other furniture, removing old paint and varnish, scars and scratches, re-painted, re-glued, and refinished.

"Assistants were provided for our kindergarten classes, which otherwise could not have been re-opened. We received help in carrying on our recreational program, and in the preparation and serving of hot lunches for the children.

"Later on we constructed several building additions primarily with WPA labor, and the work done was most acceptable and satisfactory. True, the stringent regulations and so-called red tape were at times disconcerting, but this was an administrative shortcoming rather than an operational short coming of the workers. It is a safe estimate that our school district benefited to the extent of $150,000 from the WPA effort.

"In 1940 we entered upon the ambitious undertaking of constructing a gymnasium at Dishman. Application was made to the WPA for labor and some materials, as well as the State Department of Social Security for additional financial help. The applications were approved, and the project was completed during the early summer of 1941. The gymnasium was a 70′ x 90′ brick structure with necessary auxiliary facilities of shower, locker room, and toilet facilities. It served not only as a means for an expanded physical education program, but also as a community center for young and old.

ORCHIDS TO JOHN PRING

"An interesting incident occurred in connection with the construction of the gymnasium at the Dishman School. Late in the fall of 1940, we discovered that it would be impossible to complete the project if additional funds could not be obtained. The board felt that an election to authorize a special levy would be inadvisable, since the employment situation in the area was still quite unfavorable. Some of the larger industries were operating on a part-time basis, dividing the time as equitably as possible among the employees.

"There was only one possible source, it seemed, from which additional funds might be obtained, namely the State Department of Social Security.

"A formal application, containing all data pertinent to our situation, was prepared and mailed to Olympia. We felt, however, that a personal appearance before the officials of the department, including Governor Martin, would be much more effective.

"In early December, 1940, two members of the board, John Pring of Opportunity and Dr. Neal E. Bayne of Orchard Avenue (a dentist), and I went to Olympia to confer with Mr. Graham, the director of Social Security, and Governor Martin.

"Mr. Graham was not at all optimistic about the outcome of our application for additional funds although his attitude was very sympathetic and understanding. From his viewpoint, however, further assistance seemed quite out of the question.

"At this point, the governor abruptly and unceremoniously entered the room.

"It was characteristic of Governor Martin to act informally and rather bluntly at all times, although I considered him easily approachable and democratic in the real sense of the term.

"After a brief discussion of the political situation (Mr. Langlie had just been elected governor), he abruptly asked, 'Gentlemen, what can I do for you?'

"John Pring presented our case in a salesmanlike and very convincing manner, Neal Bayne and I adding an occasional word.

"The governor turned to Mr. Graham and said, 'We can help them, can't we, Vern?'

"Mr. Graham was dubious, unless some of the allocations that had been made should be nullified for failure to provide matching funds. The governor and Mr. Graham commented on such cases and in the end, we were promised the funds requested both for Dishman and the West Valley gymnasiums.

"'We won't let you down, Gentlemen,' the governor bluntly observed.

"Both Dr. Bayne and I congratulated Mr. Pring for his expert presentation of our case. He had procured many thousand dollars for the district.

The War Years

"The gymnasium project at Dishman was one of the last major jobs of the Works Project Administration. The war in Europe had created a tremendous demand for industrial products from this country, and our own state of unpreparedness in a world of uncertainty, strife, and aggression made it imperative that we set our house in order, lest the armed strength of the dictator overwhelm the democratic nations of the world.

"The country's manpower was soon absorbed in this gigantic task. Unemployment decreased at a rapid pace, and a new era had set in. Soon our young men were to become a part of the mightiest military force in history that once again was to join the other liberty-loving nations in a fight for the preservation of justice and freedom.

"In February, 1942, my good friend and co-worker, Dr. Bayne, passed away. Mr. A.E. Lacroix of Orchard Avenue was elected without opposition to fill the vacancy on the board.

"He was extremely enthusiastic in the promotion of anything the schools could do in furthering the war effort. He worked tirelessly to induce the school personnel to purchase war bonds, and with good success.

"The literature which he faithfully distributed among our personnel, the conferences and talks which were almost a daily occurrence, and the casualty lists which included more and more of our own local boys made a deep impression on all of us and spurred us to greater and greater effort.

"For the first time in many years, we were now facing the problem of teacher shortage. The younger men teachers either enlisted or were inducted into the service. Others, both men and women, left the profession for more remunerative employment in defense plants. The policy of excluding married women was suspended, as was the policy of employing only one member of a family for work in the schools.

"Another difficult problem confronting us was our inability to purchase new textbooks and supplies. Orders often remained unfilled for months, and some items were not obtainable at all. In the face of a rapidly growing enrollment, the problem became exceedingly grave. There was an acute shortage of desks, but none could be purchased. We scoured the county for surplus desks in schools whose enrollments had not been affected by the war, and were able to obtain approximately one hundred, so old and dilapidated that many of them had to be reconditioned before they could be used

"Our building facilities were becoming more and more inadequate. Every available bit of space was being used, and in one building more than fifty per cent of the children were occupying emergency rooms. In the brief space of four years the grade school enrollment had increased by 457 pupils and no additional rooms had been provided. To carry on instructional activities under such conditions was extremely difficult, but the teachers never grumbled; they worked faithfully, and the results obtained were surprisingly good.

"The most discouraging nature of the unfavorable situation was the inability of many patrons to understand the reasons for our predicament. The telephone would ring at frequent intervals, and too often some irate parent at the other end would berate the administration for gross negligence in not providing books, supplies, and proper room facilities. All we could do was adopt a philosophical attitude and console ourselves with the fact that the majority understood and appreciated the magnitude of our difficulties.

"In the spring of 1945, the war was seemingly approaching its termination. Italy was tottering, the Germans were retreating on the western front and suffering great losses in Russia, and MacArthur had made his promised comeback in the Pacific. Indeed, the end must be near, and peace would make possible the acquisition of materials and man-power to effect improvements in our facilities on a major scale. A tremendous amount of work was pending."

A Custodian Praised

[From *History of Orchard Park Schools and West Valley High School,* by Arthur B. Ness and printed for the West Valley School District, 1950. (See article, "Orchard Park and West Valley Schools," Vol. I.)]

During the school year 1925-26 [the West Valley District] was in a more favorable position with respect to building facilities than we had been for a considerable period of time. By readjustment in boundary lines the [crowding at the] Parkwater building was relieved, and by transferring the first four grades from the Orchard Avenue School we were able to set aside space where the children could play in inclement weather. The Millwood School had been relieved of the high school department, making more space available in that building than could actually be used at the time. The only building in the district where no improvements had been effected was at Dishman, and several years passed before any major changes were made in that building.

As essential as well constructed and roomy buildings are in the educative process, the absence of beautiful surroundings is a distinct liability. Lawns, shade trees, and shrubbery are necessary to insure the proper atmosphere. Our school grounds had been sadly neglected. Except for the high school, there were no lawns and shrubs to beautify the grounds of any of our buildings; no sidewalks to the entrances had been provided, and sand and dirt was tracked into the corridors and rooms making the maintenance problem extremely difficult.

On April 10, 1926, it was proposed to the board that this situation be corrected.

On May 14 the preparation of lawns and the planting of shrubs were authorized. The hard ground around the various buildings was plowed and harrowed; a large quantity of fertilizer was applied, and by the time school opened in the fall, there was a good, healthy stand of grass around the buildings where sand, gravel, and dirt had held sway for years.

Shrubs were planted around the bare walls of buildings, walks to the entrances were built, and railings constructed to keep young and old from nullifying the work that had been done.

The man in charge of this improvement program was W. O. Elmquist who began his work as custodian in 1920. Mr. Elmquist was a most conscientious and reliable man for whom my respect and admiration grew as the years passed by. Being in charge of the custodial corps, he enjoyed the trust and confidence of all who worked with him.

He was extremely fair in all his dealings with his co-workers; he never assumed the role of boss; and no offense was taken at his suggestions. He insisted, however, that an employee do the work assigned to him, and that the work be done properly.

I remember but one instance when Mr. Elmquist lost his patience. A man had been employed as custodian in one of our schools, and his work and general attitude were reprehensible. He completely ignored Mr. Elmquist's guidance and advice, assuming, no doubt, that he knew as much as the boss, or probably more.

Finally, however, Mr. Elmquist's patience came to an end. One day, he came to the office and bluntly recommended that the man be discharged. His recommendation was promptly complied with. So far as I can recall, it was the only time Mr. Elmquist recommended the discharge of an employee. We all felt that if a man couldn't get along with Mr. Elmquist, he couldn't get along with anybody.

Everybody held Mr. Elmquist in high regard— custodians, teachers, administrators, the board, and above all, the children. His quiet, unassuming manners, and his efficient and faithful service made him one of the most appreciated members of the entire school personnel. If anything went wrong in a building, Mr. Elmquist was summoned, and the difficulty was attended to without delay. Sometimes I felt that the custodians imposed upon him, and that relatively minor tasks could and should be done without calling Mr. Elmquist.

The faithful performance of his duties can probably be best understood by his unsurpassed devotion to the tasks which would insure the greatest comfort for the teachers and the children. During the cold winter season, it was a common occurrence for Mr. Elmquist to get out of bed at three or four o'clock in the morning and make the rounds of the schools to see that the necessary temperature was maintained to prevent damage to water pipes and radiators. He seldom said anything about his early rising; he had certain duties to perform, and their performance knew no limitations in hours and labor.

Mr. Elmquist retired at the end of the first semester of 1944-45. A big banquet was held in his honor; teachers, administrators and directors, past and present, were there to pay homage to this good and faithful servant who had occupied such an important place in our school system for more than twenty-four years. He was now past the three-score and ten mark, and despite my entreaties to continue a while longer, he felt, and justly so, that he deserved a rest.

Mr. Elmquist and rest, however, are incompatible; he will continue to be occupied with various tasks until old age and health call a halt.

School at Edgecliff

[From *A History of Orchard Park Schools and West Valley High School*, written by Arthur B. Ness for the West Valley School District in 1950. Ness was superintendent of the West Valley School District in 1925 when West Valley High School was dedicated. (See Article, "Edgecliff Sanatorium," Vol. I.)]

The Edgecliff Sanatorium for tubercular patients lies within the boundaries of the [West Valley School] District. Young and old, suffering from this disease, are admitted to the institution for proper care and treatment. It is under the jurisdiction of the county commissioners, and Dr. Frank Miller is the head physician and medical director of the hospital.

A number of children of grade school and high school age are patients at the sanatorium. The question of affording these boys and girls an opportunity to continue their schooling had been a problem for the commissioners for some time. An effort had been made to provide some classroom work, but the success of the experiment apparently was not what the county fathers had anticipated.

On August 31, 1927, Mr. O. W. Young, then commissioner, requested that we [West Valley School Board] assume the responsibility for the educational guidance and direction of the young patients at Edgecliff. We would receive the apportionment money, and the county would pay the differential between these funds and the total annual cost of educating the boys and girls at the hospital. The board agreed to try the experiment for one year.

It was discovered that the lady who had been in charge of the educational work at the institution did not possess a teacher's certificate. I considered this very unfortunate, for she was a fine lady, interested in the work and well liked by the children. She was apprized of the requirement, and cheerfully agreed to withdraw in favor of someone who had a certificate.

The classwork at Edgecliff was at first confined to the elementary pupils. They met at stipulated hours, as per Dr. Miller's established daily schedule for his patients, in an upstairs room designed for classroom work. The room was unheated and the windows were open in both warm and cold weather. During the winter months children would work at their desks or at the chalk board with mittens on their hands, and otherwise garbed in woolen sweaters, overcoats, caps with ear muffs, heavy warm shoes, and similar winter accoutrements. They seemed to be very comfortable and happy in these surroundings, and the teacher, similarly dressed, did not mind the frigid quarters. It would not have been a very desirable place, however, for a teacher who could not work effectively in an environment where the temperature fell below 80 degrees above. I have known such teachers.

The work was subsequently expanded to include boys and girls of high school age. Teachers from West Valley would meet with the Edgecliff students at specified hours following their regular classes in the high school. The young patients proved to be very good students, and many of them completed the required work in a much shorter time than ordinarily prescribed. They had no extra-curricular activities and social functions to infringe on their study hours, which so often are a bane to regular high school students.

It was quite an event when the first student from Edgecliff received her diploma. We were all very happy and proud, especially the student.

A considerable number of young patients have graduated since that time, and many of them, upon recovery from the disease, have continued their schooling in higher institutions, or have obtained positions in various fields requiring graduation from high school. We have always felt that our efforts at Edgecliff have provided very gratifying results, and the work of our high school teachers certainly has meant much in the lives of these boys and girls.

Sometimes tragedies occurred, as occur every-

where. It was my custom, at the opening of school in the fall, to interview the students at Edgecliff whose education had been interrupted by the disease. I was usually received with smiles and enthusiasm.

I remember one of these interviews very distinctly. A young girl had just been admitted, and I proposed that she continue her high school work. She was a junior. She seemed somewhat apathetic, arguing that she would prefer to join her class in her home high school and graduate from there. However she was willing to think the matter over.

A little later, I spoke to Dr. Miller about my interview with her. Dr. Miller informed me, with that genuine sympathy which is one of his many good characteristics, that his young patient would be lucky if she recovered from her sickness. He felt that a little work would do no harm.

She subsequently enrolled for a very light course, and in two years' time she had satisfied the requirements for graduation. She could not attend the regular commencement exercises, but we arranged to hold a little private ceremony at her bedside.

The chairman of the Board, a couple of teachers, the president of the senior class, the girl's parents and some other relatives and I were present. It was a memorable occasion for all of us. The young girl was very happy and proud; her parents cried. I have wondered if they knew that their daughter was never going to get well.

A year later she passed away. Her high school diploma was never of any practical value to her, but she had experienced the great satisfaction of receiving it, and she knew that there were teachers and others who remembered her, who had her welfare at heart and who rejoiced with her in her pride of accomplishment, sincerely hoping and praying that soon she would be herself again, ready to go out in the world a little better prepared for the future and its promises.

The work at Edgecliff has continued until this day. It has been greatly expanded, and the young patients, unfortunate victims of the treacherous malady, have the opportunity to continue their school work, preparing themselves for the day when they would hear the cheering words: "You are well enough to go home."

The Hutton Settlement, A Valley Landmark

North of the Spokane River off Upriver Drive at E. 9907 Wellesley on 364 acres of lush Valley farmland are the buildings that make up the Hutton Settlement. It is currently on the National Register of Historic Places.

The Settlement was founded November 1, 1919, by Levi Hutton to provide a home for children deprived of a normal family through no fault of their own. In 1924 the Settlement sheltered in its four three-story cottages an average of 78 children, 59 of whom were full orphans. Today many of the 30 residents are dependent children who for some reason cannot live with their biological parents.

The education of the children is, and always has been, a primary concern at the settlement. That concern is spelled out in the inscription over the entrance way: "The child is father of the man." The residents attend West Valley schools for their formal education, but learning is a constant in their daily lives. The house parents on the staff are frequently accredited teachers and emphasize "the teaching family." Goals for their charges are good citizenship, a high sense of morality, respect for self and others and an understanding of financial and ethical values.

Originally, the Settlement had its own Sunday School, but today the children attend neighborhood churches.

In 1921 a Boy Scout Troop was organized.

As recently as 60 years ago the settlement had its own dairy barn and livestock and the children raised their own food. In 1934 there were 54 children living there. The girls canned 4,613 quarts of fruits and vegetables while the boys assisted with the raising of crops. The settlement raised enough hay, alfalfa, and silage to feed 16 cows and the work horses on the place. It was called "a model farm operated by families of boys and girls living in attractive brick cottages." Children still raise sheep and weed the gardens and complete chores before they play.

The grounds are equipped with an auditorium, tennis courts, an Olympic-sized swimming pool, basketball courts, and extensive vegetable and fruit gardens.

May Arkwright and Levi Hutton

Levi William Hutton was born on a farm near Fairfield, Iowa, on October 22, 1860. His father died when Levi was only one year old and his mother died when he was six.

His uncle raised him on his farm, but at eighteen years of age he ran away from home. His first job was as a tie splitter with the Northern Pacific Railroad. By age 25 he had been promoted to engineer.

At Wardner Junction (now Kellogg, Idaho) the mild-mannered Levi met outspoken May Arkwright, the illegitimate daughter of an itinerant preacher, who ran a boarding house there. The two married in 1887 and settled in Wallace.

Ten years later, staked by friends, they paid $880 for a 3/32 mining share. On Friday the 13th, in 1901, a huge silver, lead and zinc vein was discovered on the claim and what became the Hercules mine paid out over $25 million. Some of Levi's partners in the mine were well-known Spokane names: August Paulsen, Charles Reeves, Frank Rothrock, and the Day family. They were influential in bringing Levi to Spokane where he built the Hutton Building.

May Hutton is an historical figure in her own right. She became embroiled in the women's suffrage movement, was the first woman to sit on a jury in Washington state, the first woman to make a speech at a presidential convention, and the first woman to register to vote in the county.

She died in 1915 and four years later, Levi founded the Hutton settlement. He is said to have explained that he wanted kids to have good homes so they wouldn't have to be a wandering orphan like he was. He stipulated that none of the 319 acres could ever be subdivided and the Board of directors would consist entirely of women, appointed for life.

When he died of complications from diabetes in 1926, Levi's will specified that the bulk of his fortune go to the settlement. Today it is one of only a handful in the country that accepts no state or federal money. Other than gifts and a small amount of fund raising to satisfy tax requirements, the entire operation is funded by real estate.

Hutton Settlement is the legacy of a rich man who for most of his life was very poor.

The Hutton monument for May in Fairmont Memorial Cemetery is made to look half-finished.

It is said that Levi once explained that a half-finished memorial was appropriate for a woman whose life was only half-finished. May died at 55 years of age.

Spokane Valley Schools, 1941-1942

District	School	Principal
39	Saltese	Children transported
40	Vera	Mrs. Jennie Cheney
63	East Trent	Mary Hanly Berglund
71	Chester	Ernest Pintler
78	Liberty Lake	Kathleen Ryan
113	Greenacres	Harry Lowden
118	Trent	Harold Hoffman
128	Lone Fir	Mrs. Pearl Wright
143	Orchard Park	A.B. Ness, supt.
	Millwood	L.E. Anderson
	Dishman	Mayme Williams
143	Orchard Ave.	Elva Russell
	Orchard Cent.	Mrs. May Rogers
	Pasadena Pk.	Mrs. Nerisse Jackson
162	Opportunity	E.F. Cash
201	Central Valley	John J. Crabb
	H. S.	Sig T. Hanson, Vice Principal
202	West Valley	Hobart F. Rowlands
		A. B. Ness, supt.
303	Foothills	Roscoe Duff
348	Otis Orchards	Mrs. Elzora Gorman
		Mrs. Lucille Baump, grades
		Ben F. Low, supt.

Recreation And Entertainment

"If there remains any doubt in the minds of motion picture producers that the public intends this form of entertainment should be cleaned up, the demand for the resignation of Will Hays as Movie Czar should wake them up. The public is fed up with dirt in the films and in much of modern writing."

[Editorial, *Spokane Valley Herald,* July 14, 1934]

DANCE PAVILION AT LIBERTY LAKE SURROUNDED BY ICE
In the '40s and earlier the resort closed in the winter. Often ice eighteen inches thick
formed on the lake. Chunks were cut and saved in sawdust to be used for cooling
milk, food and drinks when the weather warmed up.
Courtesy of Helen Damascus.

Recreation and Entertainment

CHRONOLOGICAL HISTORY

1921

With 28 members and 20 instruments on hand and regular practices, the band at **Opportunity** was a full-grown band. The band was fortunate in securing the services of **Prof. J.F. Seely**, an experienced band man of Spokane, who used to play at the old Columbia Theater.

1922

Magnolia Chapter of the **Order of Eastern Star** was organized at **Millwood.**

The **Trentwood Community Club** began the erection of a community hall 42' x 90'.

First All-Valley picnic at **Liberty Lake.**

1924

July 4: The biggest crowd ever at **Liberty Lake**, estimated at 14,000 people. Trains alone brought 9,000.

As a result of a meeting held at **Wheeler's Grocery Store** in **Greenacres,** organized baseball was assured for the Valley, for the coming season. Five clubs were already signed up including **Post Falls, Rathdrum, Greenacres, Millwood** and **Jack Tire** from **Dishman.**

A.T. Dishman built the **Appleway Dance Pavillion** and amusement center at **Dishman.**

1925

J.A. Vogt, said to have established the first fruit stand along the **Appleway**, is developing his land east of **Dishman** on the **Appleway** into a park: baseball diamond, merry-go-round, swimming pool.

Dishman converted his **Appleway Dance Pavilion** to a roller skating rink. "People are tired of dancing," **Mr. Dishman** told the *Valley Herald.* "The dance business has been overworked with halls everywhere. On several evenings all 200 pairs of my roller skates have been in use."

1926

Charles Stillwell purchased **Liberty Lake Park** and **Dreamwood Bay** from **Lou Hurtig.** He painted the buildings silver, renamed it **Silver City.** "The resort took on a carnival atmosphere and the beautiful gardens were neglected," wrote Brereton and Foedish in *Memories of Liberty Lake,* p.27.

1926

Eight communities entered the *Herald's* horseshoe pitching contest.

A **Rifle Club** was formed with **Harry Larned**, president.

1927

Carl and **Clifford Anderson** bought the **Empire Motion Picture Company** at **Opportunity.**

1928

J.G. Heatherly began holding picture shows in the **Dishman Arena.** Two years later his circuit included **Rathdrum, Post Falls, Rockford, Elk, Fairfield,** and **Plummer. Millwood** was also included though not as a regular date. All seats were 10¢.

1929

August 10 : Max Schmelling gave an exhibition in the **Dishman Arena.**

1930

The **Hi-Way Pavilion** at **Argonne** and the **Appleway** in **Dishman** opened in the former **Dishman Dance Hall.** The proprietors and owners were **Dutch Groschoff** and **Norm Thue,** musicians. (See article, "Norman Thue.")

Dr. Charles A. Ham and **Mrs. Mildred West** opened **Shady Nook Miniature Golf Course** at the **SE** corner of **Argonne Road** and **Broadway.** It offered 18 holes, each hole planned to develop a special facility needed in "big golf." Located in an apple orchard, it was supposed to be the most difficult miniature golf course in the Valley.

1931

Liberty Lake Park was purchased by the **Damascus Brothers** and **Pete Lambrose.** They sold it in 1947 but repossessed it in 1951.

Spokane Valley Golf Club was formed.

A new $6800 **Otis Orchards Community Clubhouse** was built. It was half the size of the 1930 building that was destroyed by fire.

The **Izaak Walton League** took special interest in trying to build **Liberty Lake** into the fisherman's paradise it once was. They spent considerable money widening and improving the water intake from the river.

1932

August: The second All-Valley Dance was held at **Silver City, Liberty Lake** with music by Mann Brothers' ten-piece orchestra, proceeds went to buy music for the All-Valley Band.

July 29 (*Herald* Ad): At the **Appleway Theater, Opportunity,** Alfred Lunt and wife, Lynn Fontaine, Friday and Saturday in their first talking picture, "The Guardsman," plus an Our Gang Comedy and news reel showing the Republican National Convention. Admission 15¢, small kiddies 10¢.

July 23: **Hi-Way Pavilion** for lease by **A.T. Dishman.**

1933

W.J. Schafer of **Chester** opened a winter resort, **Ski-More,** at **Schafer Springs,** south of **Dishman.** He also bottled and sold "mineral" water from the mineral springs on his property. (See article, "Orrin and Stella Torrey.")

1934

Harold Johnsrud, son of **Mr.** and **Mrs. I.T. Johnsrud** of **Orchard Avenue** is author, director, and actor in a New York play, "Trip to Pressburg," starring Pola Negri.

June 9, *Spokane Valley Herald* Ad: Annual All-Valley Dance at beautiful Silver City, Liberty Lake. Fine music by Mann Brothers' 10-piece orchestra. Beautiful surroundings, good time for all. Ladies 15¢, Gentlemen 40¢.

1935

August 30: **Playfair Race Course** came into being. The Spokane Interstate Fairgrounds in the Valley were leased from the Parks Department by a Spokane corporation, the **Spokane Fair and Racing Association**. The grandstand was refurbished and a 16-day season operated.

1936

Annual Barn Dance at **The Garden** —hay, lanterns, rube costumes, free cider, music by **Juanita Clark's Mountaineers**. Gentlemen 40¢, Ladies 25¢.

1937

The first **Inland Empire Regatta** at **Liberty Lake** was marked by thrilling performances of boats going up to 55 miles per hour.

The **Pinecroft Recreation Center** was planned. It never materialized although WPA funds were procured. (See article, "Jackson and the Pinecroft Development," Volume I.)

An area dancing craze. In Spokane and the Valley 14 dancing schools emerged, teaching from tap to acrobatics.

1939

J.E. Hutchins opened the **Dishman Theater**, built by **A.T. Dishman**. (See "Dishman and the Dishman Brothers," Volume I.)

1941

Central Valley's Douglas Field was lighted for night games. It was the first lighted field in the area. The student association was the sponsor and furnished much of the labor.

1943

T.O. Dunbar bought **Johnny's Bowling Alley** at **Opportunity.** The Alley reopened October 6, 1944, with interest in bowling at a new height.

From the **Inland Empire Paper Company, Millwood** purchased for $2000 the mill's dump just east of the Town Hall on **Frederick**. It was developed for a park after **WWII**. The paper mill had its own park.

1944

December 12: The last chapter of "Captain Winslow" will be shown at the **Dishman Theater** Saturday. No more Saturday matinees.

1945

Valley Country Club, including a nine-hole golf course, was located on a 50-acre site on the north shore of **Liberty Lake**.

Swimming pools opened at the **Dishman Grade School** and **West Valley High School**.

1945   Because of numerous requests, the **Dishman Theater** again is scheduling matinees. The regular billings will be shown with a serial, "Adventures of Smiling Jack."

Ski-Mor, a winter playground built and operated by the Torreys and Schafers on the east face of Browne's Mountain during the Depression. Left: the ski jump, right: parking area for cars. 1935-36 *photo, Courtesy of Earnie Sprow.*

Fun Times and Paid-for Entertainment

At the turn of the century, entertainment was largely home-made and free, generated by family, church, or school. By the late twenties, movie houses, skating rinks, dance halls, and shows at the Fairgrounds and even in neighboring towns were becoming part of a "normal" life style.

[From Fred Coddington's informal autobiography:]

One Saturday we drove to Harrington to see the annual Mule Show. One barn in the town stabled over one hundred mules. Farmers brought in mules from the surrounding areas to demonstrate skill in handling them. There were contests to show single animals and strength of teams. Four twenty-mule teams competed. They had highly polished silver plated trappings on harnesses that glistened in the bright sunlight. Each mule in the team was matched for size and color. The teams pulled four heavy freight wagons. The brakes on the last wagon were set, skidding the wheels and giving the mules something to pull. There were prizes for the best looking team and the most skillfully driven team. But the biggest money went for the tightest turns in a figure eight contest. The mule skinners wore fancy western outfits with embroidered silk shirts and cowboy hats.

We visited the big barn after all mules were in their stalls. Farmers were forking hay into mangers and dishing out oats into special containers. One mule started braying at the far end of the building. Others took it up along the line. Soon the din was deafening.

Every spring the merchants in Spokane had a Sportsman's Tourist Fair. It was set up under the elevated tracks of the Union Pacific and Great Northern Railroads. Several blocks just west of the U.P. Station were enclosed with draped canvas. Trees were brought in to create woodland scenery and even streams flowed in canvas beds. Speckled trout swam in the streams and live ducks played in and out of the water.

All kinds of boats, tents and camping, hunting and fishing equipment were displayed. Often bear cubs were on display, climbing dead trees, and wrestling one another. The Forest Service exhibited forest animals in cages, including faun deer. They demonstrated how to identify different forest trees. Fishermen showed fly tying techniques.

One afternoon in 1928, our first year in high school (Lewis and Clark), Frank Miller and I left immediately after seventh period and headed for the Liberty Theater next to the Fidelity National Bank Building. We saw a new talking movie picture, "The Jazz Singer" with Al Jolson and sound by Vitaphone. It cost 50¢ admission, but it was worth it!

Vitaphone had some kinks that had to be worked out. The lips of the actors were not always synchronized with their voices. But the days of silent pictures were numbered.

Another friend, Bob Sandberg, and I often went to afternoon matinees at the Opportunity Theater, west of Grove's Garage. It showed only silent pictures, but they only cost 10¢.

Those matinees were habit forming because a serial picture called "Perils of Pauline" was shown before the feature picture and always left the heroine in a hazardous situation. We could never figure out how she could escape from her impossible position. The next week, sure enough, she was freed in the nick of time.

In the summer of 1929 Bob Sandberg and I rode

our bicycles to the Fairgrounds one morning. The Ringling Brothers, Barnum and Bailey Circus was getting set up for several performances. We asked if we could help with the work to earn a ticket to the show. A man let us carry water for the elephants. Those elephants drank water faster than we could carry it. Toward noon the elephants were just spraying our water over their backs. It was exhausting work, but the man gave us choice seats in front of the bleachers, beside the middle ring.

A German troop of actors brought a Passion Play to the Fairgrounds. They advertised in the paper for extras to take part in mob scenes. Bob Sandberg and I packed lunches and rode out to the Fairgrounds again. We were outfitted with shabby short gowns made of burlap. We had to take off our shoes and socks and roll up our pant legs. My first speaking part was yelling, "Hail, Hosanna, Hail!" as I scattered palm branches. Later in the play, I screamed, "Crucify Him! Crucify!" with equal enthusiasm.

At the Spokane Interstate Fair and Livestock Show, we helped launch a hot air balloon. When we arrived, men were pouring kerosene over a pile of box boards in a pit. From this five foot wide fire pit, a two foot wide trench extended thirty feet. Men dragged a sooty gray canvas bag in and centered it over the pit. Around the circumference of the flattened balloon, quarter inch ropes were attached at six foot intervals. Another rope fastened to the top center of the balloon was tied to a sand bag. About thirty boys stood around the border of the bag. Each was given one of the coiled ropes to hold. We were instructed about letting the ropes out gradually, as the balloon filled with smoke.

A man crawled down the two foot trench to light the fire. As he backed out of the ditch, we could see the center of the balloon bulging above the ground. As the edge of the balloon began to rise off the ground, we played our ropes.

When the balloon was completely lifted off the ground, the aerialist walked in under it. He was dressed in shiny yellow coveralls and wore a blue aviators' helmet and goggles. He fastened a three-foot board to some looped ropes dangling from both sides of the balloon.

After carefully inspecting the balloon from all angles, he put on his parachute packs. He tested all the release buckles on his harness. The ropes in our hands were really tugging, although the wind was only slight. Satisfied that everything was in proper order, he climbed onto his seat and grasped the tow ropes. He nodded to the man who was supervising us. The man gave us our signal, and we all released our ropes at once. The balloon and its passenger shot upward.

A crew of men climbed onto a flat bed truck. They drove off, followed by an ambulance, in the direction the balloon was drifting. The huge balloon seemed to be shrinking rapidly in the sky. The aerialist was just a yellow speck below it.

Liberty Lake

Liberty Lake was one of our favorite spots for a picnic. It was about eight miles east of us. The Interurban Electric Train went as far as the west side of the lake. Swimming facilities were good. At Neylands' Grove there was a float with a sixteen-foot diving tower.

Beyond Neylands' Grove to the south, there were some carnival concessions. Dad's bank always had its annual picnic there. Bob and I liked to ride the Thriller. It was a ring of seats suspended by chains from a high revolving steel wheel. When going fullspeed, we swung out high above the ring of spectators. Our faces often showed a definite greenish pallor when we finished that ride.

At the south end of Liberty Lake, a resort had a high wooden roller coaster slide. We could rent little toboggan-shaped sleds for 20¢ an hour.

In winter, we skated on Liberty Lake. The ice on the lake froze thick—so thick that one winter a whole fleet of Army National Guard planes landed on the ice. When there was a favorable wind, some kids carried sails while skating. Sometimes men drove their cars on the ice, towing a long line of skaters behind them. Every winter, at least one car would break through thin ice and sink to the bottom of the lake.

A Bank Opening

["Big Celebration All Day Friday," *Spokane Valley Herald,* September 11, 1930.]

With the opening of the new Community State Bank, merchants at Dishman have set tomorrow, Friday, September 12, for a community celebration and are inviting everyone in the Valley to visit them.

The particular social events of the celebration will be a big dance at the Hi-Way Pavilion, formerly the Dishman Hall, and a moving picture show in the Dishman Arena.

A thousand free tickets to the dance and three hundred for the show will be distributed through the city to patrons of the stores. A large crowd of merrymakers is expected to be on hand in the evening.

The Dishman business men are pointing out the complete shopping and business facilities of their community since the bank has opened its doors, and are urging Valley people to come in and get acquainted.

Music for the dance will be furnished by an excellent orchestra directed by Dutch Groshoff and Norm Thue, popular musicians, who opened the Hi-Way Pavilion last Saturday night.

In addition to the free tickets, free refreshments will be served and merchandise prizes distributed.

Dishman people are determined to make this a real celebration, and predict that it marks the beginning of new forward strides for their growing community.

The picture show will be "When the Wife's Away," which J.G. Heatherly of the Heatherly Circuit describes as a comedy knock-out to take the place of the fistie knock-outs frequently staged in the Arena.

J.G. Heatherly states that in the two years since he began his picture shows here in the Valley, his circuit has increased to seven regular theaters.

These include Opportunity, Rathdrum, Post Falls, Rockford, Elk, Fairfield, and Plummer. Millwood is also included though not as a regular date.

6,357 Attend Big Picnic

[*Spokane Valley Herald,* July 28, 1932]

The tenth all-Valley picnic has passed into history with the record of having been one of the best organized and most enjoyable picnics of the entire number.

While the numbers apparently fell off a little from the two previous picnics, the check this year was much more accurate than before. Boy Scouts were being stationed at each entrance with counting machines, and every possible effort made to be accurate in the count.

From 9 a.m. to 7 p.m. when the Scouts went off duty, 5607 persons entered the park (Liberty Lake) and an unofficial estimate of those going out later for the dancing in the evening was 750, according to general chairman, Dr. N.E. Bayne, making a total count and estimate of 6357, about 1000 less than the 7300 of last year.

Everything moved by the clock, with the result that there were no long-drawn-out periods of waiting for the fun to begin. The boys and girls were on hand promptly at 11 a.m. and went through their sports with evident enjoyment, while down on the horse shoe court the men tossed the shoes the entire morning, ending the tournament in a tie for first place.

During the luncheon hour the Spokane Valley Band, directed by Gus Nelson of Chester, played, much to the enjoyment of the crowd.

Following the luncheon period, the parade of decorated bicycles was held.

Other events were the women's nail driving contest, the fat men's race, baseball heave, a wrestling match, various swimming and diving events for all ages, and the town baseball game.

The heat of the afternoon made the beach very attractive, and the floats were so crowded during the water sports that the swimmers and divers stood in the water up to their knees. Due to the confusion of the contestants with the watchers on the beach, it was impossible to check on the winners in some events.

The picnic was notable for its orderliness, no drunks or trouble makers being seen on the grounds at any time.

Square Dancing at Mitcham's Barn

During World War II, the popular place to go in the Spokane area, if you liked to dance, was the Pavilion at Natatorium Park. In mid-century, especially for the square dancing set, there was the Wagon Wheel at Dartford. Then came Mitcham's Barn on Mt. Spokane, and today we have the Western Dance Center along the Spokane River on Sullivan Road.

Before the Center came into being, small groups of dancers met at churches, Whitworth College, granges, the Masonic Temple, schools, barns, the slab at Shadle, Gonzaga, and even in the basements of homes. As interest in dancing grew and attendance increased, none of these facilities was large enough to accommodate the new crop of dancers.

In the spring of 1938, Clarence Edwin Mitcham, a car inspector for the Great Northern Railroad and an avid square dancer, had a dream. He dreamed of building a dance hall on the property he owned on Deadman Creek at the foot of Mount Spokane.* The culmination of the dream was Mitcham's Barn.

In the book, *Fifty Years of Square and Round Dancing in the Spokane, Washington, Area* by Letty and Gene Kister, Cloyce and Arlene Preedy wrote about Mitcham's Barn:

"The land was undeveloped. The road to it was narrow, rutty, and almost impossible in winter—deep with mud in the spring. Thanks to the promoters of the State Park and those interested in skiing, the road later was widened and graveled. The name at that time was Macadam Road, later changed to Deadman Creek Road and now known as Mount Spokane State Park Road.

"In the spring of 1938, construction on the barn started. A team of horses was used to level the ground. A bridge was built across the creek. The trees were felled by Mr. Mitcham and his son, John, and then were peeled to become the main structure of the barn. Ridge poles, ceiling beams, floor joists, and all the rafters were made from the poles. The unused portion of the trees were sawed for lumber or used for wood.

"The maple floor was laid separate from the walls and the roof. A tall concrete footing was poured for the record turntable so the vibration of the floor would not make the needle skip.

"A massive fireplace was built on the east side of the hall. Of course, the rest rooms were outside. Also for many years the only siding was tar paper.

"On July 2, 1938, the first public dance with live music was held. In the fall of 1940 , because drinking became a problem, the hall closed to the public and in November of that year, the first club square

---

* Mt. Spokane is a popular ski and recreation destination thirty miles northeast of Spokane and north of the Valley. The lower slope is covered with pine trees. It slopes easily upward to great ledges of weather-stained granite that jut out from the mountain's sides. The summit is a bare mass of light gray granite flecked with mica. On bright days the granite appears almost white and the mica flashes in the sun. A lookout at the summit gives a sweeping view of the Inland Empire.

The residents of the foothills are often considered Valley dwellers. The mountain was first known as Mt. Carleton, then Old Baldy and in 1912 was officially named Mt. Spokane.

The Spokane Indians who had a close spiritual relation with the sun are said to have associated the mountain with the supernatural. In Jonathan Edwards' history he states that explorer Ross Cox "speaks of the chief of the Indians of the region as 'Illin Spokanee,' which means 'Son of the Sun.'"

Francis Cook, a pioneer Spokane editor and mayor is said to have purchased the mountain shortly after the Depression of 1893. He carved a rough road to its top and built a cabin there known as Cook's Cabin. In 1927 the State of Washington bought the mountain for $1.00 for a State Park. There is a photo in the Spokane history file at the city library of the Cook family enjoying the view from the summit of their mountain.

In 1931 Sonora Bruce Dodd, the Spokane woman who is credited with founding Father's Day, was instrumental in having the mountain officially dedicated as a perpetual monument to fatherhood by city and state officials. On that occasion it was called The Father Mountain.

The following year a burnished copper sun ball, four feet in diameter, was mounted on a pedestal of natural stone and concrete and placed on the highest summit by the Spokane Federation of Woman's Organizations. It reflects the sun like a beacon on a clear day.

In 1950 Binsford and Mort, Portland, Oregon, published *The New Washington*, compiled by a group of writers working under a WPA Writers' Program. This group determined that the word *Spokane* was derived from the Indian word Spehkunne (phonetic spelling) meaning sun people.

dance was held by Thad and Caryl Byrne's Do Si Do Club."

On September 2, 1964, after 26 years of keeping the Barn busy with dancing, Mr. Mitcham sold the Barn to the Howard Halls who in turn sold it to Cloyce and Arlene Preedy July 1960.

Mitcham's was small. Area square dancing was gaining popularity. The number of people dancing increased. A new hall with more space and a good floor was the dream of local dancers. The culmination of the dream was today's Western Dance Center.

Norman Thue, Musician

[By Editor Pat Caraher, *Hill Topics*, a publication of Washington State University, March, 1994.]

Norman Thue, a 90-year-old musician who started playing the organ for the old silent movies in Spokane, was honored October 9 before the WSU-Arizona State football game in Martin Stadium.

He still plays the organ on the El Katif Shrine fez trailer that participates in parades and special events, including the annual Shriners Day football game at WSU.

During the height of his musical career, Thue appeared on the Ed Sullivan and the Frankie Carle television shows. He also accompanied such artists as Sally Rand, The Anderson Sisters, Eddy Peabody, the Ink Spots, The Mills Brothers, and Elvis Presley.

In the early days, Thue filled a shift on the organ at the Liberty Theatre in Spokane and then dashed over to the Ritz for a second shift.

In 1930 after completing a degree in Music at WSU, he was offered a teaching job in western Washington, but returned to Spokane. In the Valley, he and Dutch Groshoff teamed up musically as "Dutch and Norm," a combo that played at the Dishman Dance Hall [known as the Hi-way Pavilion] and later at Lareida's. Thue also played 20 regular radio shows per week.

In 1941, Thue and a partner opened a music store [in Spokane]. Years later, when the Spokane freeway cut a path through his door, he decided to retire.

He once had an offer to move to Los Angeles to play the organ for the Dodgers baseball team in Dodger Stadium. Instead, he elected to stay in Spokane as an organist at the Spokane Fairgrounds ballpark.

Thue is known for his longtime civic work in Spokane.

Spokane Gun Club

[*Spokane Valley Today*: June, July 1987]

I had never been to the Gun Club in Green-acres—nor to any other gun club, for that matter—and didn't know what to expect.

I found 100 acres of spring-green prairie surrounded by mountains, a friendly white clubhouse at the end of a winding landscaped approach and inside the clubhouse a lot of pride. Pride, in the building which the members had fashioned out of two surplus army barracks, and pride in the membership who work hard for the club, and have won prizes and championships all over the world.

Pictures of people whom I have met in other walks of life but did not associate with the games of skeet and trap hung on the walls. There was Jerry Naimy, long-time West Valley High School teacher and published poet and Charles Libby, Jr., whose photographs often appear in *Spokane Valley Today*. I read clippings that told about former Spokane Mayor Arthur Meehan's achievements in the sport, and I was shown around the grounds by nearby Opportunity neighbors, Jean and Retired Colonel Erv Walker.

" I didn't know that you shoot trap and skeet," I said to Jean.

She laughed. "I don't. At first I came along with Erv who is a champion. The club found so many uses for me that last year they honored me with a life membership."

There are two special rooms in the clubhouse: the Skeet Hall of Fame and the Trap Hall of Fame. In those two rooms are 39 biographies, and Jean wrote them all. She also was appointed club correspondent and wrote a monthly column for *Scoreboard West, The Leading Shotgun Magazine*.

I browsed through the ponderous record books. The minutes from the year 1892 and clippings from the thirties tell the history of the club.

HISTORY OF THE SPOKANE GUN CLUB

Early records show that even before 1892 there was a loosely organized group of Spokane residents interested in the sports of skeet and trap shooting. The name they chose was the Spokane Rod and Gun Club. The group maintained trap machines on city-owned land in various locations. Sunday shoots and larger tournaments were held at the Fairgrounds and stadium. Later the traps were placed on rented property referred to as the Moran Prairie site, south of Spokane.

Following World War I, the club was granted a "revocable license" from the United States government for the use of eight acres of land on the Fort Wright Military Reservation. There the first club-house was built.

When World War II was declared, the group voted unanimously to cease activities and rent their clubhouse to the Non-commissioned Officers Association at the Fort for the duration.

Through the years the *Spokesman-Review* was very active in Gun Club activities and sponsored many tournaments. The tournament results from surrounding towns were, and still are, phoned into the paper, making it possible for it to scoop the winners.

In Spokane the war years were the years of legal slot machines in private clubs. The gun club met unofficially in various rooms in the city, installed slot machines, and therefrom earned enough money to purchase in 1948 the Greenacres site where it has grown and prospered.

The name Spokane Gun Club became official when the club was incorporated in 1912.

The club has one of the most active skeet shooting programs in the Northwest and annually hosts the longest skeet tournament of the Inland Empire, the Pacific Northwest Skeet Championships. The forty-first such event was held at the Greenacres site April 23-26 and hosted entries.

Mike Foster, junior all-American champion, is the grandson of Ed Karrer of the Gunatorium on North Argonne. Skeet and trap enthusiasts come in all ages. Ernie Gardener of the Greenacres Club is 87 years old and participates regularly. From other age groups are active participants Bob Miller and Jerry Paulus.

When I left, Jean and Erv gave me a souvenir, one of the round orange clay targets. It is a memento of a very pleasant day in a lovely Valley spot.

Transportation

"Otis Orchards is very proud of the new automobiles speeding by—Ray Fullerton's new Nash Sedan, Bob Reed's Ford Sedan, H.H. Cole's shiny Dodge, the yellow wheels on Dave Sweeney's Buick."

[The *Spokane Valley Herald*, May 14, 1920.]

WASHINGTON TIRE AND RUBBER COMPANY
The building was located on the northeast corner of Sprague and Park Road. In the teens,
Mr. Harding was superintendent and William Smith, manager.
Courtesy of DeLoss and Alice Anderson who had the first Dime Store in Dishman at Sprague and Marguerite.

Transportation

CHRONOLOGICAL HISTORY

1920

The speed limit when driving through **Dishman, Opportunity, Vera, Otis Orchards** on **Trent** or **Appleway** was 20 mph.

The **Northern Pacific** ran a two-car local train known as "The Dinky" that provided local service between **Spokane** and **Sandpoint**—to **Spokane** in the morning and back to **Sandpoint** in the evening. Service was discontinued in the '30s.

June 5: The people voted to replace the **Argonne Bridge.** Contract was awarded to **W. A. Byers.**

November 11: Dedication and renaming of the **Argonne Bridge** in **Millwood.** (See article, "Dedication of the Argonne Bridge.")

1921

The **Dishman Railroad Station** burned and was rebuilt.

A tax was levied on gasoline for the first time.

The following roads were widened 24-28 feet: **Moab** to **Liberty Lake** and the **Idaho Line**, the **Appleway** north over **Spokane Bridge**, **Greenacres** east to the schoolhouse and north to the bridge over the river.

1922

Trent Road was paved from **Spokane** to **Trent Bridge** and to the **Idaho Line** at a cost of about $250,000.

For the first time an auto reached the top of **Mount Spokane.**

Washington Water Power ceased interurban rail operation due to high costs and competition from autos.

1923

The third bridge was built at **Trent,** roadway 24', length 452'. It was designed by **Garnet** and **Davis,** of reinforced concrete, cost $93,891.57. The steel from the old **Trent** bridge was taken to **Spokane Bridge** and used to get materials across the river for the building of the south branch of the **Corbin Canal.**

1924

August 7: The 116th **Observation Unit** of the 41st **Division,** the state's first National Guard Aviation Unit, was assigned to **Felts Field.** Two hangars were erected at the **Parkwater** aviation field. (See "Felts Field," Volume I.)

Mid-20s

The Auto Interurban provided shuttle bus service between **Spokane** and **Coeur d'Alene** with many stops along **Trent Road**. Service was good with almost hourly schedules.

1925

Spokane Valley Woman's Club undertook the job of getting all roads and streets named and sign posts erected at suitable locations.

An aerial circus was held at **Felts Field**.

First municipal airport at **Felts Field**.

1927

The **Great Northern Railroad** took over the **Electric Interurban Lines** serving the Valley.

May 20: Lindberg took off from Roosevelt Field and headed for Paris.

Summer: Henry Ford rang down the curtain on the immortal Model T Ford and closed his plant to prepare for the Model A. It came out the following year. The Model B came out in 1932 for only one year. The first V-8 Ford appeared in 1933.

September 19-24: The **National Air Derby** was held at **Felts Field.** Planes flew from New York and San Francisco to Spokane. Col. Charles Lindberg, fresh from his historic solo flight across the Atlantic in May, flew *The Spirit of St. Louis* into **Felts Field**. (See article, "Felts Field," Volume I.)

1929

Newman Lake Road was paved. **Argonne** was paved from **Dishman** to **Millwood**.

Nick Mamer and **Art Walker** flew the *Spokane Sun God* on a round trip across the continent.

The area's first traffic light was erected at **Howard** and **Riverside**.

September 3: *The Graf Zepplin* was nearing the end of its round-the-world flight.

A trimotor Ford plane began airmail service between **Spokane** and **Seattle** and **Spokane** and **Pasco**.

1931

In Spokane motorbuses displaced street cars.

1932

The **Appleway** was double paved from the city limits to the concrete pavement half a mile east of Dishman at **Hardesty Road** (Fancher). The pavement consisted of 20-foot strips of concrete with a four-foot unpaved strip between.

1933

December 23: **County Engineer Scott** reported that the **Opportunity-Mica Road** cut-off at **Darknell Road**, a Civil Works Project, was progressing well. It provided work for 72 men.

1933

Art Walker of **Opportunity**, popular pilot and airplane engineer, was appointed assistant field manager for **United Air Lines** at **Felts Field**.

The concrete viaduct at **Dishman** was completed. This included widening the undercrossing and paving .2 mile of approaches. About 50 men were given work. The winning bid was $84,842.

1934

November 17: **County Commissioner J.B. Felts** met with the State Welfare Commission and it was determined that the aim should be at least 3800 men at work on relief projects by December 1. **Pines Road South** from the **Appleway** would be one of the first projects started.

Sheriff W. Miles reported to the *Herald* that drunken driving had increased more than 300 per cent in the last year. He blamed the increase on the repeal of prohibition. He said he believed there was as much or more bootlegging as when liquor was outlawed.

July 14 (*Valley Herald*): **Lt. Clare Hartnett** of **Bigelow-Johnson, Inc.** announced, "The company will take passengers for rides over the **Valley, Liberty Lake** and **Mt. Spokane** this weekend and on picnic day. A five-place Gates Day standard open plane and a Stinson closed model will be used for the flights, which will begin and end at the Valley landing field on **Appleway** west of **Liberty Lake Junction**. Cost is one cent per pound."

Northwest Airlines provided airmail and air passenger service between **Felts Field** and Chicago in only 13.5 hours.

1935

Darknell Road, an **Opportunity-Mica Cut-Off,** was awarded funds from the government to insure completion.

The four-lane **Appleway** was paved from a short distance east of **Dishman** to **Verdale**.

1936

The **Appleway** was widened to four lanes east of **Veradale** to the **Liberty Lake Junction**.

1938

Parallel parking of autos began in the Valley.

Valley roads were treated with sulphite liquid from the **Paper Mill** to keep down the dust. This process was first tried on the **Parkwater Air Field**. (See article, "Inland Empire Paper Mill," Volume I.)

1939

Thomas Bienz, president of the **Chamber,** decided north and south streets should be called "roads." The house numbers on east-west streets, to be called "avenues," were changed to conform to Spokane numbers and given Spokane street names. The **Appleway** became **Sprague Avenue; Shelley Way** became **Fourth; McCanna** became **Eighth; Campus** became **Twelfth; Saltese** became **Sixteenth**. (James Glover had named **Sprague** in Spokane for General J.W. Sprague, superintendent of the western division of the **N.P.R.R.**)

1939-40

A new 4-lane highway bridge was built across the Spokane River at the **Idaho Line**—the sixth bridge built at **Spokane Bridge.** Contractors were **Alloway** and **George;** cost, $110,000; length 511' with sidewalk on both sides.

1940

Street signs were installed on the **Appleway** and **Trent Avenues**.

The end of the **Spokane-Coeur d'Alene** train run known as the "Inland Empire Express" on the Electric Interurban Line. Passengers had connected with steamboats on **Lake Coeur d'Alene.** The last passenger off the train was **T.D. Miller,** E. 511 **Mission**, who also had been on the first run in 1903.

1941

The **Trentwood Train Station** employed a full-time telegraph operator to take care of the **Naval Supply Depot, Trentwood Rolling Mill,** and the apple packing business at **Otis.**

August 7: Several residents on **Shelley Way** (Fourth) reported losing tankfuls of gas during the night.

Work began to widen **Trent Avenue East** from 2 to 4 lanes.

1943

The **Vera Community Club** voted to place small waiting stations at bus stops.

The **Auto Interurban Company** had 35 round-trip schedules to the Valley. The Spokane Motorcoach Terminal was at Trent and Howard.

1945

Loren Lemon purchased 115 acres of the old **O'Riley** tract at **Adams** and **Saltese, Veradale,** for the construction of an air park. The air park will repair and service small aircraft, train students and arrange short charter flights.

Local residents were notified that house numbers must be displayed prominently if they expected mail delivery.

Dedication of the Argonne Bridge

[As told by Lois A. Larson.]

One morning in November 1920, Mr. Black, Music Director of the Orchard Park Schools, announced to us Millwood High School students that we had been asked to sing patriotic songs at the dedication of the new Argonne Bridge, across the Spokane River. The program would be after school.

Because it would be dark when I got home, I had to ask my parents' permission to participate. My mother and father felt that it was an honor for our school to have a part in the dedication and gave me permission.

The day of the dedication was cold and bleak. A strong, bitter cold east wind was blowing. Mother insisted I bundle up. I wore a wool tam on my head, a knit sweater under my coat, and spats that came nearly to the calf of my legs.

We students, bucking the wind, walked by twos from the high school building past the Sampson Grocery Store, over the electric railroad tracks, and past the Inland Empire Paper Mill to the new bridge.

It was to be dedicated as a lasting tribute to the local boys who fell at the battle of the Argonne Forest in World War I. The battle was still fresh in our minds. We remembered hearing that it was one of the fiercest battles fought against the Germans up to that time.

The new bridge was truly a wonder. It was *concrete* and was built straight across the river. The old wooden bridge had been angled from the steep bank on the north shore to an easier bank on the south shore and was a few feet lower than the new one. Its sides were not quite parallel. Even so, it served its purpose well and had been in constant use by horses pulling wagons and buggies and only now and then an auto.

The new bridge was the only traffic bridge between the Green Street Bridge (within the Spokane city limits), and the bridge at the Idaho-Washington state line.

We high school students were placed about midway on the bridge with our backs to the river. The speakers stood across from us and the local audience crowded onto both ends of the bridge. During the dedication I could not see or hear because the people crowded in, so anxious were they to be part of the celebration.

The opening songs were lost in the wind as were the words of the long-winded commissioners and dignitaries. The songs we sang were "America," "My Country 'Tis of Thee," and "The Star Spangled Banner." We sang one of these songs each morning at school for what were called "the opening exercises" that started the day.

By the time the dedication ceremonies were over, we were so nearly frozen that we walked stiff-legged back to the school, happy to get there and get onto Mr. Olsen's bus. After a three-mile ride, I walked about another ¼ mile home.

My mother took one look at my blue face and my stiff walking and put me into a hot tub of water and then to bed covered with woolen blankets. I did not develop the cold she feared, remembering the terrible flu epidemic of 1918.

I didn't object to the treatment because I also feared a cold— or rather the onion plaster that was Mother's remedy for a cold.

In the early days, Argonne Road north of the Appleway was called the Millwood Road; south of the Appleway, it was called the Chester Road.

Not Everyone Was Lucky Enough to Have a Car

[From the informal autobiography of Dr. Frederick Coddington.]

Across the highway from the Methodist Church [on the SW corner of the Appleway and Bowdish] were the tracks of the Interurban Electric Railway. We could catch trains there to go to Spokane, Liberty Lake, or Coeur d'Alene. Between the highway and tracks was an open wooden shelter with wooden seats along three sides for train waiting.

The Electric Railway and our bicycles were our chief form of transportation until the summer of 1924 when Dad bought a second-hand Model T Ford touring car. It wasn't perfect, but it was a CAR. Dad took the head off the engine block and ground the valves. When he got it back together, it ran well and did almost 50 miles an hour! For a month, we rode in it everywhere we went—even to church, although church was easily within walking distance. Dad drove it into Spokane every day to work at the bank, but was always careful to keep it within the 25 mph speed limit.

In the fall he installed a floor heater that conducted air over the hot exhaust manifold. In wet and cold weather, he put on side curtains. The back of the front seat had been cut out and hinged. It could be folded down between front and back seat cushions to form a bed. That came in handy for camping trips, like the one we took to Roseburg, Oregon, August 1925.

Dad wanted to see some timberland that he purchased. Dad, Mother, and John slept in a tent, but Robert and I shared the Ford, lowering the seat back for our bed. We went down the Columbia River Highway and up the coast to Tacoma. Part of the way, Dad rode on the left running board, holding the tire pump in his free hand. Mother drove. Whenever the left front tire became too soft, he had Mother stop. He pumped up the tire and jumped back on. Each pumping took us another mile or two toward our destination. We eventually reached a town where he bought a new inner tube.

In the spring of 1926, Dad traded in the Model T on a brand new Chevrolet sedan. It smelled wonderful inside. On the outside, it was light blue with lots of chrome trim. With balloon tires and shock absorbers, it was much more comfortable and smooth riding than the Model T. It had shutters in front of the radiator which let the engine warm up quickly. They were controlled from the dashboard.

On my sixteenth birthday, I got MY driver's license, even before I had a car.

As soon as school was out for the summer, I started picking strawberries for Mr. Davidheiser, saving every penny, nickel, and dime that I made for a car. Within two weeks, I accumulated ten dollars.

Happy and excited, I rode my bicycle to Dishman and entered the Brownson Motor Company office. (See article, "Brownson Motor Company.") I asked a clerk if I could see a car salesman. A man came out of the back room.

"Sonny," he said, "what can I do for you?"

"I want the best Ford ten dollars can buy," I told him.

He looked puzzled. Then he said, "I believe you mean it."

"I do mean it," I said. "I have ten dollars in this bag." I held out a bulging leather money pouch.

"Come out in the back with me," he said, "and we'll see what can be done."

I followed him.

Behind the building were the remains of about twenty Model T touring cars being gradually dismantled.

"I believe," he said, "that you should take this chassis, because it has the best engine. We'll find you some wheels for it, and a radiator. I suppose you will want two spare tires and rims?

"I think that would be a good idea," I said importantly.

As soon as we had picked out the parts, he said, "Come on inside and we will draw up a contract."

While he worked on the contract, I sorted out my

quarters, dimes, nickels and pennies. I piled them in stacks, grouped in even dollars. He made out a bill of sale and a certificate of transfer.

I rode my bicycle home to get a jack, pliers, screwdriver and wrench. I transferred the wheels we had picked out to my chassis and piled the radiator, hood and spares in the back. That evening Robert towed me home with Dad's Chev.

In two days, I had relined all the transmission and brake bands and got my car licensed.

I charged the neighborhood kids five cents to take them swimming. We went to the rapids in the Spokane River, below Carter's farm. Their nickels kept me in gasoline and gave me money for tire patching materials in giant economy sized kits. The kids helped me fix flat tires. All the tires had boots in them very soon.

In the spring of 1932, I traded my Model T Ford to Vernon Moss for his Harley Davidson motorcycle. I overhauled it in our backyard.

The constable at Opportunity heard that I had it. He came around to see if I had it properly licensed. When I showed him the parts all over the backyard, he scratched his head and told me to get it licensed before riding it on the streets.

I got it running and bought the license for it. John and I rode it to the river for a swim every afternoon that summer.

McCollum Crawford Ford

Marguerite Crawford, whose husband was Tom Crawford of McCollum Crawford Ford, reminisced recently about the difficulties of starting a business during World War II.

"No one in their right mind would have considered starting any phase of the automobile business in the early '40s," said Marguerite. "Detroit was consumed by war orders. Autos were not being manufactured for purchase by private citizens. Like other products, shortages of even used cars were at an all time high.

"But," Marguerite continued, "autos were in Tom Crawford's blood. He began pumping gas and fixing flats as a school boy in Arkansas at a local dealership. When his family moved to San Diego, California, he immediately got a job as lot boy and progressed to service manager, to parts manager, to sales manager for Pontiac.

"I was working as a nurse in San Diego," Marguerite said. "The year was 1941. I needed a new car and Tom Crawford sold me a brand new Pontiac! That's how we met. Not long after, we were married and at the recommendation of a young fellow named Fred Utter (also a salesman at Pontiac), we came to Spokane.

"Fred enticed us to come to Spokane by telling us of the beautiful countryside, the lights under the falls, of the wild pheasants, the great hunting and fishing—and that there was a Cadillac dealership for sale.

"'I'll buy that dealership if you will manage it,' Fred said to Tom.

"Tom liked Spokane, agreed to the partnership and Fred bought what became Utter Cadillac.

"In Spokane while working for Utter, Tom met Harold McCollum. Like Tom, Harold was a natural with cars. As a youngster in Espanola (near Medical Lake), he saved his money to buy old junkers to fix up. Until the right job came along, he was working as a male model at the old Kemp and Hebert store on Post and Main. (The Kemp and Hebert site later became the Palace Department Store and in 1994 is the site of Nordstrom's.)

"In spite of the fact that it was war-time and there seemed to be no future in cars, Tom and Harold became partners in a used car lot on the SE corner of Stevens and Third in Spokane.

"They did so well," Marguerite continued, "that Ford offered them a franchise. This was an honor and a prize and what they really wanted. Nothing was harder to come by during the war. Even to apply for a dealership, the applicant had to have a building. Tom and Harold had no building and saw no immediate hope of acquiring one. Few places were available.

"But they were determined. They found a filling

One of the first new vehicles after the war (1946). Tom Crawford, right, delivers a new Ford panel truck to William Schafer. Schafer will use it to deliver his bottled mineral spring water.
Courtesy of Marguerite Crawford.

station for rent on the NW corner of Sprague and Bessie. They rented it and showed it to the Ford agent and presented it as their building. The Ford dealership became theirs.

"While working from their rented filling station, they had an opportunity to buy from A.T. Dishman the frontage across the street for a building of their own.

"Again because of the war effort, problems arose. Harold and Tom needed a permit to build on their property, but few were issued and even for those few, the wait was long. They did not receive their permit until 1944.

"They finished the building, McCollum Crawford Ford, just in time to receive three of the first Fords manufactured for sale to private individuals after the War.

"People were so anxious after the war for new things," Marguerite said. "They came in droves. Looked under the hood, examined the interior, almost as if they couldn't believe their eyes. During the war, Tom used to go to Montana, anywhere, to buy used cars to sell.

"The new cars were cause for celebration. Friends and businessmen filled the showroom with flowers. There were more flowers than cars.

"At first, we had only the three cars to show. But we took orders—first come, first served. People even offered us money "under the table" to be put higher on the list.

"We stayed open until midnight that first day."

*   *   *

In 1994 McCollum Ford is doing business at that same location although there have been several changes in ownership through the years.

Memories of Early Aviation in the Valley

[From Dr. Frederick Coddington's informal autobiography.]

Airplanes and their engines were improving in their dependability.

One of our neighbors, Edgar Bigelow, had been an aviation instructor for the Canadian Army during World War I. He wanted to get back into flying. He went into partnership with a Valley businessman named Johnson. They bought several Alexander Eaglerock Biplanes, located their flying school out at the Parkwater Airport (later called Felts Field) and called their enterprise the Bigelow-Johnson School of Aviation.

Mr. Bigelow often talked to the Scouts about airplanes and got us boys interested in flying and in making flying models out of balsa wood.

In 1928 he took my friend Robert and me for our first airplane ride. We rode our bicycles to the Parkwater Airport and paid $2.50 each at the Bigelow-Johnson office. We were loaned leather helmets and goggles. We climbed onto the left lower wing step of the plane and into the forward cockpit. Mr. Bigelow checked to see that our seat belts were fastened securely. Then he climbed into the rear cockpit.

A man came out to start the engine. He called out, "Contact off!" Mr. Bigelow repeated, "Contact off!" The man pulled our propeller through two complete revolutions. The man yelled, "Contact!" and Mr. Bigelow repeated it. The man swung the blade of the propeller downward and jumped aside. The big engine started and went into a steady rhythm. The man pulled chocks from in front of both wheels and waved to Mr. Bigelow as we taxied slowly to the far end of the runway.

Before pulling onto the runway, Mr. Bigelow checked out the engine. He checked the ailerons on the trailing side of both wings and we saw the wings wiggle. A socket in the floor between our feet moved side to side. Then it moved forward and backward, and the foot pedals at our feet moved in and out. Everything seemed to be working perfectly. He checked the sky all around us. We looked

back at Mr. Bigelow and he smiled and nodded. Then he advanced the throttle and pulled into the runway. We could see the throttle lever on the left side of our cockpit move forward.

The roar of the engine was deafening and we saw the ground racing past us. Then it was dropping away from us.

The Spokane River was glistening on our left side. Everything seemed to be moving slower and trees and buildings rapidly grew smaller. We leaned over the side and the wind tore at our helmets and goggles and lips.

We flew straight over the hills beyond Shelley Lake, and soon were looking down onto Liberty Lake. We made a figure of eight turn over the lake. We recognized the resorts around the shoreline but they appeared amazingly small. We headed back to Opportunity and circled our neighborhood. Our house and chicken pen revolved slowly beyond our right wing tips.

Soon we recognized the river and the airport ahead of us and we began to drop nearer the ground. We made a sharp turn and the runway was lined up straight ahead of our propeller. We landed with a slight bounce. We could feel the vibration of our wheels and tail skid on the dirt runway. We taxied in front of the Bigelow-Johnson Hangar. Our engine coughed and died and the propeller stopped.

We had been in the air exactly fifteen minutes.

We were sorry when, because of the Depression, business at the aviation school dropped off. Mr. Bigelow took a job flying air mail for a government subsidized company. One night, when snow covered the ground outside Pasco, Washington, he crashed into an open field and was killed instantly. It was a terrible loss to our community and neighborhood. I wrote a sonnet about him for an English class assignment. At his memorial service, at the Opportunity Presbyterian Church, I read it, by request:

He's gone! The world will miss his cheery smile,
Uplifting spirit in a world of men;
He stood for honesty and faith and then
He held his place among the rank and file.

He taught men how to fly with grace and style,
A gentle man of strength, some jeered him when
He spoke of God. Reviewing his life again,
I honor him who has finished his last mile.

Oh harken, all you earthbound toilers who
Aspire for loftier vistas of this world!
Come, gather around his grave with heartfelt
    sighs
And let your solemn prayers and songs ensue.
Rejoice beneath your nation's flag unfurled,
Commemorate his freedom in the sky.

The two Fancher Brothers (for whom Fancher Road is named) owned a couple of airplanes. They refitted them with special fuel tanks and radios. One plane had a hose to lower for refueling the other. They practiced with the two planes flying close, one above the other. They lowered the hose from the refueling plane to the other repeatedly.

One morning, the Fanchers took off in the endurance plane. They carried extra engine oil and a week's supply of food and water. They flew all over Washington, Idaho, and part of Montana. They returned to Spokane every eight hours to take on more gasoline. They kept that plane in the air for over six days.

116th Observation Squadron, Felts Field, Washington

Although only the east end of Felts Field is actually in the Spokane Valley, Valley folks have always considered it their airport. They are proud of the fact that Felts is older than Spokane International Airport and they are proud of the records of many Valley aviators who served there. (For an early history of Felts Field, see "Felts Field" in Volume I.)

They are also proud of the record of the 116th Observation Squadron for which the airfield was organized and of which their own Major John T. Fancher was the first commanding officer.

It was during the '20s and '30s that the 116th operated out of Felts Field. It was at Felts that word was received that the unit was the first National Guard organization in the country to achieve full flight qualifications for every officer in the unit (many of whom were Valley men). And it was at Felts that in 1934, the most modern aircraft hangar in the country was completed.

In the late '30s, the unit was tasked by the Federal Government to take pictures of the Columbia River in order to find a site for the Grand Coulee Dam.

This photography became very important in the planning and construction of Grand Coulee Dam.

With the approach of World War II, the unit was called to active duty in 1940, and was assigned to Gray Field at Fort Lewis, Washington. From this location the 116th flew antisubmarine patrols along the Pacific Coast. The unit was abandoned in 1943, and personnel were assigned to other Army/Air Corps units.

In February 1949, the 116th Fighter Squadron was reactivated at Felts Field, home of the old 116th Observation Squadron. Officers and airmen of the 116th formed the nucleus of the new organization. The new unit flew P-51 Mustangs of World War II fame.

Gordon Knauss, who lived a block west of Park on N. Dakota, remembers, as a teen-ager in the '20s and '30s, going to the airport and helping polish the planes. For this, the pilots allowed him in the plane during a take-off and landing, but he was not allowed to go on a flight.

Communication

When Ed Olson [the Freeman Village Blacksmith] was asked if he ever watched television, he said, "I wouldn't have a TV in my house. All's you do is sit and watch it and I have to get up early in the morning."

Against the front wall [of his shop], a relic marking years of service adorns the wall. It is an old-fashioned, battery operated hand-crank telephone. Ed was on a 22 party line and the bill was less than $3.00 a year. He said a large telephone company offered to buy out the Star Phone Company and set him up with modern equipment. To his amazement it would have cost $70 a year for a business phone like he would need. "Why, the C.P. Thomas Mercantile had a pay phone that anyone could use to make a long-distance call!"

[From *Memories of Yesterday and Today, Freeman, Washington, 1885-1985*, Roberta Goldsmith.]

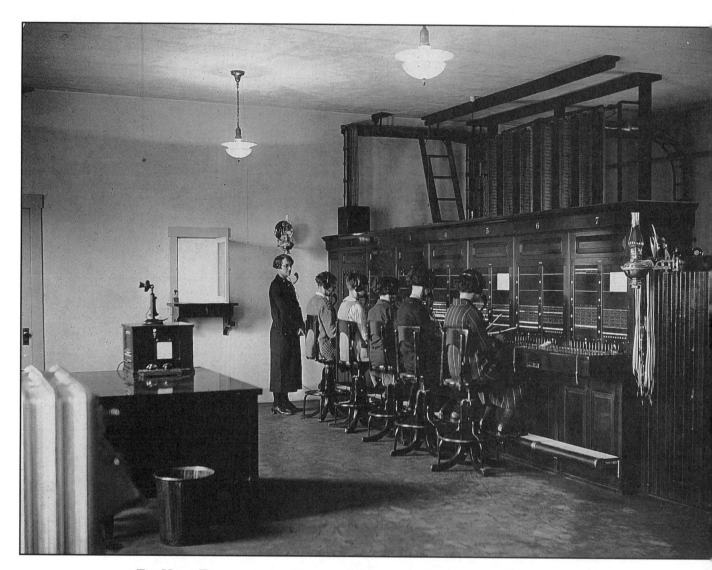

THE HOME TELEPHONE AND TELEGRAPH COMPANY, OPPORTUNITY EXCHANGE, 1925
First located in a corner of the Odd Fellows Building; in 1924 in a new building on Robie (Waller) Road
near the Appleway. Bertha Payne (Kunkel) was chief operator for many years.
Courtesy of Vern G. Payne, manager of Madison Lumber in Opportunity.

Communication

CHRONOLOGICAL HISTORY

1919   July 1: First class postage rate was 2¢ per ounce.

1920   March 24: **Nelson** and **Frolander** published the first issue of *The Spokane Valley Herald*. (See article, "A Newspaper for the Valley".)

June 25: 12 **Saltese** farmers subscribed to telephone connections. Phone lines reached the **Saltese** on August 13.

March: **Opportunity Post Office** advanced to Third Class.

1921   **Dishman** secured its own post office.

1924   Regular Transcontinental Air Mail Service was begun in the **U.S.**

A new "Orchard Office" was being constructed in the Valley by **W.J. Doust** of **Opportunity** for the Home Telephone and Telegraph Company of Spokane. The exchange began in 1911 with one small section of switchboard connected directly to Spokane on a ten-party suburban line.

April 1: **Buell Felts** became managing editor of the *Herald* and **Wilbur King**, business manager, after buying the paper from **Dunphy, Nelson** and **Mason**. Offices were transferred from the Rookery Building in **Spokane** to the **Opportunity Bank Building**.

1925   November 17: **Automatic Dial Phones** were installed in parts of the **Valley**. The old "Orchard" exchange became "Walnut."

1927   **Otis Orchards Post Office** located in a new building at the junction of **Kenney Road** and **Wellesley**.

January: New *Herald* printing plant on the **Appleway** and **Shirley Road** (**Sprague** and **Herald**) and paper published in **Valley** for first time. Paper enlarged to seven columns. **Buell Felts**, editor and publisher, tried to include the east side of the city in what he called "**The East Side Herald**."

1927

Cowles Publishing built a warehouse at **Millwood.**

July 1: **Earl Z. Smith** became editor of *Herald* after **Buell Felts'** death in a plane crash May 29. (See article, "Felts Field" Vol. I.) **Smith** continued until his death in 1935. (See "A Newspaper for the Valley" for a sample of Buell's editorials.)

May: Many Valley residents heard the broadcast by radio of Lindberg's take-off on his solo flight across the Atlantic Ocean. (See article, "Radio—Even Television.")

International Air Mail Service was available.

1929

Airmail service between **Spokane** and **Pasco.** Also a tri-motor plane began service between **Spokane** and **Seattle.**

Postmaster Kelsey at **Opportunity** reported he dispatched 10 air mail letters on a Tuesday in April addressed to points in continental Europe.

1932

E.Z. Smith became president of the Washington Press Association.

July 6: First class postage rate per ounce raised to 3¢.

1933

Walter C. Ketterman was appointed postmaster at **Opportunity.** He had been in office and clerical work all his life having been with **Spokane Dry Goods Co.** from 1919-1929 and then in the office of **Armour and Co.**

1935

Neta Lohnes Frazier became editor of *Herald* at the death of **E.Z. Smith.**

1930s

Regular television programs were being broadcast in the U.S. under commercial license from New York City, Philadelphia, Chicago, San Francisco, and Schenectady, N.Y. By 1940 there were 20 licensed radio transmitting stations in the U.S. with applications for 150 more.

1940

Mail Service twice daily in the Valley.

The **Valley** was threatened with imposition of telephone toll charges on calls to Spokane. Toll charges were dismissed because of **Chamber** activity at Seattle hearings before the Public Service Commission.

All Valley telephones were dial phones.

1942

V-Mail was instituted for use of the armed services.

1943

The postal zoning system began in 24 major cities in the **U.S.** including Spokane.

By 1951, 7000 telephones were connected in the Valley. The Spokane Valley did not have its own radio station until the '50s. Bob Swarz and Art McKelvie, World War II veterans, performed necessary carpentry chores to officially open Station KZUN in June, 1957, at S. 15 Pines Road. "This is your cousin...Radio Station KZUN" was the familiar broadcast. MacKelvie was from Zillah, Washington, and Swarz was reared in Spokane.

The Orchard Telephone Exchange

When the Pacific Telephone and Telegraph Company decided to establish an exchange in Opportunity in 1911, the Valley knew it was growing. Until that time, telephones were few and far between, a luxury not many could afford, and were connected directly to the exchange at Spokane on ten-party suburban lines.

The establishment of the Orchard office in a small portion of the Odd Fellows Hall in Opportunity on September 11, brought the telephone squarely into the Valley community and from that date on, it was accepted as a necessary household appliance. Initially, 138 telephones were connected.

The entire service by day was handled by Chief Operator Bertha (Payne) Kunkel and one other operator. A night boy handled such emergency calls as came through after the office closed for the day.

According to an entry in Bertha's scrap book, the first switchboard was a small section of a PBX board which had formerly served a Spokane hotel. Early on Bertha made note of an emergency: "the boy who took care of the board the first few nights, forgot to blow out his candle one night and awoke with his bedding on fire."

The little office was under the supervision of the Highland Office Chief Operator in Spokane. The Highland Office, on the corner of Third and Crestline, had begun operation in 1911 also, and was a three-story brick building with Mrs. Lane Truell as Chief Operator. Bertha noted in her scrapbook that "the Highland administrator made her inspections of the Orchard office on horseback!"

At first, growth at Orchard was slow. Four years after it was established, the 138 phone connections had increased only by a mere 14 new telephones, numbering only 151 on January 1, 1915. However, by the summer of 1919 the picture had changed.

Demand had increased substantially. 362 phones were in use. During that year over $40,000 was spent on providing additional facilities for the Valley by the Home Telephone and Telegraph Company of Spokane (the name of the local suburban station).

Again from Bertha's scrapbook: "At 8 p.m., May 18, 1921, a fire started in a garage west of the Orchard Office, and burned out a complete block. Bertha and her helpers, Josephine Fordyce, Olive Beedle, and Harriet Wade, worked even while the windows of their office were burning and until they were ordered to get out because some dynamite was to be set off to help halt the fire. The cables were then immediately cut and six men moved the switchboard across the street. This remark later was heard—'Strange that it took only six men to move the board out and twenty men to move it back in.'"

When Orchard opened, it had only thirteen suburban stations. By 1924 there were 750 and a new brick building with seven sections of switchboard was built on Robie (once called Waller Road). The Robie property was acquired when Bill Hart, local blacksmith, sold the land to the phone company.

Orchard, changed to Walnut in 1925, served a large area: as far east as Otis Orchards and Saltese, as far south as Freeman, and west to and including Pasadena Park, Millwood and Dishman. In 1940 dial phones were established in all parts of the Valley. An unidentified clipping in Bertha's scrap book describes the change over in this manner: "Tonight at midnight a drama with but two characters, the old and the new, will unfold. It won't be like other dramas because there will be no audience, no applause. At midnight when Walnut telephone offices change to dial operation, a switchboard which has not been silent for a single moment in 29 years suddenly will be silenced.

"Signal lamps which have been flashing for 29 years suddenly will be dark. Millions of voices which have been passing through for 29 years will no longer be heard. Operators will get down from their chairs, put away their headsets, and leave the building for assignments elsewhere in the city.

"At 12 o'clock, men will pull this gadget, twist that gadget, working silently and swiftly. Soon a clicking sound will be heard. It will be the new saying his lines in the final act of the drama, as the thousands of dial switches take over their permanent job of handling the voices of Walnut telephone users.

"Delivery of the new telephone directory was virtually completed this morning. It was sealed in a printed band which asked Spokane telephone users not to use the directory until Sunday because of more than 5000 number changes." [Both Orchard and Lakeview in Spokane were changed over at the same time.]

"The party line designations of J,M,R and W have been eliminated on the dial exchange. Work of installing the five car loads of telephone equipment which went into the Orchard and Lakeview office began seven months ago."

No jobs were lost. All people on the payroll were assigned to other offices in the city.

The customers were well prepared to handle this latest step in the march of progress. District Manager Bert H. Callison held classes in the Opportunity School to teach residents the fine points of dialing. He brought a huge dial phone to his classes at the school and allowed each person to experiment.

The first telephone service in the Washington Territory was established by Charles B. Hopkins. Shortly after the Nez Percé War in 1877, the government abandoned the telegraph line it had built from Fort Benton in Montana to Fort Walla Walla. Hopkins purchased a section of this line to establish service from steamboat landing at Almota on the Snake River to the town of Colfax with a pair of the first telephone instruments to come to the West Coast. Hopkins expanded the service to other towns in the Inland Empire. The first telephone service in Spokane began in the year 1887 under the name of the Inland Telephone Company.

The Phonograph, Radio—Even Television

[From the informal autobiography of Dr. Frederick Coddington.]

In the fall Chi Dollweig moved into our house. Chi got his nickname because he came from Chicago. He worked with Dad in the bank. He wanted to live outside the city, so asked if he could have room and board with us. Mother gave up her bedroom and shared Dad's room.

Chi invested all his money in phonograph and radio equipment. He had a fine collection of classical records and owned a beautiful Edison phonograph that played disc records. It had a silent electric motor and used a diamond needle. It also played Victor records if Chi changed the needle head and used steel or bamboo needles. My favorites among his records were a Fritz Kreisler violin solo, Liszt's "Liebestraum" and a popular song, "Marquita."

Our neighbor, Edgar Bigelow who delivered a gallon of fresh milk at our house every evening, always came in to hear recordings of "Barney Google" and "Old King Tut."

Bob Goodrich and I together financed an Old Edison phonograph that played cylinder records. We paid five dollars for it and a suitcase full of records. The suitcase had cylinders of cardboard, covered with flannel, attached to one side. They kept the records from bumping against each other and getting scratched. The machine had a horn-shaped brass speaker that moved along the record with the diamond needle. We had some very good records including "A Lemon in the Garden of Love." That was an aria from the opera, "The Spring Chicken." Even better was Matt Keefe's "Yodel Song."

We received *Boys Life* magazine every month. Robert found plans in it for building a crystal set radio. He bought insulated wire, terminal posts, crystal, cat whiskers, slider rod, and earphones. He followed the directions carefully and when finished, received audible signals in the earphones. The music or voice was not loud but it was clear.

When Chi moved in, we learned more about radio. He had bought the first 8-tube super heterodyne set in Spokane. He set it up on our living-room table and placed his storage batteries on the floor beside it. We helped cut two long poles in the woods south of Chester for an outdoor antenna.

One we planted by the chicken house and the other on our roof. The lead-in wire came through a tiny hole drilled in a front window frame.

Chi experimented with different types of loud speakers. One winter night he tuned in a powerful station in Schenectady, New York. He sent a telegram to the station: "Coming through loud and clear."

We heard it read over the air waves that same night.

When the Snyders moved into a house in our neighborhood, they brought with them a bell-shaped radio that ran off alternating current. On warm summer evenings at 7 p.m. they set it in an open living-room window. Our whole neighborhood assembled on their side lawn to listen to "Amos and Andy" broadcasts.

In 1927 one night in May, people were glued to their radios. A young unknown aviator called Slim Lindberg had taken off from New York, headed for Paris. He was somewhere over the Atlantic Ocean in a one-engine land plane. He had taken no radio, so he could carry more gasoline. The prayers of a whole nation, that night, were for his safety.

The next morning, electrifying news came through that he had landed safely at Le Bourget Field in Paris. The whole world was wild with enthusiasm. He had thoughtfully taken along a letter of introduction to present to French officials. Charles August Lindberg immediately became the idol of everybody.

That fall we visited Spokane. We were waiting at Felts Field when the *Spirit of St. Louis* circled our airport. It came in for a perfect three point landing. It taxied past the huge waving and shouting crowd.

Despite the Depression, we got a floor model electric radio for Christmas. We began to listen to favorite programs after our homework was finished. My favorites were Sherlock Holmes stories advertising Washington Coffee, and "Death Valley Days" advertising Twenty Mule Team Borax.

Even in those days, boys were working on the problems of television. One boy in our Science Club experimented with producing a television-like image. I never learned how his experiment turned out, but twenty years later, television is working!

A Newspaper for the Valley, Spokane Valley Herald

[From the *Spokane Valley Herald Anniversary Edition*, March 23, 1945.]

The *Spokane Valley Herald* celebrated its 25th anniversary March 3, changing the volume number to 26 and starting No. 1. The founders of the paper published the first issue on March 24, 1920, Harry E. Nelson and Karl Frolander being the first publishers.

The first issue was distributed free and was an eight-page tabloid. Three issues were published under this set-up to May 7, 1920, when the first full-size six-column paper was published through the Western Newspaper Union's weekly service. Harry Nelson (see "Harry Nelson, 'Mr. Spokane Valley,'" Volume I) continued to be associated with the publication as associate editor and R.W. Mason took over as the editor, with offices at 326 Rookery Building, Spokane. J.R. Dunphy's name appeared in the masthead as publisher with the November 26 issue and R.W. Mason and Harry Nelson continued as editors.

Interior of *Spokane Valley Herald* building at 10104 E. Sprague, built in 1926 and remodeled in the '50s. Rudy Brandvold is operating a linotype acquired at the time of remodeling. Old linotype in background. A very modern *Herald* building was built in 1971 at First and Farr. *Courtesy of Patricia Smith Goetter.*

FELTS AND KING TAKE OVER

On April 1, 1924, Buell Felts and Wilbur King became publishers of the *Herald* and for the first time located offices in the Valley at the Opportunity Bank Building. This association continued for a short time until Buell Felts became sole editor and publisher. During the latter part of 1926, a new printing plant was constructed to handle the printing of the *Herald* which until the first week in 1927 had been printed elsewhere. The building is the same as is now in use and was financed by selling bricks in the building to subscribers. With the first issue printed in the new building, several changes were made, among which was the enlarging of the size of the paper to seven columns and the reduction of the subscription rate from $2.00 to $1.00 per year.

EARL Z. SMITH BUYS *HERALD*

On May 29, 1927, Buell Felts, publisher of the *Herald* and a lieutenant in the air service in the first World War, was piloting an airplane on a Sunday excursion when motor trouble apparently caused the plane to crash, killing the publisher and his passenger, E.E. Baker. (See Vol. I, "Felts Field.") The entire Valley paid tribute to the popular publisher; all schools, business houses, and banks closed for his funeral. His wife, Genevieve Felts, continued the publication of the *Herald* for five weeks after Buell's death and with the July 1, 1927, issue, the late Earl Z. Smith presented his first issue as editor and publisher.

IRVING SMITH TAKES OVER

Mr. Smith continued as editor and publisher of the *Herald* until his death, August 30, 1935. The interest of the paper passed on to his wife, the late Violet M. Smith. The elder son of the Smiths, Irving, succeeded his father as publisher of the *Valley Herald* and was joined by his brother-in-law, Marc Gillespie, as business manager. Neta Frazier, who had served for several years previous as associate editor, became editor.

This management continued until January 14, 1938, when Mr. Gillespie sold his interest in the *Herald* to Mr. Smith. The late G.R. Scott at that time joined the staff as business manager and Mrs. Frazier continued as editor.

Irving continued as publisher until July 1942, when he entered the C.P.T. program to train as a flight instructor. As of that time this management had responsibility for publishing the *Herald*: Charles Vaughan, editor and advertising manager; Tom Vaughan, publisher and manager; Mrs. Esther Gnagey, news editor; Ralph Brownlow, operator and printer; Al Poe, press and floorman; Mrs. C.R. Scott, subscription department; Jerry Vaughan and Gerry Snow, folders; Jeanne Stanley, addressograph; Aaron Bowers, bookkeeper.

At the time of Buell Felt's death, his widow, Genevieve (Collins) Felts, collected his editorials into a booklet. This is from that booklet called *Buell's Editorials:*

BALANCING THE YEAR'S BOOKS

Like everyone else in business, we have been busy these evenings with our books, balancing accounts and taking stock of the year's business. Like others, too, ours has had its up and downs, the books show.

While I was considering that fact and dreaming of a business that would always show a steady gain with no ups and downs, the decorations on the fireplace mantel caught my eye. It's a custom at our house to put the Christmas cards we receive on the mantel where we can enjoy them and the pleasant associations they recall. The collections this year seemed larger than in years past. I left the account books to read the names again.

Sure enough, there were several cards from new friends we had not known a year ago. Brother editors we have met and come to know as friends since last Christmas. A business firm or two we have had pleasant dealings with during the year. The old friends were there with greetings a little warmer, their cards seemed to say, than ever before. Obviously, we had gained in friendship for the year, made new ones and strengthened the old.

Balancing the gains in that department of this business of living against any losses the books showed in our other endeavors, I found the whole account quite satisfactory.

Neta Lohnes Frazier, Author, and Editor

Neta Lohnes Frazier, who became editor of the *Spokane Valley Herald* in 1935, was also an author. She worked for the *Herald* for 15 years; and after retirement, devoted her talents to the writing of teen-age books that became national favorites.

By-line Denny, written in 1947, won a Literary Guild Award and was the first of a distinguished list of "Frazier books" that followed. It was based on Neta's experiences at the *Herald* and her readers said the characters were suspiciously like people they knew as Valley neighbors and *Herald* employees. In an interview for the *Herald*, November 1, 1978, Neta said, "The book just about wrote itself. It took only six months to write and was immediately accepted by a New York publishing firm [The Thomas Y. Crowell Company]. It became a Junior Literary Guild selection."

Neta was a native of Michigan. She was raised in a strict Methodist home—"under lock and key," she often said. By the time she was ready for college, the family had moved to the Valley and then her life began—when she "went away to school." At Whitman College she worked on the college newspaper. However, after coming to the *Herald*, she soon found that she knew almost nothing about community newspaper work and said she learned "by doing." That was also true of her writing. She was a member of Spokane Writers for many years and there "we learned from each other."

After college she taught for a short time. That career was interrupted by the Depression. She lost her job when she won her husband. During the "lean" years, school boards did not look favorably on married women working. One income per family, they determined, was all the economy could handle. Neta, like many other woman teachers, was "let go" so that a man or unmarried woman could fill the vacancy.

She began at the *Valley Herald* in 1927 as editor for the newspaper's neighborhood correspondents. Her salary was 30¢ an hour for a work-week of four days and one night, the night that the paper was put together by the small staff. "We all learned to do everything," she said. That "learning everything" eventually led to her being prepared to fill the editorship when the editor, her neighbor and friend, E.Z. Smith, died in 1935.

Her husband, Earl Frazier, taught at North Central High School. Although he did not lose his job during the Depression, his salary was cut like all teachers' salaries at the time, making her income from the *Herald* an important family supplement.

By 1942, when her daughter and two sons were grown, Neta was ready to leave the *Herald* and concentrate on writing *By-line Denny*, a book she had thought about for some time.

In addition to *By-line Denny*, teen-agers of that generation fondly remember *Stout-Hearted Seven*, based on the true story of the orphaned Sager children and their long journey between Missouri and Oregon (nominated for the Young Readers' Choice Award); the biography, *Sacajawea, The Girl Nobody Knows*, which she considered "possibly her best," and the *Little Rhody* series.

Valley residents of all ages enjoyed her *One Long Picnic*, which came about because of an interview with pioneer Seth Woodard. During the interview, Seth told Neta that migrating across the country had its difficulties for the grown-ups, but for the children "it was one long picnic." It, like many of her works, was laid in the Valley she knew well and loved.

On April 18, 1990, Neta celebrated her one hundredth birthday at Riverview Care Center where she instituted the AAUW annual used book sale.

Jerome Peltier, Historian

Jerome Peltier had his finger in just about every area pie dealing with preserving local history. With the Reverend Wilfred P. Schoenberg and Richard T. Lewis, he was co-founder of the Pacific Northwest Indian Center. He was chairman of the history committee of the Eastern Washington State Historical Society and Museum. He was the first treasurer and a trustee of the Spokane Indian Health Center. With Thomas Teakle, he founded the Spokane Corral of the Westerners, a local organiztion of history buffs and scholars. Westerners International honored him signally by naming him "Living Legend #16." With sister Mary Elizabeth Dunton and Mrs. Fabian Smith, he founded the now defunct Fort Wright World War I and II Museum and was a founder of the Realistic Art Association.

But let's begin at the beginning...

Jerome Peltier was born in Clocuet, Minnesota, in 1911. He remembers well the first book he ever read, *Dr. Rabbit and Tom Wildcat*. "I read it to pieces," he said.

The family came to Coeur d'Alene by train when Jerry was fourteen years old. In his own words, "Then and there I fell in love with the West. From the train, I saw Indians dancing at Mandan, N.D. and cowboys riding the range in Montana. And these wonderful, wonderful Rockies!"

Shortly after settling in Coeur d'Alene, he attended a Mass at the Cataldo Mission. The great Father Cataldo spoke in the Selish Indian language to an overflow crowd of mostly Indians. After Mass, those who wished to speak to Father Cataldo formed a line. He asked me where I came from. When I said that I came from far away Minnesota, he said he had come farther—from Italy. He laughed and also told me that he had more recently come from California, the Northwest being his last hope for failing health. Hale and hearty, he laughed again.

This contact with Father Cataldo and the Indian language awakened an interest that eventually led to Jerry's writing two books about the Coeur d'Alene Indians.

When the Paulson Building was being constructed in Spokane, his father became a carpenter on the job. After it was built, he was named maintenance manager. Jerry and his father at that time lived in the old (bus) Terminal Hotel across from the City Hall, then located between Howard and Wall. Jerry enrolled in Kinman Business School and found out for sure that "those were not the kinds of books I wanted to have my head in."

He got a job at John W. Graham Co. as packer in the warehouse. He remembers well the wooden packing boxes of those days. "I had to size up every shipment and order each box made to fit the goods. I became so good at it that Graham transferred me to his fourth floor sample room, a real honor. I later became credit manager. I spent my spare time browsing in the book department. Those were the Depression years. I could afford only to look.

"I knew John W. Graham on a first name basis. He lived halfway up Monroe Street, in a house with beautiful gardens. He loved flowers and on his European trips often bought flowers in Paris and Holland and sometimes shared them with me.

"He once told me that he had not really intended to settle in Spokane—was on his way to the coast when he ran out of money, stopped off in Spokane and found a job with book and office supply salesman, Sylvester Heath. Heath was burned out in the great Spokane fire of August 4, 1889. Heath decided not to reopen his business and loaned John W. $399 to set up the business in a tent across the street from where the *Review* Building is today."

While at Graham's, Jerry met many book lovers and history buffs, some of whom became his lifelong friends. Among these were William D. Allen, who owned the Book Nook in Spokane across from Pete Jacoy's, and George W. Fuller, a regional historian who headed Spokane's public library system for many years.

When Fuller died in 1937, his widow sold Jerry 23 pioneer letters her husband had collected including one by John McLoughlin and another by

Henry Harmon Spaulding. That was the beginning of his collection of original manuscripts and memorabilia.

He traded books with A.W. Patterson, a brother of Robert who founded the Crescent. J. Howard Stegner, a historian whose mother operated a grocery store at Trent, and Seth Woodard, for whose family Millwood is named, were among his Valley friends. (See Volume I for more about both of these pioneers.)

In 1937 Jerome married LaVerle Boyer whom he met at a picnic in Coeur d'Alene Park when she was fifteen. They had three children.

"I left Graham's in 1947 and in 1950 LaVerle and I bought Clark's Old Book Store at W. 831 Main." Jerry owned and operated that business until 1978. "During those years we were burned out, flooded out, and changed locations five times. In the last move to 318 Sprague, we moved 60,000 books."

During the '50s and '60s Jerry's articles appeared regularly in the *Spokesman-Review*. The supplement that he wrote about the Spokane fire is considered the most complete written account of that event. He had published eight books and is currently working on two others. He was named distinguished author of the year by the Eastern Washington Historical Society in 1985. The same year AARP awarded him Outstanding Volunteer of the Year because, with his many other community services,

he spent hours visiting local nursing homes cheering and aiding the residents.

Works published by Jerome Peltier are as follows:

Banditti of the Rocky Mountains about the Henry Plummer gang of Virginia City and Bannock, Montana.
Manners and Customs of the Coeur d'Alene Indians
Warbonnets and Epaulets, about the Steptoe and Wright Indian campaigns
A Brief History of the Coeur d'Alene Indians
Madame Dorion, the story of an Iowa Indian heroine who came to our Pacific Northwest in 1811
Antoine Plante, 1852 settler of the Spokane Valley
The Diary of Edmund Cavileer Hinds, his overland journal to California in 1850 and his experiences in the gold fields, edited by Peltier
Black Harris, famous mountain man and trail guide
The Fur Trade Was Equitable in the Far West

The last six titles are printed and published by Ye Galleon Press, Fairfield, WA., and may be obtained there. Jerry is hard at work doing final revision on two more books: *Felix Warren*, stage coach owner, and *The Custer Fight*.

The Senior Times: How and Where It All Began

Jim Osman's grandfather, Nate Osman, followed the railroad west "about 1880" and settled in the Saltese-Mica Peak area where he farmed. By March 26, 1922, when Jim was born, his immediate family lived on ten acres near what was then known as 16 ½ Street and the Appleway, now Blake Road and Sprague Avenue. There his parents, Ralph and Merna, raised their six children: Helen, Earl, Lewis, Lois, Gary, and Jim.

To help with family finances, when Jim was ten

years old he delivered the *Spokane Press*, little realizing that newspaper work was eventually to be his claim to fame.

"My unforgettable memory of that time is the severe winter of 1934," said Jim. "The wind blew so hard and the snow was so deep that south Sullivan was blocked with snow drifts. The crust was frozen so hard that I rode my horse on top of the snow to deliver my *Press* papers. I could see only the tops of fence posts."

The family farmed the property until 1939. "We kids got 25¢ a crate (24 hallocks) for picking strawberries, 35¢ for raspberries, and 10¢ a box for picking apples," said Jim. "We worked out. I worked for R.B. McCabe, Easter plowing 10 acres with a single bottom plow. Times were hard. My mother's parents were so poor that they saved their potato parings for seed.

"I remember the year the Opportunity Bank failed. My father had made $28,000 in apples . Sidney Smith convinced him to put the money in the bank. The next day the bank failed. Only ten per cent of the lost money was ever recovered—and not until four years later."

The $250-per acre irrigation fee became more than the Osmans could afford. Ralph and Merna decided then and there that "the Valley was becoming too densely populated to raise six children" and traded their property for acreage in Usk, Washington. Jim was seventeen years old.

In Usk the family continued farming and ranching.

Jim had played the sousaphone in the Central Valley High School band. When he volunteered for the Army in 1941, he was accepted as a musician.

During World War I, to entertain the troops, a man named Johnny Walker organized a group of performers into what was known as the "Yard Bird Club." It was the forerunner of the USO. The group was so well received that during World War II, Johnny recycled the idea at Fort McArthur where he and Jim Osman were stationed. This time Johnny called the group the "Original Yard Bird Club."

In 1942 Jim became a member of that performing troupe. He was in the show "Hey, Rookie" which was the predecessor of the famous "This Is the Army." Both shows were later made into movies. Jim wore a wig and long underwear and did a ballet dance that his family to this day tease him about.

In California he got his first whiff of newsprint. A buddy of his who worked on the *Los Angeles Examiner* frequently took him into the newspaper building. Jim was fascinated with the wire service and says he believes much of today's hi-tech communications are based on that old method of wire communication.

Jim's war experiences took him abroad. In Europe he was wounded and still deals with shrapnel in his knee that partially disabled him for life. In the Philippines he contracted, at different times, malaria and hepatitis. He was discharged from the Army December 23, 1945, while in the Philippines.

Immediately after the war he married his first wife, Teresa, and lived in St. Paul, Minnesota, her hometown. There his two children were born. Teresa died soon after the birth of their son and Jim returned to the Cusick-Usk area where he worked for Diamond Match.

In 1950 he met his second wife, Eileen Naccarato from Priest River. They came back to Sandpoint, Idaho, in 1951. Jim had not forgotten how fascinated he had been with that L.A. newsroom and found a circulation job with the *Spokesman-Review*. In August 1952, he was made district manager of circulation.

Sadly the *Review* terminated him at age 53. Reason: he was too old to work. This, coupled with the fact that his mother and father were old and knew little about the benefits that were available to the aging, plummeted Jim into the career for which he will always be remembered in the Valley and surrounding areas.

In 1973 at Hayden Lake he began a paper for seniors. He called it the *Senior Review*. It is still in existence although in order to move back to the Valley Jim sold it only a year after it was started.

When an apartment he was managing in the Valley became vacant, he was referred to HUD and the Office on Aging. That Office had received a $20,000 grant from the government to put together some form of communicator for senior citizens. Those who knew about it did not feel competent to do the job.

By chance, in October 1975, Jim heard of the dilemma and that the Office on Aging was seeking someone to put together a paper "similar to the *Senior Review* that was so successful at Hayden Lake."

"I started that paper!" said Jim. He was hired on the spot.

By January 23, 1976, he had 5000 papers called the *Senior Times* on Spokane streets.

Today Jim also publishes *Senior Power*. Together the two senior papers have a circulation of 100,000. He couples his newspaper work with educational forums on aging, providing a much needed service to what he calls "The Great Inland Northwest."

Leo Oestreicher,
Early Day Photographer of Mt. Spokane

Leo Oestreicher was a much loved Valley photographer. In 1923 he came to the Spokane Valley to attend Spokane University. While still attending school, in 1925 he bought a small building on Walnut Road near the campus and began taking photos professionally. He hired University students in various capacities at his photo laboratory.

For thirty-five consecutive New Years Eves, from 1929 until 1964, usually with friends or half-a-dozen college-boy volunteers, he climbed Mount Spokane to take photographs of snow blown trees. He sold a full page of his snow scenes to the *Spokesman-Review* Sunday rotogravure page every winter.

The New Year's Eve climb and the photographs became a tradition that the entire city and Valley looked forward to.

In Dr. Frederick Coddington's autobiography, he tells of a New Years Eve that he spent on the mountain with Leo.

"The first year that I went along (1932), the snow was reported to be very deep. To keep the snow out of our shoes while climbing, we applied wrap leggings over our pants and would tie on burlap sacks around our legs over our shoes when we started to hike. The top of each sack would be gathered above the bulge of our calf muscles, making us known as Pucker Footers.

"We prepared vegetables and beef for stew and packed them in salt sacks. We carried bread, butter, syrup, pancake flour, coffee, shortening, eggs, bacon, and fruit in small sacks. Leo took along an extra pound of photographer's flash powder in addition to his cameras. With bed rolls and skis, we felt loaded down for a long hard climb.

"We went as far up the Mt. Spokane Road as our truck would take us. Then we tied on our gunny sacks, shouldered our packs, and started climbing. It was about dusk. As a full moon rose, we were climbing in a fantastic fairyland of snow-covered trees and glistening moonlight. Occasional frost crystals, almost one-and-a-half inches in diameter, reflected the moonlight as we moved on. Like huge silent ghosts, the trees formed grotesque shapes against a black starry sky and cast blue shadows along our path.

"We arrived at Cook's Cabin and found a fire already burning brightly in the big stone fireplace. The caretaker and his wife had known we were coming.

"We filled an iron kettle with snow and swung it on its crane over the fire. When it was boiling, we dumped in our meat and vegetables. It soon filled that large guest room with a tantalizing aroma. While the stew cooked, we unrolled our blankets over fresh straw strewn away from the fireplace.

"After filling ourselves with the stew, we started for the top at 11 p.m. The big stone cabin at the top was well stocked with cord wood. We built a roaring fire in the mammoth fireplace and warmed ourselves again.

"A little before midnight another party of climbers joined us. They had climbed the north side of the mountain. When they pulled off stocking caps, we were delighted to find that they mostly were girls. Two men had climbed with them. One had brought a fancy chromatic harmonica and added sparkle to an already sparkling experience.

"Precisely at midnight, we went out with Leo to set off his flash powder.

"It illuminated a large area of the bald spot on "Old Baldy" and was visible in Spokane and the Valley. The illumination carried our New Year's greetings to everyone celebrating at home.

"Feeling literally on top of the world, we returned to the warmth of the fire, the harmonica, and girls teaching us the Virginia Reel.

"The girls had brought some cookies; we made a kettle of cocoa, and all had a delightful impromptu party.

"On New Year's day we skied back down the roadway to our truck and day-to-day living that had seemed far away while we were on the mountain top."

162

THE SPOKANE VALLEY WITH MT. SPOKANE IN THE BACKGROUND.
Photo by Leo, Courtesy of Joan Schwisow.

Leo remembered photography when it was a big, bulky view camera with the black cloth hood.

"In those days," he said, "the magnesium-powered flash gun was the only artificial light that could be used to expose on the slow film available. I poured the explosive powder into the flash pan and extended it over my head. A charge was set off by a primer similar to a shotgun shell detonator or by a spark from a flint. A ball of fire would emerge from the pan to everyone's delight and I would open and close the shutter. If the subject moved during the process, his image was blurred for posterity."

During Leo's year and a half as a student at Spokane University he saw the need for someone to take pictures for school annuals and for local people. Thus began Leo's Studio and Camera Shop.

In 1951, he sold the Studio business to Lawrence Morgan, a portrait photographer, and devoted his time to his two other businesses, Leo's Photo Supply and Leo's Camera Shop. He retired in 1961 and moved to property near Valhalla Point, on Lake Coeur d'Alene. He died at the age of 87 in 1990 at his Coeur d'Alene home.

For information about Mt. Spokane and Cook's cabin, see "Square Dancing at Mitcham's Barn."

163

Medicine and Health Care

"In the early decades of the present century, the [Spokane County Medical] Society represented a profession that had become generally complacent in its status. By and large, most of its members were committed to their patients and gave their services liberally. Charity was an inherent part of medical practice...The Welfare State was yet to be established. Doctors met the need for medical care of the indigent while preserving the dignity of their patients. Doctors were affluent and, in the public eye, revered.

[From "A Very Brief History of the Spokane County Medical Society" by Lawrence Pence, M.D., *Medical Bulletin*, Volume 62, Number 3, Fall, 1989.]

Medicine and Health Care

CHRONOLOGICAL HISTORY

Until **Valley General Hospital** was established in 1969, Spokane continued to be the health care center for Valley residents. **Bob Nelson** says that **Karl Frolander,** one of the founders of the *Valley Herald* had the first "so-called drug store, probably in the **Odd Fellows building** and that he sold out to **Dr. Hopkins,** who had his office in the back of the drug store on the corner of **Appleway** and **Pines**." **Katharine Krell** remembers Dr. Hopkins in 1927 treating "Mother for scarlet fever, my sister for scarlet fever and measles and me for measles—all at once." Others remember Dr. Hopkins making house calls. **Dr. Walker** is also remembered making house calls. (See "Dr. Walker.")

1921

Dr. Charles B. Ward II and **Dr. Arthur Betts** opened an office for the practice of diagnostic radiology on the second floor of the first **Paulsen Building**. The second **Paulsen Medical and Dental Building** was built in 1929.

1924

Summer: **Dr. John Finney** moved to Spokane. He recommended early ambulation for surgery patients long before it became the established practice in World War II.

1925

Dr. N.E. Bayne, Dentist, had his office on the 2nd floor of the **Brown Building** in Millwood.

Late 30s

J.E. Halpin located his pharmacy on **Sprague** in **Opportunity** just off **Pines Road**.

1932

First meeting of the **Spokane Medical Auxillary**.

1933

"The **Spokane Medical Service Bureau** was founded to enable poorer people to afford adequate medical care. The original coverage offered by the MSB was limited to groups of 25 or more employed males, each earning less than $150 per month. The premium was $1 per month and included doctors' services, hospital services paid in full, and all prescription drugs paid in full. At this time office calls were $2, hospital rates were $2.75 per day and tonsillectomies cost $12.50." *Medical Bulletin*, Volume 62, Number 3, Fall 1989, p.79.

1934

As a precaution against the spread of infantile paralysis, **Orchard Park** and **West Valley School Boards** postponed the opening of school from September 4 to September 10.

1934

December 4: **Vera School** was closed for two weeks at the order of the county health officer when it was discovered that fifty-one children were at home with measles.

1937

Dr. Elizabeth White, first woman president of the Deaconess Medical Staff, began her practice in Spokane. She charged $3 per visit, the going rate, and never changed it for the thirty years of her practice in Spokane.

Dr. John W. Epton and his wife Kathryn arrived in the Valley and rented a home from the Dibbles, corner of **Argonne** and **Broadway**. Dr. John had offices in the Paulson and Fernwell buildings in town but made house calls in the Valley. The **Eptons** lived in many locations including an apartment over **Rice's Meat Market** and at E. 12624 **Appleway**. According to his wife, "John was dedicated to his profession, often being paid in vegetables and fruit if at all."

1939

Stella Torrey opened a maternity home at E. 11105 Sprague. **Dr. Epton** delivered babies there.

Redford Hall on the old University campus was purchased by **Mr.** and **Mrs. T.A. Hunt** for operation as a home for the aged. It was known as "Hunts Haven of Rest."

1940

The Spokane Emergency Hospital was on the second floor of the Old City Hall under the care of a county health officer, Dr. Arthur Lein. The injured were brought to the City Hall Emergency Room in the police "paddy wagon," a grey converted van. This was used as well to transport patients to one of the three hospitals. After the war, each hospital developed its own emergency room.

1942

Dr. John Epton built his home with a medical office at N. 7 **Walnut Road. Dr. Charles Kyle** joined him there after a few years. **Dr. Epton** rented the office to **Dr. C.R. Manley** after Pearl Harbor when he went into the service as a flight surgeon. He won the Air Medal for 14 flights over Tokyo. When **Dr. George Velonis** joined the group, **Dr. Kyle** left. **Dr. Velonis** had served in the European Theater of the war. **Dr. Manley** had been a medical missionary to India for a number of years.

1943

Fort George Wright Regional Hospital and Convalescent Center opened at the Base. It was a 300-bed red brick building erected to care for air corps personnel. The hospital cared for those stationed at Geiger Field, Fairchild Air Base, Fort George Wright, and their dependents. The hospital was destroyed by fire of unknown origin July 8, 1967.

Baxter General Army Hospital, a 2000-bed cantonment-type hospital opened north of the Spokane River and west of the city. It was closed and dismantled after the war.

1944

March: **Dr. and Mrs. James Aldrich** opened a new 35-bed Community Hospital with modern equipment in the old **University Administration Building** at E. 10410 Ninth, University Place.

1944

Dr. C.R. Manley was joined in practice by **Raymond E. Stannard. Dr. Stannard** had been a missionary to China for 15 years serving under the American Foreign Baptist Missionary Society. He spent six months in a Japanese prison camp in Shaoking. His wife and six children arrived in the Valley with him.

November: A $12,000 19-room small animal veterinary hospital was opened by owner, **Dr. George C. Mank** of **Orchard Avenue**, on **Sprague Avenue** near **Hardesty Road**. It had the latest in X-ray, surgery and dispensary equipment.

1945

November 23: **Dr. C.R. Manley** invited the public to an open house at new offices at **9404 E. Sprague** across from the **Valley Creamery**. He had hoped to return to the mission field but was not permitted to do so because of unsettled conditions abroad.

December 21: **Dr. Epton**, recently returned to his office in **Opportunity** after serving in the South Pacific, told the *Valley Herald*: "If only some of the people who were in strikes in the war plants could have been in my place, and have seen the large number of planes going out on missions in the morning, and only a few coming back, perhaps they could have given more thought to going on strike. I saw Valley boys in action at Iwo Jima and held them in high esteem for their courage and bravery going into battle from which many did not return." He wore proudly his gold lapel button signifying honorable discharge.

A 1921 fire, fought by a bucket brigade and water from a near-by irrigation ditch,
destroyed most of the Opportunity Block except the Odd Fellows Hall. The buildings
were wooden, but rebuilt with Mica brick after the fire.
Courtesy of Orville Kinkade.

Joseph John Walker, M.D.

[As remembered by his daughter, Mary (Walker) Michaels, 1994.]

When we moved to the Valley (about 1921) there was already a Dr. Walker in Opportunity. He moved away soon after my father opened his practice. I am sure he was not intimidated by my Dad, but chose to leave at that time coincidentally. There was another doctor at about the same time—Dr. Fishleigh—but he did not stay long either.

Dad's first office was in Opportunity but it burned with the rest of the business section. At the time of the fire, Mother was attending the last PTA meeting of the year in the third floor auditorium of the old Opportunity School. She saw the fire from the window, took her Hupmobile touring car to the fire and loaded Dad's smaller equipment, books and chemicals into it and took it all to our house at 12th and Pierce.

Will Larned, our neighbor (uncle to present day Harry Larned), took his truck to the fire and along with others brought the heavier equipment and furniture to our home.

Dad's office was in our home until he opened a new office in a new Opportunity structure known as the Knight Block. Doctor Hopkins came to Opportunity quite some time afterwards.

Almost all illnesses were attended to at home, $2.50 a visit no matter how far the doctor traveled. Office calls were $2. Tonsillectomies were done in the office, $25. Babies were delivered at home, $25. Serious cases were taken to the hospitals in Spokane. I remember my father often went to attend patients in the hospital twice a day although transportation was not easy. He went via the Apple Way, the best road during hazardous weather. After a long, cold trip on a winter's night— no heat in the car, no automatic window wipers, no snow tires, traveling 35-40 mph on unplowed, snowy roads— he would return home, chilled to the bone and say, "What this Valley needs is a first class hospital and it will have one some day, just you see."

About our house, which still stands. It is the Dutch colonial at 12th and Pierce. It was built by a mason named Vinge of interlocking tiles made at Mica. The tiles have air passages in them. The theory was that the air would act as insulation for both heat and cold. It worked just fine! Our house was always warm in the winter and cool in the summer.

The basement is made from granite blocks that were rejects from the granite quarry off Dishman-Mica Highway. They were free for the taking, but we had to pay 25¢ per load to have them hauled. They were delivered by a horse-drawn, heavy farm wagon, driven by a man named Strom. He had previously worked in the mines in Kellogg. The house cost approximately $8,000 and was designed by a friend of the family, Mr. Richardson. He had no formal architectural training. The tall split leaf birch in the front yard and the Norway maple were prizes from Apple shows. We had ten acres of fruit trees that I loved. That house saw many happy times!

Dentistry at Opportunity

Bertha (Payne) Kunkel was chief operator at the Opportunity Orchard Office of the Pacific Telephone and Telegraph Company for twenty-eight years, from 1911-1939. Dr. W.H. Allen's dental office was on the corner of Sprague and Robie in Opportunity in front of the telephone office. Bertha kept a scrap book. In the scrap book on a '30s page was this undated clipping, source unknown, about the progress of dentistry in the Valley:

The thought of the dentist's chair carries dread to many, due to the fear of grinding on a tender tooth.

Dr. W.H. Allen of Opportunity, realizing much of this fear is the result of a too vivid imagination, at the same time admits filling or pulling teeth in the past has not always been pleasant for the patient. The advance of science is making the visit to the dental office little of an ordeal, he said.

Dr. Allen explained the recent installation of an automatic analgesic machine by which the patient can administer to himself a harmless gas that relieves not only all actual pain of dental operations but also all fear of it.

Dr. Allen, among the first to install this machine in the Inland Empire, said the machine was invented in England and used 1,800,000 times in a clinic there before being finally perfected so it could be operated by the patient while the dentist worked. The apparatus consists of gas-filled cylinders beside the dentist's chair from which a rubber tube leads to the patient's chair with an adjustment at the head. This connects with a half-rubber sphere which fits over the patient's nose, from which the gas is inhaled.

Attached in another tube leading to the machine is a bulb that lies in the patient's lap. As the dentist works, at the first indication of pain the patient presses the gas bulb and inhales gas until pain ceases. As the patient senses the pain before the dentist is aware of it, the patient can gauge how much gas is needed to stop or prevent the pain.

"As the gas is harmless and an analgesic rather than an anaesthetic, in that it does not render the patient unconscious, there are no ill effects if more than the required amount is taken," said Dr. Allen.

The Opportunity dentist stated he had good results with the machine, particularly with children in fear of the dentist's chair. One whiff of the gas removes fear of it, in his experience.

An accompanying photo shows Miss Myrtle Johnson of Opportunity with a nose piece strapped to her head. She is smiling.

Halpin's Pharmacy, Oldest Drugstore in Opportunity

[*Spokane Valley Today*, May, 1993]

Rick Ericksen was all smiles when he told me in a recent interview that Halpin's employees had purchased the business known as Halpin's Pharmacy and Treasure Room, E. 11406 Sprague; and, except for improvements such as the new carpet soon to be installed, the business would "stay the same. We will still offer the high quality merchandise and service customers are used to," he said.

From among the 35 store employees (now the new owners), four have been selected on the basis of seniority, experience and training to act as a man-agement team. They are Rick, who is chief buyer; Ron Gill, chief pharmacist; Jo Ann Dietel, buyer for cosmetics; and Dan Higgins, buyer for housewares.

Frank L. Terhaar and Gary Christiansen, previous owners, are looking toward retirement. However, under the new contract they will continue working in the store until the current debt is retired. That is estimated to happen within the next six years.

Frank joined the company in 1954. In 1969 he and Gary, a longtime employee, formed a partnership and purchased the store from J.E. Halpin.

Halpin's is the oldest drug store in Opportunity. It has changed locations three times and expanded at least seven times since the business was started in the late '30s by J.E. Halpin. The original store was located on Sprague just west of Pines in the old Opportunity block. (See Volume I, "A Place Called Opportunity.") In addition to drugs, it featured a soda fountain.

The soda fountain has gone by the wayside, and the present store has many additional departments: the Treasure Room (a gift shop), pharmacy and sundries, housewares, cosmetics, jewelry, the Christmas shop, electronics, cards, grandfather clocks, and the Baby Bath Shop.

Ray Gist, hired by Halpin as chief pharmacist in 1940 immediately after graduation from WSU, said "things have changed. There is a lot more book work. We used to fill the prescription, ring up the money and the transaction was complete. Now there are countless forms to be filled out and new drugs come onto the market all the time. I came over to get a prescription for my wife the other day and had never heard of the drug."

Yes, there are new things at Halpin's—even new ownership; but, emphasizes Rick, "customers will find that the courtesy and service are the same as when I first began working here as a 19-year-old janitor and delivery boy while attending University High School, in 1966."

Orrin and Stella Torrey, Blacksmith and Mid-Wife

[*Spokane Valley Today*, June-July, 1988. (At the time of this interview, Orrin was deceased. Stella is now (1995) deceased.)]

I don't know of any couple in the Valley who are credited with as many "firsts" as Orrin and Stella Torrey.

Before there was a ski resort on Mt. Spokane, the Torreys and their parents, the W.J. Schafers (for whom Schafer Road is named) operated the first area Olympic-size ski jump, a toboggan-run, skating rink, and lodge on the east face of Browne's Mountain just beyond the present-day Ponderosa. There Orrin designed the first area rope tow, using a Chevrolet engine for power.

Before there were medical complexes, rescue units, Minor Emergency Clinics, health cooperatives, and even before Spokane Valley General Hospital, a sign at E. 11105 Sprague with a stork on it announced the MATERNITY HOME operated by Stella with Orrin's help.

There was the Schafer-Torrey mineral spring water business and Torrey's Blacksmith Shop at E. 6809 Sprague where from 1932-1960 Orrin built the first Opportunity firecart, repaired artificial limbs, put rubber tires on wooden wheels, and supplied engine parts when they were not available during the war.

As if these projects did not keep the Torreys busy enough, behind the Torrey Maternity Home were the Torrey rental locker boxes, a smoke house and a meat preparation department.

"We started married life in the Depression years," Stella said, "Those were hard times. We had to be creative."

Stella was born at Edwall, Washington. The family, hoping to grow apples, moved to the Valley when she was ten years old. Among her earliest memories is walking one and a half miles to the old Chester School each day—in winter with her legs wrapped in burlap to keep warm.

On their Valley property the Schafers had water problems from the start. They dug several wells before they found water that did not smell of iodine and sulphur and was not foul tasting. The apple trees, subirrigated by the mineral water, died. So the Schafers tried dairying. But when the cows drank the spring water, they went dry. Other water, not tainted with minerals, had to be provided for the cows.

But the best water on the land for human consumption came from the mineral spring. An ailing World War I veteran employed on the farm discovered that he got the same healthful effect from drinking that water that he had gotten from a famous French spa to which he had been sent for treatment. A relative, recovering from a long siege

173

of illness, also experienced the recuperative powers of the water. Schafer began to bottle the water and sell it locally and in the city.

From 1920 until 1960, the familiar mineral water truck with its one hundred gallon tank made regular stops in the area. A firm believer in the powers of the Schafer spring mineral water was Eli Hutton, of the Hutton Settlement.

There were four Schafer children. They helped with the dairy by milking and caring for the cows, cleaning the barn, and delivering milk. Stella was the oldest. She and a brother did most of the delivering in the Spokane area before school in the morning. So that they could continue delivering when they went to high school, they were enrolled at Lewis and Clark.

Stella longed for college. Knowing her parents could not afford it, she hired on as a maid for Dr. Peter Reid of Spokane. He became aware of her talent for medicine and urged her to go into nurses' training.

In 1914 Stella enrolled at Deaconess Hospital where she was able to work for her room and board and $5 a month to cover incidental expenses. She graduated and when a friend became ill, filled in for her in a Salvation Army Hospital in Denver. She stayed there three years, caring for about eighty pregnant unwed girls per year. Thus were sown the seeds that would blossom into the Spokane Valley Maternity Home.

In the meantime Orrin Torrey, who is remembered as "a genial giant with a heart to match," was receiving his "basic training" on the family wheat farm in Odessa. There he learned farming, marketing, and how to repair farm machinery. He and his mother migrated to the Valley.

In 1931 Stella also returned to Spokane and became a nurse at Deaconess Hospital where she had received her training. She soon met Orrin, married him, and promptly lost her job. During the Depression, one breadwinner per family was thought to be sufficient.

The couple moved into a house at N. 18 Pines Road. Orrin earned the $25 per month rent money by working at the box factory next door. Stella recalls the electric train depot next to the box factory on the northwest corner of Sprague and Pines.

In 1934 twin girls were born to the Torreys and in 1936 Orrin and his father-in-law developed Ski-Mor. It was an active resort until 1942 when it closed because snow "always seemed to come at the wrong time. It would snow during the week," said Stella. "We would load up on hamburger and goodies for the weekend crowd, then it would chinook. We would be eating hamburger for weeks. Later a ski resort opened at Liberty Lake. I think it was in the '70s and I remember that they imported snow."

When our twins were five years old, a friend asked to pay for maternity care in Stella's home. Dr. Epton (the doctor in charge) agreed, and soon two other expectant mothers were enrolled with Stella. As fate would have it, all three babies were born on the same night, and Stella was in business. Unable to buy equipment because of worldwide war shortages, a pressure cooker became the sterilizer, a strainer and cloth were used for applications of ether, and Orrin built the delivery bed (and also one for Deaconess Hospital).

The new business was a success and soon the Torreys had to move to larger quarters at E. 11105 Sprague where Taco Bell is today. "A man named Steinke built our corner fireplace in barter exchange for mother and baby care, " said Stella. "He built many rock houses in the Valley—the group near the entrance to Newman Lake is still standing. He was remarkable. He could look over a rock, put it on his knee, hit it and it would break."

Torrey's Blacksmith Shop was a landmark for twenty-nine years. The doors closed on September 1, 1960, when Ed Jensen, then owner, moved to larger quarters at E. 6305 Valleyway. Stella's Maternity Home closed in 1950 when she retired.

"Now," said Stella, "it seems good to have nothing much to do."

Business and Industry

"Any casual observer must be impressed by the growing number of new business establishments opening in the Spokane Valley. Some of these represent large investments in capital outlay. This can mean but one thing, namely, that these shrewd business men have confidence in the growth and stability of the district. These investors are convinced that the Spokane Valley has a fine future and they express a willingness to participate in the continued growth of the community. It is, therefore, incumbent upon the residents of the Valley to reciprocate this expression of confidence by giving cheerful cooperation and patronage to these new concerns wherever and whenever possible. The Valley should move ahead as one unbroken unit, respecting the rights of everyone, but preferring the local business man or merchant when he can deliver the goods and services."

[Editorial, *Spokane Valley Herald*, November 9, 1945.]

Business and Industry

CHRONOLOGICAL HISTORY

1921

Steps were taken at **Opportunity** and **Dishman** to organize a **Spokane Valley Bank.**

The **Standard Stoneware Plant** at **Chester** began the production of pottery and stoneware.

Frank R. Salter transferred his cider plant from **Veradale** to **Dishman** and opened an ice cream manufacturing plant there.

John and **Elsie Dean's Store** purchased from **Terry Grant** opened in **Otis Orchards** on the corner of **Kenney** and **Gilbert roads.** Gas pumps were added.

Neil Brother's Grain Company bought **W.P. Myers** warehouse in **Opportunity.** (See article, "A Turn of the Century Big Businessman," Volume I.)

A two-story brick and concrete Masonic Temple was built at **Millwood** by Myers and Telander.

1922

Spokane Valley State Bank and **Millwood Mercantile** moved into the ground floor of the **Masonic Temple Building.** On the second floor was the lodge hall where community activities were held.

William John Schafer began to bottle and sell the mineral water from **Schafer Mineral Springs** in the foothills just south of **Chester.**

Charles E. Taylor built a 26-room hotel at **Newman Lake.**

C.E. Johnson erected a brick building in the **Opportunity Block** to replace a frame one that burned. The frontage was 100' on the **Appleway,** 60' deep.

Lulu Raymond, N. 203 **University,** became an agent for the N.Y. Life Insurance Co. Her son **Harry Raymond** was a county commissioner.

Martin Kalez built a saw mill at **Liberty Lake** employing 20 people. 20 million feet of timber were taken from the property before the mill caught fire and burned to the ground.

1922

L. E. Solum and Sommerfield formed a partnership to sell groceries and meat in Opportunity.

Fire destroyed Reinemer's General Merchandise and the Tom Bienz Drug Store in Dishman. They moved into the building occupied by Johnson's Sporting Goods.

1923

February 10: Lynn Brownson and Arthur Johnson opened a new automobile company in Dishman in the building later occupied by Appleway Chevrolet. (See article, "Brownson Motors.")

The building Dishman touted as the "capital building" or "skyscraper," a 3-story "business block" on the corner of the Appleway and Argonne with five storerooms and eight apartments was barely finished when it burned. Thereafter it was known as "The Ruins."

1924

Harold G. Anderson moved to the Spokane Valley from the Gonzaga District and purchased the land that was to become the Early Dawn Dairy. (See article, "Early Dawn Dairy.")

1925

The brick and tile Brown Building in Millwood was completed on the site of the old Millwood Hotel. Owned by George Brown, Paper Mill superintendent, it housed a pharmacy and drug store on the first floor and Dr. N.E. Bayne, dentist, on the second.

"Mr. Photographer," Leo Oestheicher, had accumulated 70,000 negatives and was in business on Walnut Avenue near Spokane University. (See article, "Leo Oestreicher, Early Day Photographer of Mt. Spokane.")

The Pringle Garage was remodeled and enlarged. Automatic gas pumps were installed. Closed about 1950.

The Greenacres Branch of Potlatch Lumber moved to a site at Corbin Addition in Greenacres.

1926

The Byram Block in Millwood replaced the old Byram Building that was built in 1912.

A new business center was fast developing at Corbin Addition to Greenacres.

Inland Empire Paper Company doubled its production of news print and added 150 employees.

The Fruit Growers State Bank at Greenacres moved into a new building at Center and Appleway.

1927

E.G. Pangborn and J.W. Walker bought the Liberty Sewing Station at Dishman.

1927

The **Dean Store** and **Post Office** moved to a new building at the corner of **Kenney** and **Trent**.

The **Triple X Root Beer Barrel** opened east of **Pringle's Garage** facing **Trent** in **Otis Orchards**. **Hank** and **Lillian Kile** were the proprietors. It was the first hamburger stand in the Valley. In the thirties it was licensed to sell beer and became the first tavern in **Otis Orchards**.

Joe Falco took over the management of a sandwich and produce stand in **Dishman**. Son **Joe, Jr.,** and Grandson, **Louis,** continued the business, which became **Falco's Garden Center**.

Thomas Bienz, owner of **Dishman Drug**, moved it into a two-story brick store at the **SE** corner of the **Appleway** and **Chester (Mica) Road**.

1928

John Pring, Sr., became a salesman for **Appleway Motors** on the northeast corner of **Argonne** and the **Appleway** where the Farmers and Merchants bank is today. He purchased the dealership on May 1.

The **Inland Empire Paper Mill** was built at **Millwood**.

Jack's Diner, later **Knight's Diner**, in 1947 **Wright's Diner**, from 1955-1994 the **Town and Country Restaurant**, opened on the **NW** corner of **Trent** and **Fancher**.

1929

A.J. Dick opened the **Dishman Barber Shop** with a beauty parlor and hemstitching shop adjoining.

Lee Sowers had the first barber shop in **Otis Orchards**. It was east of **Halloran's Store** facing **Wellesley**.

Charles F. Krieger and **Lynn J. Brownson** started the **Dishman Majestic Company**.

Hausfield and **Olson** started an auto business in **Opportunity**.

Ruff Coble bought the **Valley Cash Meat Market** at **Opportunity**.

October 24: Stock market crash ushered in the Depression.

1930

Darby Fuel Company was located at 7309 **Appleway, Dishman**. **Hunter Darby** also built many Valley homes.

C.E. Mecum opened a clothing store in **Dishman**.

J.F. Brod erected a store in **Dishman**.

Louis Berland opened an ice plant in **Dishman**.

1930

Sidney Smith, opened the Valley's first real estate and insurance office in Opportunity. It was in a small building near the tracks of the old Inland Empire Electric Line. (See article, "Sidney Smith," Volume I.)

The Community State Bank opened in Dishman. C.H. Tart was president. It combined the Community State Bank of Valleyford and the Fruit Growers Bank of Greenacres.

On land that was the Channon Price home, Doc Dockendorf operated a service station until 1949.

1931

The Opportunity State Bank, which had opened May 31, 1919, closed.

The International Cement Plant at Irvin, begun in 1913, was producing an average of 215,000 barrels of cement a day from rock mined at Marble and Boyds, WA. In the late '30s this company supplied cement for work on Grand Coulee Dam.

1932

C.W. Pearson opened a tea room, "Sunshine Cottage," at Vera.

Dishman State Bank closed following a run precipitated by the closing of the Union Park Bank in East Spokane.

Torrey's Blacksmith and Metal Shop was located at E. 6809 Sprague. (See article, "Orrin and Stella Torrey.")

Valley residents voted that there be no beer or wine sales in the Valley.

George Pierce opened his garden store where the Valley Creamery now stands.

Dishman Community Creamery was opened by J.B. Chaney.

C.F. Schimmels had a blacksmith shop in Dishman.

R.W. Straight opened a flour and feed store on the Appleway in Corbin Addition adjoining Beck's Garage.

1933

The Spokane Valley State Bank at Millwood applied for Federal Deposit Insurance, as did most banks in the country.

1934

Morrison Brothers Seed Company's main warehouse burned in one of the most spectacular fires in Valley history. Thousands watched the flames which could be seen for miles. The three story building collapsed in one hour and a half.

Mr. and Mrs. J.D. Foote of Spokane purchased the Brownie Lunch Room at Opportunity from Florence Sandstrom. It served dinner from soup to pie for 25¢.

1934

W. A. Yeager bought the **O'Brien Garage** and changed the name to the **Newman Lake Garage.**

December 22: The **Community State Bank** at **Dishman** paid a 10% dividend bringing total reimbursement to 50% on deposits when bank closed.

February 10, 1934: **Wilbur Peters' Father** opened his hardware store in a portion of the **Knight Block** in Opportunity. **Wilbur** took over in 1946 and son **Gary** in 1981.

W.O. Bartholomew of **Opportunity** took a long time lease on **Jack's Place**, owned by **Jack Pierre**, at the corner of **University** and the **Appleway**, to handle a full line of groceries, gas, and feed.

Valley barbers decided that beginning February 3 on weekdays, shops would be open from 8 a.m.- 6:30 p.m. and on Saturdays from 8 a.m.-8 p.m. Price of a haircut: 35¢.

Dishman Community Creamery, after opposing a state ice cream code for a number of weeks, agreed to conform by raising the price of ice cream from 30¢ to 35¢ a quart.

1935

Ed Anderson and **Kenneth Marchesi** bought the **Osbun Mercantile** at **Greenacres** and named it **Greenacres Mercantile.**

1936

Brown Metal Works of **Spokane** moved into the **Spokane Valley Growers Union Warehouse** at **Opportunity**.

Ben Jacklin and son, **Lyle,** co-founded **Jacklin Seed** and bought a warehouse in **Dishman**. (See article, "The Jacklin Brothers.") **Arden** joined the company after WW II. By 1938 the company doubled the capacity of its plant. In 1941 the company opened a **Dishman** store.

C.R. Longfellow opened **Packard Sales** at **Dishman.**

Robert S. **Hartley** opened the **Valley Cleaners.**

Washington Brick and Lime and Sewer Pipe Company moved its mortar plant and sales yard from Spokane to **Dishman.**

Dishman Trading Company erected a 100' x 50' building .

December 24: **Decker** and **Amy Alice Lakin** celebrated their golden wedding anniversary. **Decker** founded **Lakin Milling** and had his business on the north side of the **Appleway** across from the **Opportunity Block.**

Gertrude Lambert built a real estate office in connection with tourist cabins at **Dishman.** This was the beginning of Valley motels.

F.R. Salter built store rooms and the **Adams Drive-In Market** at **Dishman.**

1936

Ed Halpin bought from **E.C. Paul** the **Opportunity Drug Company**, located just west of the **Appleway** and **Pines**. (See article, "Halpin's Pharmacy.")

1937

H.L. Geesey and **H.W. Fairbanks** bought the **Dishman Trading Company** from **A.T. Dishman; Lee Joyner, Jim Ashley** bought the **Brownson Motor Company** in **Dishman; B.H. Fischer** took over the grocery department of the **Valley Cash Market at Opportunity**.

Safeway built a supermarket at **Appleway** and **Willow** in **Dishman**. **Jay Bobbitt** with 3 clerks and 2 butchers operated the self-service store, one of the largest in the **Safeway** system.

1938

Zono Feed Store at 1831 E. Sprague became **Aslin-Finch Feed Store**. In the spring of 1946, **Aslin-Finch** built at 5618 E. Sprague.

T.G. Sandow opened a service station at the corner of **Appleway** and **University**.

Hazel Carley opened her food store and restaurant at **Opportunity**.

R.W. Strandberg bought **Vera Red and White Store** from **Ralph Owen**.

1939

John Radinger and **George Johnson** took over the **Sather** and **Evanson Dodge and Plymouth Company**.

J.F. Brod sold the **Rexall Drug** at **Dishman** to **University Pharmacies, Inc.**

M.B. Mitchell and **R.W. Cruver** bought the **Dishman Motor Company**.

Tony Close built the **Casaloma Motel**. It had 20 apartments, a grocery store, and a meat market.

Bergan's Dishman Store opened in a new location at **Chester Road** and the **Appleway**.

Jack Finch and **Fred Aslin** bought the **Milltowm Feed and Supply Store** at **Millwood**.

James W. Fox operated the **Fox Milling Company** on the **NE Corner** of **Sprague** and **Pines**. Son, **Jim** took over the family business after college. In 1984, it was sold to **Darigold** and expanded with plants at **Deer** and **Medical lakes**. The store at **Sprague** and **Pines** was eventually sold to **H. Douglas** who made a deal with **Albertson's** (who currently occupy the property.)

The acreage where **Spalding Wrecking** is today along I-90, was used by **Dolph** and **Max Spalding** for storage for their Spokane business.

1940

Unemployment still acute.

1940

Turner Lumber and Fuel Company opened at **Opportunity** on the north side of the **Appleway.**

Hagen Cleaners And Laundrymatic, family operated, opened in **Opportunity.**

The **Thue Dime Store** opened at **Dishman.**

Jack Martin began a **Ready-Mix Concrete Business** at the **Dishman Gravel Pit.**

Fred Hoffman started the **Valley Mart** in **Dishman.**

F.M. Somerfield and **E.J. Carscallen** opened a real estate and insurance office in **Opportunity.**

1941

Appleway Motors Company of which **John A. Pring** was manager moved to E. 8500 Sprague Ave.

William Coddington, Opportunity, became assistant manager of the **East Side Branch** of the **Old National Bank,** located at E. 2114 **Sprague,** succeeding **Earl Hovig, Orchard Avenue.**

The Caloric Furnace Company of Spokane of which **A.E. Knight** was a member, took on the sale of the Kelvinator, an iceless refrigerator for the home. The manufacturer's guarantee "read like a fairy tale, though they say they stand ready to back it up." (*Valley Herald*)

W.F. Strahorn erected a supermarket next to the **Orchard Avenue Grocery** on **Park Road.**

Walter Ottomeir bought the **Chester Store** and **Service Station.**

John Goldbach bought the old **A.T. Dishman Granite Quarry** (started in 1889) from the **Empire Granite Company,** who bought it in 1909.

1942

Dan Giboney opened a men's wear store at **Dishman.**

Thornhill-Carey Funeral Home bought the **J.B. Felts** home for a Valley location.

Dishman Safeway was converted into apartments.

D.J. Blackmer and **Walter N. Voelker** opened **Valley Electric and Repair** at **Opportunity.**

Karl K. Moore built a 19-unit bungalow court in the **Orchard Avenue District.**

Guy Hart opened a dry goods store at **Opportunity.**

1942-45

As war industry moved into the area, so did people. This brought about the opening of many small businesses such as **Judy Learn's** and **Dorothy Kingrey's Ladies Ready To-Wear** in **Dishman** and **A.S. Johnson's Western Auto Store** in **Dishman**. There were also many buy-outs: **William A. Stuart** of **Veradale** bought the **Opportunity Plumbing And Electric Company** at **Opportunity**, **A. C. Townsend** bought the **First Avenue Poultry** at **Opportunity** from the estate of **Lee Foedish**. There were many others, too numerous to name.

1944

Ray Korte opened his super modern food market in the remodeled **Opportunity General Store**.

Tom Crawford and **Harold D. McCollum** began a **Ford Motor** franchise on **Sprague Avenue in Dishman**.

Lynn Brownson opened a new Firestone store at the Ford showroom of **Brownson Motor Company** building in **Dishman**.

The long awaited opening of **Johnny's Bowling Alley** in **Opportunity** took place.

Mr. and **Mrs. Charles Leonard, Opportunity,** bought the bakery in **Dishman** from **George Hunt** of Newport. **Bert Lomax** was a previous owner.

1945

Mr. and Mrs. Logan Jorgens, Veradale, purchased **Opportunity Gardens** at **Sprague** and **Pines** from **John Ochs**.

Bill Fox and **Kae Sowers** who own the **Opportunity Grain** and **Feed Company** purchased the **Anderson Berry Ranch** south of the **Appleway** and east of the **Opportunity Grade School**. They hoped to erect a farm service store there.

January 1: **Carl's Supply Company, Inc.,** moved into the **Appleway Motors Building, Dishman** and handled a complete line of **John Deere** farming implements, electrical appliances and was a Good Year tire distributor.

Oscar D. Reinemer

[*Spokane Valley Herald*, September 11, 1930]

A real pioneer among Dishman business houses and merchants is the Appleway Mercantile Company, owned by O.D. and E.C. Reinemer.

The date of Oscar's entering business at Dishman was March 2, 1918, when he opened a grocery store at the corner of Argonne Road and the Appleway, adjoining the Dishman building now known as "The Ruins."

Associated with Mr. Reinemer were Raymond Dishman and John Safranek, who had the meat department.

In the fall of 1922 the Dishman Building, remembered by residents as a handsome, three-story structure, was burned in one of the most spectacular fires the Valley has experienced. Following the fire, Mr. Reinemer bought the interest of his partners and built the brick building which is the present location of the Appleway Mercantile.

The Dishman Drug occupied half the building until March 1928, at which time Oscar took over the whole building, doubling the floor space.

Elroy C. Reinemer, his brother, acquired an interest in the business in 1925, and has since then had charge of the meat department. One additional salesman is employed.

Six weeks ago Oscar Reinemer took another step in the progress of Dishman, when he built the new bank building on his property adjoining the store.

This new structure is one of the most attractive in Dishman, having a front of tapestry brick and terra cotta, with large plate glass windows. The interior is light and cheerful, the walls being a soft green in tone, with a red tile floor. The floor space has been divided to provide for the equipment of the bank, private office, etc.

In this, as in other ways, Mr. Reinemer has shown his faith in the Valley, having invested both in business and property. Last fall he built an attractive new modern home on the hill a little way north of the highway.

Oscar has always been one of the dependable workers in every enterprise for the upbuilding of Spokane Valley. He was president of the Chamber of Commerce last year, and continues his work for Valley progress since his term of office expired.

Brownson Motor Company

[*Spokane Valley Herald*, September 11, 1930]

A little over seven years ago, on February 10, 1923, to be exact, Lynn Brownson and Arthur Johnson, two young men of the Valley, opened a new automobile company, using half the Opportunity post office building as an office for the first week.

Then, having secured the local Ford agency, they leased a building at Dishman, now occupied by the Appleway Chevrolet Company. Besides the two proprietors, there was one mechanic to do repair work. The company was known as the Johnson-Brownson company. At the end of four months, Mr. Brownson bought his partner's interest in the firm, since when it has been the Brownson Motor Company.

"We now have 33 employees on our payroll," said Mr. Brownson, "and we expect our year's business to total $600,000."

When Mr. Brownson acquired the Ford agency, he was the youngest Ford dealer in the United States, and is still one of the three youngest.

Last year his company, and incidentally the town of Dishman, won national recognition when the Brownson Motor company came in first in the Pacific Coast district of the Firestone contest, and second in the entire United States.

Mr. and Mrs. Brownson have an attractive house on Walnut Road, with grounds beautifully landscaped, including a large wading pool for the children and a tennis court which affords much pleasure to the entire neighborhood.

APPLEWAY CHEVROLET COMPANY, 1930
Looking east at the corner of Argonne and the Appleway in Dishman, where Farmers and Merchants Bank is today.
Courtesy of John Pring

Appleway Chevrolet and the Pring Connection

Appleway Chevrolet, once called Appleway Motors, is one of the oldest Chevrolet Agencies in the Northwest.

It was founded by Charles Stevens on the northwest corner of Appleway and Argonne Road. John A. Pring, Sr., joined the dealership as a salesman and with $1000 saved and $4000 borrowed, purchased the dealership May 1, 1928. His partners have since included his son, John (Jack) A. Pring, Jr., and grandsons, Timothy and Bradley.

The dealership John Pring purchased in 1928 was a small, two-car showroom. One year later the stock market crashed and the Depression hit the country. The Opportunity State Bank failed and the Dishman Bank, opened only two years before, failed. John recovered only twenty cents on the dollar of the sum that he had managed to save. It took courage to keep going, but he often said that it was learning how to weather bad times that made for good times later on.

He weathered the bank failures and by 1941 the business had outgrown the original showroom and moved to new quarters at the present location, E. 8500 Sprague Avenue. The land was purchased from A.T. Dishman and the original building was erected for $40,000.

Two months after opening at the new location, Pearl Harbor was bombed and World War II began.

186

Car dealerships were without cars to sell. John, in debt from construction costs, knew he needed to produce revenue. Because of the influx into the Valley of workers in war related activities, a big need developed for housing. John bought 40 acres of wheat land just south of Mission, platted 120 lots and built houses for less than $4.50 a square foot. He sold them to young families on easy terms for $100 down. The addition became known as Mission Addition. The homes sold for approximately $5000. He later became a developer of the Chester Hills and Chester Heights.

John A. Pring, Sr., died on July 22, 1992, at age 86. "A visionary man, he believed in the Valley and its potential for growth," said his son Jack.

Jack reminisced further about his father's life: "Dad was born in Lewiston, Idaho, in 1906 and raised on a cattle ranch . At the age of 12 , he drove a team of 16 horses from Lewiston to Walla Walla to work in the harvest fields. He later worked the rodeo circuit riding bucking horses. He was a man of the old school. Later in life he was an airplane pilot. He was in six airplane crashes, one in 1934 at Felts Field caused his deafness, but that didn't keep him grounded. He used a hearing aid, read lips, and bluffed a lot. Today we would probably say he was kind of wild. Just a tough old-timer in the real sense of the word.

"He played polo at Playfair Race Course in the '30s. I would go down there and watch him. That's a big part of the reason I bought the track in 1981," Jack said. "He loved the Valley, said it was the only place to live and worked for it—its schools and communities—seeming somehow to know what the Valley would become."

The Jacklins and the Grass Seed Industry

[Excerpts from "Memories—'85, '89, '93" by Arden Jacklin. Used with permission of Don Jacklin, January, 1995.]

My father, B.H. [Ben] Jacklin, moved his family from Ashland Junction, Wisconsin to the Spokane Valley in 1926. We located in Corbin Addition, the second house east of Barker Road on the north side of Sprague.

We were poor. We left Wisconsin with no money. However, on the train out we did have a big hamper of fried chicken, bread and cookies prepared for us by Grandmother Jacklin. And Bert Whealy, the manager of the Spokane Seed Company with whom B.H. had been promised a job, sent us transportation money.

What a trip it was. I well recall that we three sons, Lyle, Owen, and I, had impetigo and were all painted up with gentian violet. We were lively grade schoolers, and were gently but firmly avoided by the other passengers.

Times were not good and the new development of homes in Corbin Addition, where we settled, were not selling well. B.H. and my mother, Coral, bought our house for $25 down and $20 per month. What luxury it seemed to us! It had electricity, running water and flush toilets, none of which we had back on the farm. And B.H. bought a used Model T touring car; we were more used to horses, wagons, and buggies.

After two years, Spokane Seed Company de-emphasized seed peas and B.H. was hired by Frank Sloan as manager of the Washington-Idaho Seed Company at Bonners Ferry, Idaho. Large acreages of seed peas were then grown in the Kootenai Valley.

Mr. Sloan contracted to grow peas for the Blue Mountain Cannery on annually rented ground in Dayton, Washington; so he shut down the Bonners Ferry Plant.

B.H. accepted an offer as manager of the Morrison Brothers Seed Company at Dishman, Washington, owned by Ned and Norton Morrison. The Jacklin family moved into the old "Dishman House" just

JACKLIN SEED COMPANY, DISHMAN, 1937
North side of the paved two-lane Appleway, west of viaduct.
Courtesy of Don Jacklin.

north of Sprague Avenue on Willow Street, after living briefly in both Orchard Avenue and Opportunity.

When we sons were in grade and high school, B.H. shared his dream with us about some day having our own seed company. He never lost sight of that dream.

Lyle, Owen, and I all went to Washington State University and majored in agronomy. I graduated in January 1934 and began working with the then Soil Erosion Service in the Department of Interior. By 1936 my mother, Coral, had died and B.H. married Emma Moeller. We boys, B.H. and Emma decided it was time "to go" [with the dream.] I could send some money for expenses to my brothers and they could work out, at least part-time.

We began our partnership, formally signed March 1, 1936. It was capitalized at $25,000, with considerable indebtedness.

Our first warehouse at the "Old Dishman Place" measured 15 x 30 ft. Two carloads of "hand picked seed peas were milled on foot treadle belt sorters and shipped to canners in Wisconsin. Of course, for a successful business, considerably more volume and a much larger plant were necessary.

B.H. contacted A.T. Dishman informing him of our needs. A.T. said, "We need your business here and I'll finance your warehouse if you'll build it." Ten percent interest was charged on the loan.

B.H., Lyle, Owen, a cousin, Gale West, and carpenter Ivan Sies from Bonners Ferry, Idaho, built the warehouse. A.T. provided money for materials as they were purchased, keeping track on the back of an envelope he carried in his shirt pocket, and adding it up when the building was completed.

A bank account was set up with the Washington Trust Bank and bankers Fred Stanton and Frank Guse. The Jacklin-Washington Trust banking connection continues to this day [1995].

We contracted with Palouse County farmers to increase seed pea production with company-owned seed stock varieties. The combine-run sacked peas were milled, sorted, hand picked, bagged, and shipped from the Dishman plant to canning companies in Wisconsin where high quality planting stocks could not be grown.

Because garden varieties of bush beans and seed peas could be grown in the Spokane Valley, a marketing outlet was established with the S.D. Woodruff Company for sales in Connecticut and Florida. The Jacklin Company began contracting, leasing, buying, and farming land in the Valley to grow seed for processing and shipping eastward.

During this time, a cattle operation was introduced. In the beginning, there was considerable open range in the Otis Orchard area and eastward where grazing cattle were tended by a cowboy who stayed right with them. Later for a feeding operation, a farm was purchased south of Otis, bordering the Spokane River which later expanded and moved to a ranch between Ross Point and Rathdrum. This project was not a good money maker and was abandoned in favor of horses and ponies. B.H. was a good trader. When two carloads of Indian ponies from British Columbia became stranded at the Old Union Stockyards, he bought them for "a song" and sold them at a good profit to riding academies on the coast of Washington. The die was cast. The company was into the Welsh pony business.

[That venture collapsed when the market collapsed, taking down with it the Jacklin venture.]

Meanwhile, the seed and pea and bean business prospered. During the war years of the early '40s, there was great demand for edible peas and beans for the armed forces, as well as for our Allies. The company became deeply involved in that production, supplying foods on government contracts.

We outgrew our quarters and wished to expand. During World War II lumber purchasing permits were available only for essential uses. Retailing of seeds and supplies was not an essential classification. However, regulations did not prohibit tearing down a used building and reusing the lumber.

A man named McCallum owned a large old abandoned apple storage warehouse in Opportunity. It was well built. There were two layers of good pine and fir boards on each side of the studs; the roof joists supplied many board feet of good reusable lumber; there was dimension stock from the heavy floor joists—just what was needed for a store building.

Jacklins bought the apple warehouse, tore it down and used the lumber to build a three-story high, 70 x 50 foot building in Dishman.

THE TRANSITION YEARS
FROM BEANS AND PEAS TO GRASS

I worked as an agronomist for the Soil Erosion Service, later renamed The Soil Conservation Service from January 27, 1934, to December 28, 1941. Much of my time was spent in erosion control with forage species and their role in crop rotation. This interest and experience in the use and production of grass and grass seeds I brought to Jacklin Seed Company. Also, this enabled the company to establish and operate a complete and extensive retail garden and field seed store in Dishman.

While I was still with the SCS, samples of many kinds of grasses and legumes were supplied by SCS to Smith Hughes instructors for demonstration planting in Washington and Idaho. One of these sets was received by P.K. Jones at Mead High School, and plots were planted on the Chris Brand ranch on Peone Prairie.

B.H. and we boys were impressed with the growth there and saw the potentials for seed production.

In the spring of 1942 with the cooperation of Karl Paulson, we planted two varieties of these grasses for seed production measurements on Orchard Prairie, north of Millwood. The two planted were blue wild ryegrass and chewings fescue. The fescue yielded well and in the spring of 1944, row crop seed production fields of "Olds" creeping red fescue were planted on the Karl Paulson and Ed Zurlinden farms on Orchard Prairie and on the Ernie Worthington farm on Pleasant Prairie.

We also planted several kinds of forage grasses for seed production on Jacklin's Otis Orchards farm. The plantings were successful, and so began the grass seed growing industry. Jacklin's bought and leased land on Pleasant and Peone Prairies for production. They initiated farmer contract growing and the "prairies" rapidly expanded in the production of creeping red fescue.

During this time, Jacklin's also bought dryland wheat land bordering State Line, Idaho, drilled one of the earliest private wells to irrigate that land, and planted it to grass for seed production.

After a few years of growing fescue seed, baling and hauling off the thrashed straw, Karl Paulson decided to try burning the grass stubble. Seed yields increased spectacularly. Open field burning had begun!

KENTUCKY BLUE GRASS

Ed Geary of Klamath Falls, Oregon, had successfully grown and marketed heavy bushel weight, high quality Kentucky bluegrass seed. Seed stock was obtained from him and planted at Jacklin's State Line ranch. Also, seed stock of Delta Kentucky bluegrass was obtained from Canada.

Within two years, Merion Kentucky bluegrass was released by the Greens Section of the U.S. Golf Association and Jacklin's jumped on it hard. The Spokane and North Idaho area became the world's largest producer of Merion and growers had a heyday.

While the exciting new business of growing grass was developing, Jacklin's still carried the seed pea and bean business, but with decreased emphasis. Soon all bean seed activities ceased, and the land converted to grass seed production. Then all seed stocks of peas were sold and contract growing discontinued. Jacklin Seed company devoted its main energy to grass seed.

The business was incorporated in 1959. In 1972 it merged with Vaughan Seed Company. Now of Post Falls, it is one of the Inland Northwest's most prominent companies. It has made significant contributions to the growth of Kootenai County by building Riverbend Commerce Park in Post Falls, and contributing significantly to the business recruiter, Jobs Plus of Coeur d'Alene.

In 1989 Jacklin Seed completed work on a new 22-acre park-like research center on a low bluff overlooking the Spokane River in Post Falls.

Seed World, November 1988, listed Jacklin Seed Company as one of a handful of industry "giants," a leader in the seed industry.

Thornhill Funeral Home

In 1907 pioneer orchardist James B. Felts built a graceful family home on his orchard site at E. 10300 Sprague Avenue. Three great paned picture windows flooded the soft carpeted elegance of the living-room with light. The wallpaper was light beige with a colonial theme. Scattered about were several floor lamps, tasteful wall pictures, and plants. At the far end of the room was a cozy brick fireplace edged with ivory woodwork and mantel.

In 1942 Harold Thornhill purchased the home from George Felts and his mother, who were living there at the time. Harold had started a funeral home in Spokane in 1934. Valley residents, aware of his expertise, urged him to offer mortuary service in the Valley. The Felts place on Sprague was an ideal location and the tasteful home was the ideal building. His family lived in it only two years when Harold announced that he would open Thornhill's in the Valley, the first ever Valley funeral home. He also agreed to provide 24-hour ambulance service—likewise, the first in the Valley.

Harold remodeled and expanded the Felts home, adding a 29-foot addition in the front. The apple storage barn formerly used to store the bountiful crop produced by the ten acres of orchard around the home became the funeral home garages. During the first summer what later became the front lawn was planted in watermelons because Harold had no time to plant grass. It is said that a huge crop of melons, some almost 20 inches in length, resulted from the virgin soil.

When the Felts home became the Valley funeral home in 1943, Harold built a spacious ranch style home for his family next door. A large cottonwood tree planted in 1907 still graces the property, now Lamonts and the University shopping complex.

Harold came from a long line of funeral workers. His father, Perle Francis Thornhill, and his grandfather, Bryant Thornhill, both had been in the furniture and undertaking business in Idaho and Spokane. Perle Francis was born on Barker Road in Greenacres January 1, 1882, but graduated from high school in Portland, Oregon. He was trained in undertaking work by a professor of embalming and followed his father Bryant who, at the time, had a funeral home in Kellogg, Idaho. Perle subsequently sold his interests to his brothers in 1935 and moved to Spokane after his son, Harold, opened Valley funeral home.

Harold was born in 1907 and attended the University of Idaho and the California College of Embalming. The funeral home in Spokane that he opened in 1934 was called the Mission Funeral Home originally, but later became the Thornhill Funeral Home.

Today Thornhill's Funeral Home is located at S. 1400 Pines Road. Geneva, Harold's wife, was always an active partner in the operation of Thornhill's Valley Funeral Home.

Real Estate: Alvin J. Wolff, Sr.

[Excerpts from the autobiography of Alvin J. Wolff.]

My earliest recollections are of the family home at 434 W. Buckeye on the north side of Spokane. A block to the north was beautiful Corbin Park, named for D.C. Corbin, an early community pioneer. The park had earlier been our city's race track and fairgrounds.

In 1924 the "management" of our family [Drs. Jesse and Edith Wolff, parents] sought a neighborhood more conducive to the goals they dreamed of for their children. Where more land translated into more opportunities to keep our shoulders to the wheel of busy-ness. And so to Orchard Avenue we did go.

Our home was almost new. The builder, William Sillman, was an apple farmer as well as a home builder. Poor Mr. Sillman was later blown to Kingdom Come having made the mistake of carrying dynamite in his car.

Our Orchard Avenue home sat on an acre of irrigated Spokane Valley apple orchard (six miles to town). Fifty-six Wagner and Jonathan apple trees were there. Never since have apples of the flavor of those entered my mouth.

The Spokane Valley contained rich soil with lots of rocks. We were constantly removing the large rocks and stacking them as fence lines or using them for building foundations.

Most important to my parents was the suburban environment. It let children enjoy the benefits of responsibility with plenty of chores to assign to us unsuspecting kids.

I learned of an opportunity to enter business. Yes, I became a merchant newsman. More than a hundred customers who were to pay fifteen cents a week for six evening deliveries.

These were the Depression years, the paper boy couldn't help but be aware. The route covered an area including several subdivisions of land for homes begun in the early and mid '20s, some finished, others finished just enough so the owner could get along until times improved. As the paper boy who got into most of these homes once a week to collect for the paper, I watched failed businesses, lay-offs, and cutbacks and shared these experiences in ways one never thinks of today.

But everyone had faith and knew there was a future. We felt it was just a matter of time and doing and learning to prepare for it.

We were brought up to "amount" to something and to be proud of who we were. We were encouraged to be what we wanted to be. We were aware of the struggle of grandparents, the will of parents to improve their lot in life to something beyond those who had gone before. We were taught this took "doing on our part" and translated into understanding what opportunity meant.

At home in Orchard Avenue there was always time to have fun. We fed animals and knew they lived because we fed them. The home we lived in was always warm because we cut, chopped, and stacked the wood to heat it and we fed the furnace as it got colder.

Distractions from radio and television didn't

exist. Radio was just getting started and we heard it only on special occasions like hearing about Lindberg flying *The Spirit of St. Louis* across the Atlantic Ocean, or the Dempsey-Tunney fight. In the late twenties and into the thirties we could hear comics like Eddie Cantor or Amos 'n Andy. Later President Roosevelt told us how he was going to make things better for all of us. Being able to hear a radio broadcast was an "event" and the entire household (often neighbors) put aside whatever they were doing and gathered around the radio set in absolute silence and listened in awe.

When I attended West Valley High School not nearly as much real estate was used to park cars as today. Normally four to six cars belonging to teachers and staff and maybe there would be two student cars. We didn't know the words *parking lot* although there was an area designated for cars, mostly to enable the one and only brand new school bus to make its way to the front of the school house to load and unload students.

Gasoline cost eight cents a gallon, oil fifteen cents a quart. Tax on gas was one or one and a half pennies. Service stations were full of service, washing windows, putting air in tires, checking for air and water together, and a quick check of all functioning parts.

Summers following high school and at college vacation time each of the [three] Wolff children [Erma (Mrs. Robert N. Arick, died in 1985), Lionel and Alvin] attended Kinman Business University. J.I. Kinman was a patient of our [optometrist] father. Until the school moved many years later, there were always pictures on the wall of the Wolffs and many others who had become successful in regional and Spokane business. Kinman became Trend College in recent years and finally passed out of existence in 1994.

In 1933 President Roosevelt made an announcement that would forever change the northwest. Congress had approved the construction of Grand Coulee Dam. For the owners of millions of acres of arid land in Central and Southern Washington state it meant a brilliant future. The Wolff family with much preparation had the old 1928 "Victory Six by Dodge Brothers" overhauled for the trip (a hundred miles or so each way), valves ground, new tires, so the family could see, before it happened, the site of the great dam and all the acreage to be reclaimed from desert wasteland to productive

farms. By the time we got there, a hot dog stand was already at the site at the river's edge 200 feet below the present road that crosses over the dam.

My grandfather, Sigfried, had been born in Germany. We were listening to the radio when the announcement came of Hitler being elected to power in 1932. Grandfather's great concern left a vivid memory with me. He knew well he was hearing a forecast of doom.

The local airport was less than a mile from our Orchard Avenue home. We frequently went to the airport, walked through the hangars, looked at the planes, climbed up and even got in to feel and touch. Arthur and Hertha Klein, sponsored in this country from Germany, could not believe such liberties were allowed. Remembering the circumstances they had fled from, they looked for the police to come and remove and arrest such trespass.

It was being drafted into the Infantry in 1941 that forced me to face the fact that I needed to make some decisions about the path my life would follow. My grandfather was an optician, predecessor of the present day professional in optometry. My father followed in his footsteps and was schooled and licensed in the profession, as was my mother. My parents were more than willing to support, in every way, any desires I had to continue what seemed to be the family profession. But I did not accept their challenge even though I served an apprenticeship in that profession.

After many interesting assignments in the military, my career in the Army included application of my optical knowledge. I ran the only mobile optical unit (a unit of the Fifth Army) which served troops from Africa to Italy and Southern France and beyond as the war moved north. In this capacity we ground lenses into their proper prescriptions, "made" a few bifocals, cut and shaped lenses into frames and fitted them onto the faces of those who wore them.

I consider my military experience a turning point in my life as a result of the varied responsibilities imposed on this draftee-become-officer. I was involved in things of great magnitude. As a captain, I ordered materials directly from manufacturers in the States and dealt with millions of dollars worth of equipment and helped bring it to function. Our unit was small and independent. As a senior officer, I acted as commander and was called upon to be

Alvin Wolff, Sr., stands in front of the early home of the Alvin J. Wolff Company, an attachment to the east end of a Texaco Station located on the southeast corner of Sprague and Farr, present site of Home Base. The company moved into a new structure in the spring of 1954 one block east at 11305 E. Sprague. It was the first commercial building in the Valley that allowed parking between the building and the street. *Courtesy of Alvin J. Wolff, Sr.*

informed on matters concerning my troops. I found it necessary to challenge a superior officer in a matter of supply and survived without being court martialed because my mission proved to be for the benefit of the service. I sat in meetings with full colonels and generals and learned to make moral choices and to deal with people.

I came out of the service motivated and ready to take hold of my life and settle down and be a breadwinner.

Christmas 1945 found me in Texas to claim my new bride, Jane. We promptly returned to Spokane and soon after to the Valley. While working days, I re-enrolled in law school at night with a goal to using law in real estate or using real estate in a law practice. A job with the then "Dean of Commercial Real Estate," the late Ralph W. Watson, brought about my decision to make real estate my chosen field.

By 1948 there were 10,000 people in the Valley, many of whom were in need of housing. There were very few rentals and no apartments due to the shortage brought on by World War II.

I used a big chunk of my wartime savings to pur-chase a 1941 Packard 6. Nothing like a roomy Packard to show families real estate.

In 1949 I manned my first real estate office alone —desk space in the Valley Chamber of Commerce's rented office, a little house across from the present Valley Washington Mutual Bank. Five years later at 11305 E. Sprague, the Alvin J. Wolff Co. built a brick office building—the first commercial building set back far enough to enable client parking in front, on a paved parking lot. At that time the railroad ran between us and four-lane Sprague Avenue.

By 1976 when I stepped aside, the company had a staff of 70 associates in various assignments.

When Alvin retired, the Wolff Companies (as known today) was the oldest existing real estate firm in the Valley. It had evolved from a one-man business to involvement in property management, residential and commercial sales, subdivision development, the construction of hundreds of houses and apartment houses, and a mortgage company.

Alvin Jr. (Fritz), present owner of the companies, has gradually changed the company's emphasis in keeping with the demands of change and growth in the Valley and the entire Spokane area. The company no longer sells single family homes. It specializes in multifamily (apartment) development and management and real estate investing.

Fritz continues the fourth generation of Wolff's who have contributed to the Valley community during the last one hundred years.

Valley Garbage Service

January 10, 1995, *Spokesman-Review:* "10,000 specially designed garbage carts costing from $38.40 to $42.99 to be used with three previously purchased specially designed garbage trucks that cost $145,000 apiece!"

Mark Gillespie should hear about this. After all, garbage collection was his idea in the beginning:

Early in Valley history each township had its own dump. The Opportunity dump was located at Mission and Bowdish where the Senior Center is today. Later it was moved to Nineteenth and Pines. The Millwood dump was where the town park is today. The Greenacres dump, just east and south of Greenacres on Henry Road, is the one being considered for capping today. It was used until 1970 when the Mica dump was opened.

In the late 1930s a young man named Mark Gillespie was working out of town as a salesman for the Union Oil Company. When he came home weekends, his family job was to bundle up the week's garbage and take it to the township dump. Going to the dump, to put it mildly, he considered darn inconvenient.

"Why can't there be some kind of garbage collection?" thought this creative and inconvenienced young man.

He bought 1000 garbage cans, loaded them a few at a time in a pick-up, and went door to door leaving a garbage can at each place that would have one.

"Try it for a month," he said. "I'll pick up your garbage once a week and haul it to the township dump for you."

The cost at first was $1 a month. But when in a short time the 1000 garbage cans had found homes, the price was raised to $1.25 and Valley Garbage became an official business. The date was June 1940.

Every new business has its headaches and Valley Garbage was no exception.

At the Pines private dump, garbage was burned. This was about the time that houses were being built in Opportunity Terrace. The ladies complained of the fly ash from the dump soiling the clothes that they hung out to dry on lines in their yards.

They took their problem to County Commissioner Grant, who agreed to put in a landfill on the hill east of Henry Road in Greenacres in exchange for the Opportunity site. This was about 1949 and was the beginning of the county getting into the garbage business.

Enter Hector McIntosh on the scene. For twenty years, about 1921-1941, Hector had owned the Boston Garage, at the corner of Main and Brown in Spokane. He wanted to try farming, sold his garage and for one year farmed near Phileo Lake in Spangle. Edith, his wife, didn't like farming and wanted better schools for her two sons. So back to Spokane the family came. By that time (1943) Valley Garbage had expanded and had two pickup trucks, an old International and an old Reo. The beds of both trucks had been enlarged by adding wooden side boards so they could haul more. (Unloading was done by shoveling.) There was enough business to hire help. Hector was in the right place at the right time.

Mark Gillespie hired him to drive a garbage truck. The company was working out of Mark's residence at 14817 E. Sprague where a Steel Fence Siding Company is today.

In 1946, to help the company in a financial crunch, Mark sold a quarter interest in the business to Hector and the trucks from that time on were parked behind the McIntosh home at 10800 E. Sprague just west of the Appleway Florist.

The company subsequently bought the property at 11720 E. First where the Valley Garbage Service is today (behind the present Opportunity Post Office, originally built as a neighborhood Safeway Store).

The Greenacres dump was used until about 1970 when the Mica dump was opened.

The office building of the Valley Garbage Service was built in 1955 by partner Hector McIntosh. "Hector was always the brawn of the partnership, running the trucks and maintaining them and Mark was the brains, running the business end," said Herb McIntosh, Hector's son. "When I was first married, I lived in the little house just west of Valley Garbage which my father encouraged me to buy for $600. "

Today Dewey Strauss is part owner and manager of Valley Garbage. His family came from Davenport and settled in Opportunity in 1942 when he was ten years old. Dewey bought Hector McIntosh's share of the Valley Garbage Service in 1960.

The new carts and trucks haven't reached the Valley yet but when the time comes, I'll bet Mark Gillespie will be hovering around overhead with his eyes bulging saying, "Times sure have changed!"

Opportunity Furniture: A Result of World War II

[*Spokane Valley Today*, August, 1988]

Only fifty years ago, the south side of Sprague Avenue between Union and Fox was Mrs. Anderson's raspberry patch. And Sprague was the dusty two-lane road known as the Appleway.

Today there is so much traffic in that area on six-lane Sprague that it is difficult to turn into the post office across Fox Road or the Sinclair Station or the Century Loan Pawn Shop or Spear's Better Home Furnishings which now occupy the block.

The exciting growth began with World War II.

In 1941 James William Fox, father, and James Wesley Fox, son, purchased the seven-acre block of berry patch from Mrs. Anderson and farmed it briefly.

Trentwood Aluminum Rolling Mill and the Naval Supply Depot at Velox on Sullivan Road, and other war-related area activities were bringing people by the carload and trainload to the Valley. Most of these newcomers were young singles and families starting to put down roots. It was not unusual for servicemen and war workers to dig a basement and live in it for several years while slowly completing the upper level of their houses-to-be. Demand for inexpensive furniture and second hand furniture was great.

For the purpose of selling floor covering and furniture and appliances to the many new residents, James William Fox tore out the raspberry patch and built a concrete block building on the Fox Road corner of his property. Richfield Oil made a deal with the Foxes for the Union and Sprague corner and built a service station where Sinclair is today.

Among the newcomers were Gideon Korus, an X-ray technician stationed at nearby Farragut Naval Training Station, and Carl Kappen, a government policeman at Galena Air Base in Spokane.

After the war, Gideon did not return to Philadelphia, PA, where he had previously been a record coordinator for the Immigration and Naturalization Service; and Carl did not return to the Black Hills where he had managed a J.C. Penney store for twelve years. Both found employment in the Spokane area—Gideon with the State Employment Service and Carl with the local J.C. Penney.

In 1948 the two men met at Redeemer Lutheran Church in the Valley. Both had noted that the floor covering business at E. 11803 Sprague was for sale. One day over lunch they decided to buy the business. They chose the name Opportunity Furniture for their new enterprise and sold new and used furniture and appliances. The partnership lasted twenty-five years until both men retired.

At first the pair had no truck. They delivered from a four-wheel trailer made from a Model T Ford. Later they traded Gideon's car for a truck.

Said Gideon, "It was mostly learn as you go for Carl and me. But the Lord blessed us and we enjoyed a good business life. We were highly under-financed, but we put our minds to it and worked hard. We were congenial, always divided things equally—even a gift of chocolates—and made sure we each had one and only one day off."

Gideon, because he had attended business college in his native North Dakota, became the bookkeeper. Both watched their pennies.

Gideon remembers only one time when he was late for work. "It was TWINS!" he said.

Said Carl, "I'll never forget one customer from Priest Lake. He bought a used daveno. He came back the next day and told us he found a box of jewelry and old coins in the built-in drawer. After that, we examined our used furniture more carefully.

"We had a wonderful partnership, Gideon and I. When we retired in 1973 and sold the store, I missed Gideon more than I missed the business. Gideon taught me a lot."

Both Gideon and Carl served as elders at Redeemer Lutheran Church and followed the old tradition of keeping their store closed evenings and Sundays. One day a lady called wanting an appliance delivered on Sunday. They refused. "You don't want business very badly, do you?" she said in a huff.

A week later a woman came in and bought a washer, dryer, and freezer. "I'm the lady who called about Sunday delivery," she said. "When I thought it over, I admired your conviction."

The partners said they had very little trouble with thieves. They remembered, however, one Saturday when a roll-away bed apparently rolled away from a sidewalk display.

Gideon and Carl sold the business to Jerry Mauer and Rudy Paetal, who discontinued the used furniture section of the business. They operated the NEW furniture store for ten years until Jerry became ill, and sold out to Spear's Better Furniture.

The Foxes, who purchased the raspberry patch in 1941, also owned and operated Fox Milling on the corner of Sprague and Pines.

WORLD WAR II

"We humbly and profoundly hope that this is the last war and that we are approaching an era of world peace that will last forever."

[Editorial, *Spokane Valley Herald*, August 14, 1945.]

Page of Dedication

Please list the name of your war hero/heroes on this page. Paste in clippings, photos, and add your memories. This will be the most important page in this history.

World War II

CHRONOLOGICAL HISTORY

I began this chronological outline by including the boys and girls from the Valley who participated in the armed services during World War II. The list was soon engulfing the entire book. At West Valley High School alone there were more than 700 names on the service roll. I decided it would be better not to list anyone than to leave some out. Therefore, there are no individual war stories as such in this volume. Service records are mentioned only in a larger context.

However, the stories of those in the armed forces are a vital part of Valley history and should certainly be included. I am assigning that writing to you readers. Please use the opposite page to write YOUR hero's history and add photos and clippings to your writing. That record will be a cherished family keepsake. Then please turn back to the dedication page and read it again. This book is dedicated to your hero and all the heroes of World War II. As you read this chapter, know that all readers are remembering the bravery and courage of OUR heroes.

1939 September 1: Germany invaded Poland. **WWII** began.

1940 August 27: The U.S. Draft Law was enacted.

November 5: President Roosevelt was elected to an unprecedented third term.

Postmaster Chester Bennett of the Valley was taken prisoner at the fall of the Philippines and passed away in a Japanese prison camp.

1941 March 11: The U.S. Lend Lease Act was signed.

December 7: The Pacific War began with the Japanese attack on U.S. and British posts at Pearl Harbor and Malaya. The next day the U.S. declared war on Japan.

The Valley began to experience rationing, war-time shortages, and the effects of government controls by the **OPA.**

The Defense Plant Corporation decided to place an aluminum rolling mill at **Trentwood** on land owned by **Jessie Steinke** and her husband. The mill was completed in 1942. The first carload of finished aluminum was shipped from **Trentwood** February 27, 1943. When the mill opened, it employed 450 residents.

1941

December 11: Germany and Italy declared war on the United States. The U.S. took reciprocal action.

December 23: Wake Island fell. U.S. troops arrived in Australia.

1942

Daylight Saving Time began as "War Time" when **FDR** ordered clocks set ahead to save energy.

In the Spokane area, including the Valley, there were over 22,000 Victory Gardens.

March 30: MacArthur was appointed Supreme Commander Southwest Pacific Area; Nimitz was Commander-in-Chief Pacific Command and **CINC** Pacific Ocean Area.

First American Army Air Force plane flew "The Hump" airlifting massive supplies from India to China.

The **Walter Steinkes** came to what would be the **Trentwood** site of the **Velox Naval SupplyDepot**. They built a large rock barn, had 40 cows, a new house, new chicken houses, cleared rock off the land, dug a well for irrigating 160 acres, and "had used it only once when the Navy came and told us we had to move."

Naval Supply Depot contractors received "Go Ahead."

1943

September 12: Eisenhower assumed post as Commander-in-Chief Allied Expeditionary Force (for Northwest Africa).

Acute labor shortage in the Valley due to war-time building and industries.

Campfire Girls in the area collected and sold grease and salvage to help purchase a Red Cross ambulance.

May 17: The **Dishman Ration Board** opened to help hold prices down and assist in stabilizing both the cost of living and prices in general. Volunteers made surveys of the prices of cigarettes, men's work apparel, and used durable goods at restaurants, grocery stores, shoe shops, dry cleaners, garages, and locker boxes over an area of 800 square miles. Nationally during WW II prices rose only about 30% compared with 61% in World War I from July, 1914 to November, 1918.

December 18: Evening slippers with trimming of gold or silver leather were released from rationing.

All Valley Veterans of Foreign Wars met and formed a local group at the **Opportunity Town Hall.**

Valley Community Club passed a resolution against the sale or leasing to Japanese of any land in the Spokane area.

1943

December 23: New B and C Gas rationing coupons were each worth five gallons of gasoline, not three gallons as the old coupons were. Residents did not get more gasoline however, just fewer coupons.

December 16: **West Valley High School** placed four gold stars on their service flag for former students who gave their lives for their country and stars for four who were missing in action.

The old apple packing house at **Union** and **First** became an Army Ordinance Depot during the war. Many local folks worked there.

The United States $12,000,000 **Naval Supply Depot** at **Velox** was opened.

1944

Valley residents with garden flowers were again asked to donate them to patients at Baxter and Ft. George Wright hospitals and to the chapels at Geiger and Galena Air Fields.

Giboney's Men's Wear was officially certified as the Valley's rationed footwear distributor. The store stocked No. 3 footwear for industrial workers and type No. 4 for farmers. Both types conformed to **OPA** requirements.

The **Ed Biersdorfs** received a thrill when their son, Bill, radioman with the infantry at Camp Roberts, phoned long distance having won the call on the Gary Sims radio program in Hollywood.

Mrs. R.T. Vivian of **Pinecroft** turned in $226 to the Red Cross, earned by making and selling pot holders.

Jack Hood of **Opportunity** wrote of the invasion of Europe: "When we made our landing we found the water was sometimes five or six feet over our heads... My watch stopped the very minute we hit the water."

August 1: The **Rolling Mill** was given its first renewal of the Army-Navy "E" award for increased production, maintenance, less than 5% absenteeism, and war bond purchases. The "E" award was an incentive award given to industry during the war.

January 13: **H.J. Collins,** District Fuel Rationing Representative of OPA, announced that householders in the Valley should not have used more than 44% of their total yearly oil ration.

January 16: Eisenhower assumed duties as Supreme Commander, Allied Expeditionary Force.

February 3: Both sides of the Valley, having tallied more than $30,000 at the end of the week, were running neck and neck in the race to sell their war bond quotas in the Fourth War Loan drive.

April: The **Valley Chamber of Commerce** went on record as sponsoring a

1944

post-war planning committee to find and make jobs for returning servicemen as they were discharged from the armed forces. **Sig Hansen** became chairman of the **Spokane Valley Citizens' Committee for Post-Victory Employment.**

June: To help farmers get the workers they so badly needed to help harvest crops, the OPA issued supplemental gasoline rations both for city dwellers to go into the fields and for migratory workers who will follow the harvest.

Lt. Louis S. Means of **Millwood** told an unusually large group of **Kiwanis Club** members about his experiences in a German Prison Camp.

October: "Shoe rationing will continue indefinitely but coffee will continue to be unrationed," stated **Dave S. Cohen**, District Director of the OPA. "The coffee stocks are nearly three times as great as when coffee rationing started so allotments are no longer necessary."

Mrs. Albert Bogen, War Chairman of the Veterans of Foreign Wars Auxiliary, began a campaign to collect junk jewelry to be sent to service personnel in the South Pacific to be used by them as barter with the natives.

September 29: **Valley People** were asked to continue in the national program to convince people to open their homes to workers in vital war plants to relieve the critical housing shortages in the area.

November 7: Roosevelt was elected to a fourth term as U.S. President.

September 29: Pupils at **Trent School** bought $380.55 in war bonds during the week. Their goal was to buy an Army jeep within the year.

The number of ration points required for butter was boosted to 16. That meant that civilians would have to spread the precious stuff a little thinner.

Again the **West Valley Schools** have gone over the top in the sale of war bonds and stamps, securing $40,084 in the sixth War Loan Drive. This makes a total of $62,432 sold since September.

November 10: *(Valley Herald)* **H.C. Collins**, district fuel rationing representative, stated today that crankcase oil drained from gasoline engines, and fuel oil which has been reclaimed from used lubricating oil, are under the rationing program.

The quota of new passenger automobiles for rationing in November was the lowest to be given since rationing began. It was a 35% reduction from the October quota necessary to make the remaining supply available as long as possible for essential purposes.

1945

(Ad in *Valley Herald*): "The post-war home is here! You can order a three-room home on Monday and it will be set up and ready to move into by Wednesday on your own Valley property. You don't even have to own your own property. Simply buy a house and the **Jenses Camp** will rent you a lot immediately. **Mr. Jenses** has received four carloads of the round-top steel quonset huts used in construction of the Alaska Highway."

1945

The **Dishman Victory Sewing Club** made 95 pairs of convalescent slippers and five pairs of curtains for the recreation room at the Baxter Army Hospital in Spokane.

April 12: Roosevelt died; Truman succeeded him as U.S. President.

May 7: All German forces surrendered unconditionally at Rheims.

May 8: V-E Day proclaimed.

The **Chamber of Commerce** instituted a "Take Care of Returning Veterans" Campaign.

August 6, 9: U.S. atomic bombs fell on Hiroshima and Nagasaki.

September 2: V-J Day. Japan signed the Instrument of Surrender. There was a giant street dance in Spokane.

The Trentwood Aluminum Rolling Mill on Sullivan Road, General Machinery Company on Freya, and the Ordinance Depot in Opportunity were recipients of the coveted Army-Navy "E" award for outstanding production of wartime materials. The award consisted of a pennant for the plant and pins for employees. The award presentation ceremonies were usually attended by military, civic and plant leaders and employees with a military band present. General Machinery maintained the Trentwood and Mead aluminum plants when they were turned over to the government by the Aluminum Company of America after the war. Right of the podium: Lt. Laurence Boutwell, Resident Inspector of Naval Materials; holding banner on the right: E.J. Simon, president of General Machinery.
Courtesy of Larry Boutwell.

Rationing

During World War II, shortages of everything—even "necessities"—brought about complete changes in life style on the home front. Prices rose dramatically and some items, such as a new car, were next to impossible to obtain. By 1942 there were critical shortages on the home front of meats, fats, oils, dairy products and processed foods.

To bring about an equitable distribution of the available goods and to curtail the spiral of rising prices, in January 1942 the War Production Board was implemented and local ration boards were soon set up. Nationally these were under the jurisdiction of the Office of Price Administration, known as the OPA.

On May 17, 1943, a ration board opened in the Valley at Dishman to serve the eastern portion of Spokane County. It was headed by Chief Clerk Dwight Higgins and Board Chairman A.J. Treibel. The day-to-day work was done by a corps of loyal volunteers. When the office closed September 28, 1945, after 27 months of operations, the *Spokane Valley Herald* reported that the volunteers had contributed 15,642 hours for the cause. The local activity was known as the War Price and Rationing Board.

Rationing ended nationally on some commodities August 24, 1945. On that date the OPA removed canned fruits and vegetables, fuel oil, stoves, and gasoline from the list of rationed commodities. Gasoline rationing had started May 15, 1942. Car owners were given an A, B, or C stamp to place on their windshields. This determined how much gas the driver was allowed, depending on how critical his driving was to the war effort. Meats, fat, oils, butter, sugar, shoes, and tires were rationed until the office closed.

Old-timers praise the work of the Board saying, despite complaints, misunderstandings, criticism, and some "cheating," it successfully "held the line against inflation in the Valley."

A national survey was made of price control in World War II compared to World War I. Up to September 1944, there had been a total rise of a little over 30% in prices nationally over the preceding four years. During World War I between July 1914, and November 1918, when the Armistice was signed, the cost of living rose 61%. Similar comparisons could be seen in industrial prices. According to the *Valley Herald*, March 23, 1945, the total rise locally between August 1939, and September 1944, was a little over 25%. During the 61 months of World War I hostilities, prices rose locally over 106%.

From all accounts available, the rationing board was welcomed in the area and dinners of gratitude were held to honor the workers. Ration books and stamps, used for such critical items as sugar and gasoline, were considered a necessary bother.

The posted precepts of the Board were:

1. Buy only your share of what is available.
2. Know the ceiling price of every purchase. (Ceiling prices were imposed on some items to keep prices stable.)
3. Refuse to pay more than ceiling.
4. Report all overcharges to War Price and Rationing Board or OPA District Office.

The Kinkades, Father And Son

In Volume I, page 162, the second paragraph under the title, "Carl Goffinet," reads as follows:

"Carl Goffinet recalls Grove's Garage next to the IOOF Hall and a man named Kincaid who was chief mechanic."

Since the publication of Volume I, I have found the son of the "man named Kincaid;" and have learned that his name was spelled Kinkade.

He was Paul Kinkade and his son is Orville Kinkade. They have quite a story.

Both Paul and Orville have left their marks on Valley history, but in very different ways. Paul was the mechanic at Grove's Garage. Orville early-on said he didn't want anything to do with mechanics. He also said (when it looked like the United States was going to get involved in World War II) that he didn't want to be in the Army, crawling around in the muck and dirt. He wanted to be in the air where the environment was clean.

Alleen and Paul Kinkade came to the Valley in 1913 from Illinois. Their three children, including Orville, attended the old Opportunity Grade School on the southeast corner of Pines and Bowdish. Orville remembers buying groceries at the Myers Store on the southwest corner of Pines and Sprague and attending the Baptist Church on the corner of Appleway and Union.

While Orville was in grade school the family spent some time in California. There he had two experiences of note: (1) his father took him to the 1932 Olympics in Los Angeles; (2) one day while playing marbles, the earth began to shake and his marbles were flung sky high. He remembers his dad taking cover under a fire truck being repaired, shouting, "Earthquake! Earthquake!"

Later after a brief stay in Coeur d'Alene, the family returned to the Valley and bought a house at S. 118 Pines Road. Paul, as we know, found work at Grove's Garage, but he always dreamed of owning his own repair shop. In 1941 he was able to buy Kinkade's Auto Repair at the southeast corner of Pines and Sprague. In 1947 this was sold to Harvey Banks of Veradale and Paul built a more modern shop at S. 122 Pines Road next to his home. It also was called Kinkade Auto Repair.

In 1939 when Orville graduated from the old Central Valley High School at the bend in the Appleway where Greenacres Junior High School is today, war clouds were forming. To escape the Army, he began to take flying lessons at Felts Field. These were paid for by working at Gillespie's fruit orchard at 25¢ an hour. By the time Orville enrolled at Cheney a year later, the government was offering free training to boys who would enroll in a Civilian Pilot Training Program at Felts Field. Orville enrolled and took all four of the courses offered: Primary, Basic, Advanced and Instrument Flying.

At Felts, he looked longingly at the big P-36 fighter planes on the ramp and said over and over to himself, "I gotta fly one of those."

His two years of college training at Eastern Washington State College made him eligible to be an aviation cadet before Pearl Harbor. After Pearl Harbor, he became a full-blown member of the Air Corps and went on active duty January 18, 1942. He had his physical at old Fort George Wright where Spokane Falls College is today. His training began all over again: Primary, Basic and Advanced—this time in California and Arizona. Upon graduation as a 2nd Lieutenant August 27, 1942, he was sent to the East Coast where he made the transition to piloting fighters, first P-40s and then P-47s known as Thunderbolts. The Thunderbolt was one of the Air Force's fastest and most heavily armed fighter planes.

Orville was shipped to Europe on the Queen Mary and became a member of the Eighth Air Force. After thirty-three missions over Germany, during a mission over the Rhine River in Holland, he was shot down in a ball of flames November 5, 1943. Bullets pierced both his left leg and arm before he bailed out and landed in shallow water

In the '20s and '30s Grove's Garage was the center of the small business block that formed in Opportunity on the south side of Appleway between Pines and Robie. Left, Paul Kinkade, chief mechanic; right, Mr. Grove.
Courtesy of Orville Kinkade.

where he sat in a little rubber boat that was part of his parachute pack for six hours, waiting for the Germans to capture him.

PRISONER OF WAR

German marines picked him up and took him to a hospital on the coast of Holland. He remained there as a Nazi prisoner for three months and then for 15 months was a Nazi prisoner at Stalag Luft No. 1 Prison Camp. He was freed when the Russians liberated the prisoners there May 4, 1945, four days before V-E day. He arrived home June 30.

Orville also served in the Korean War, flying missions as a night pilot.

During his twenty-four years of service in the Air Force, he received many awards including the Distinguished Flying Cross, the Air Medal, and the Purple Heart. He retired from the Air Force in 1965, attaining the rank of Lt. Colonel.

Orville and his wife Arlene are back in the Valley today.

That is the story of the man and his son "named Kincaid" with one brief addition: Roy Pierce, son of pioneer George Pierce, wrote that his father "often shot pool in the basement of the IOOF Hall, along with Glenn Downing (Washington Water Power), Frank Maxey (orchardist), John Hossfeld (bookkeeper), and R.P. 'Paul' Kinkade."

The Story Of Trentwood

[Facts for this story are from issues of *Alcotrend*, published by the Aluminum Co. of America, Trentwood Works, 1945.]

The Valley had little experience with "big" business. Most of its businesses had sprung literally from grass roots. The Paper Mill in Millwood was the largest Valley employer through the '30s and once settled into the little town it established, both the mill and the company-town residents were totally "Valley."

In 1941 when the Defense Plant Corporation announced that it planned to place an aluminum rolling mill in the Valley, the Valley had to rethink itself. Alcoa (Aluminum Company of America), the company that would build and operate the plant under government contract, was a giant in the aluminum industry. The new mill was expected to employ 2500 workers!

In January 1942, what seemed like only a minute after Pearl Harbor, a delegation of government representatives and building experts visited the Spokane area and selected a flat piece of ground on Sullivan Road covered with last year's wheat stubble as the location for what would become the Trentwood Rolling Mill, largest aluminum rolling mill in the western United States.

Ground was broken the following March.

Over 5000 men came on the job, many of whom stayed on after construction to help operate the big plant. Furnaces were erected and the first aluminum rolling ingot ever cast west of the Mississippi was poured on November 24, 1942.

The remelter began shipping ingots to eastern plants for rolling on December 7, 1942. Roofs were still to be built over much of the south end of the plant.

On February 15, 1943, the 112-Inch Mill went into operation and on February 27, the first plate was shipped. It was cold in the plant. The thermometer was hugging zero outside and people were working in their mackinaws because the heating system was not ready for operation. In March the 4-Hi and Flat Mills were started. The 120-Inch Mill started

rolling in May. The Continuous Mill sprang to life on all five stands in June and Trentwood was on its way to becoming one of the nation's great producers of aluminum sheet for war.

The plant consisted of 52 acres of joined buildings under a single roof. It cost more than $47 million and was so large the workers used battery powered carts to get from one part of the plant to another.

From *Alcotrend*, October 5, 1945: "The story of Trentwood is a story of people. Men from farms, stores, the woods, mines, service stations, banks, and other industries. Women who had worked before and women who hadn't. Boys on summer vacations, or just out of school. Soldiers and sailors on furlough. Very few knew anything about aluminum except that it was light and bright and made good cooking utensils. But they learned in a remarkably short time to cast it, roll it, and do the thousand and one things necessary to production and maintenance. For their efforts, they won world-wide acclaim and the recognition of the Army and Navy departments.

"Three hundred and two Trentwood Alcoans went into the service. Four gave their lives for their country. The plant was humble in their memory and proud to have worked with them.

"When the end came, a mighty armada of fighting planes had gotten their tough aluminum hides at Trentwood. Had all the sheet produced at Trentwood gone into the manufacture of B-17's alone, a gigantic air force of 25,000 planes could have been built. Actually, Trentwood sheet was shipped at one time or another to every aircraft manufacturer in the nation. Thousands of pounds of the metal went to England and Russia.

"On September 14, 1945, the last ingot was rolled at Trentwood and rumbled and crashed to the coiler at the end of the run-out table. The plant closed for a victory celebration. A full chapter was completed and added to the voluminous history of World War II. It was a long chapter of miracles—of miracle men and women and of a miracle metal that drove the enemy to mortal defeat—the result of terrific aerial bombardment made possible by the 375,000,000 pounds of aluminum sheet produced at Trentwood for war use. Most of that monumental production had gone into aircraft.

"Every month in its over two years of production, the men and women of Trentwood Works met every production demand made upon them for Army and Navy material.

"With every person straining at the wheel, output rose to 120 per cent of rated plant capacity in the month before V-E Day. Company records for sheet production were broken by practically every department in the plant. Four Army-Navy "E" awards for excellence in production were the culminating recognition for a job very well done.

"This exemplary war production record had started only three years before in a stubble wheat field in the Spokane Valley.

"When the war ended, among the jetsam left stranded was $793 million worth of government built, war surplus aluminum plants; giant installations resting in silence. Trentwood in the Spokane Valley was one of these.

"The Permanente Metals Corporation of which Henry Kaiser was president had long been interested in aluminum. It had first tried to enter the industry in 1941 and had proposed building an aluminum reduction plant in the Pacific Northwest. That failed; but after many negotiations, in July 1946, Permanente Metals leased from the government both the Trentwood Rolling Mill in the Spokane Valley and the Mead Reduction Plant in Spokane. Not long afterwards the corporation changed its name to the Kaiser Aluminum and Chemical Corporation. By 1964 Kaiser Aluminum (of which Trentwood was now a part) was 121st of the nation's top 500 industrial firms according to *Fortune* magazine.

"Trentwood, at that time, sat on 525 acres with nearly 65 acres under roof. It employed approximately 1700 hourly and salaried employees and had capacity that could be developed to produce up to 569 million pounds of aluminum sheet and plate products annually."

COMMISSIONING OF THE NAVAL SUPPLY DEPOT, VELOX, DECEMBER, 1942
Warehouse in background. Front row L to R: Lt. Cmdr. Barner, Lt. Cmdr. Wright, Lt. Cmdr. Jones, Lt.
Parks, Lt. Fisk, Lt. Welliver, Lt. Hill, Lt. Evans, Lt. Daum, Lt. Bamber, Lt. Cannon; (standing) Lt. Cmdr.
King, Lt. Johnson, Ens. Tilley, Ens. Gibb.

A Naval Supply Depot for the Spokane Valley

At the height of World War II, the Navy Department saw a need for Inland Supply Depots—points of storage for coastal activities whose warehouse space and facilities were inadequate to serve the demands of the fleet. These depots also could be supplemental supply bases in the event that coastal stations were bombed. It was imperative, the Navy decided, that such a depot be located in the Inland Northwest.

VELOX

Velox was the name of a railway whistle stop in the Spokane Valley, approximately twelve miles from Spokane city center. Lying between the Spokane International Railroad on the south and the Northern Pacific Railroad and State Highway No. 2H on the north, it had excellent, for those days, transportation facilities. Also, four major railroads serving Seattle and points East converged nearby in the city of Spokane: the Northern Pacific; the Chicago, Milwaukee, St. Paul and Pacific; the Union Pacific and the Great Northern, making Spokane the railroad center of the area.

Hemmed in by the Cabinet Range of the Rocky Mountain Cordillera, the topography of the land was excellent also. There was less than ten feet variance in the slope of the terrain in the vicinity of Velox. This comparatively level topography, the good transportation facilities, excellent foundation and drainage conditions and the fact that Velox was the only mile tract of land available within a fifteen mile radius of Spokane combined to make it the Navy's choice for the proposed Inland Northwest depot.

On May 14, 1942, Clifton, Applegate and Henry George received a Letter of Intent from the Bureau of Yards and Docks, naming them prime contractors of the proposed Naval Supply Depot at Velox in the Spokane Valley. This was the contractors' "go ahead" signal.

A crew was assembled and only two days later car after car of coverall clad workmen turned off the highway at Velox and drove through the uncut wheat toward the depot site. On this same day, May 16, the first shovelful of earth was turned on the new project. Hundreds of workmen milled through the wheat field, using the backs of their saws as scythes to cut down the wheat and clear a path for the foundations of the first temporary buildings.

In less than a week the pounding of hammers, buzzing of electric saws, and mingled voices of brick layers supplanted the neighing of horses at plow time and the scraping of harrows along wheat rows. Sounds that had for so many years been natural to the Spokane Valley gave way to the vibrations of progress, in later months to seem the natural thing.

Whitehouse and Price, Spokane architects, were hired by the Navy to design the depot, and Lt. Cmdr. H.G. Clark (CEC) USN was appointed Officer-in-Charge of Construction. When the contract was nearly completed, Lt. Cmdr. Clark was relieved of his duties by Lt. Cmdr. M.W. Kehart (CEC) USNR.

Lt.(jg) I.J.Herring (CEC) USNR was the Resident Officer-in-Charge of Construction. Assistant Resident Officer-in-Charge of Construction was Ensign Richard S. Cannon (CEC) USNR, later to become Public Works Officer of the commissioned depot.

During the construction period three shifts of workers were employed, with a peak of 4895 employees on the payroll. Many of these employees were doing construction work for the first time, having spent most of their lives on farms in Washington and Montana. In spite of this fact, only three deaths were charged to the job, and the injuries received at work were minor ones. For a project the size of the construction of the depot, this was considered an admirable safety record.

Material delays were experienced throughout the construction period. No sooner had the contract been let than a heavy rainfall in the entire Northwest area halted logging operations, making lumber, already a high priority item, almost impossible to obtain. What little lumber was available was procured first of all for the immense Naval Training Station to be constructed at nearby Farragut, Idaho. The foundation for that installation was being poured at about the same time the contract for the Naval Supply Depot was let, and Farragut had been awarded a higher priority rating than the Depot.

Steel also was a critical item. The difficulty in obtaining prefabricated metal parts for the heating plant caused considerable delay in the completion of that building.

In spite of all the delays, work progressed remarkably well, due largely to the excellent cooperation between labor and management. At all times morale was high and the workmen were as interested in getting the job done as the contractors. Many of them, bitten by the construction bug, got Navy fever and joined the Seabees when the Depot was completed.

Seven months after the contract was started, the Depot was commissioned with an underrun of over one million dollars realized on the contract.

Captain Joseph E. McDonald (SC) USNR proceeded to Spokane on September 1, 1942, as Supply Officer-in-Command of the Depot. Assistant Supply Officer-in-Command was Lt. (jg) Charles H. Parks. Frank Elliot, civilian administration officer, and Lt. Parks established temporary offices in the Hutton Building in Spokane (since the Depot Administration Building was not complete) and began recruiting civilian personnel for the Depot August 15, 1942.

On September 15, Captain McDonald and his staff of four naval officers (all men) and thirteen civilian employees (four men and nine women) moved from offices in the Hutton Building to the accounting office of the then completed Administration Building on Depot premises. The balance of 1942 was spent in expansion. As buildings were readied, they were immediately occupied.

The cold weather started early that year with the first snowfall in November, the forerunner of a tough, cold winter. It caught the Depot without adequate heating facilities. The Administration Building had to be heated by an old boiler set up in an adjoining shed. In the storehouses, heat was obtained from miscellaneous oil and electric heaters. Warehouse No. 3 used an improvised heater constructed from an old engine, and heat for the three officers' quarters was obtained from an old threshing machine engine.

It was during this period that the duty officers' room was completed and furnished with department store furniture, ordered sight unseen. Because the bed was too short and too narrow, the duty officer welcomed the opportunity of checking the warehouse doors and keeping the heaters glowing.

By New Years Day, 1943, the Supply Depot at Velox was ready for commissioning. It was the beautiful day of a hard winter. Ceremonies were held out of doors on the front steps of the Administration Building. Assembled were 150 civilian employees, fifteen commissioned Navy officers, a platoon of Marines (stationed as guards on the Depot), an African-American band from the Naval Air Station, Pasco, and civilian guests: Mayor Sutherlin and Chamber of Commerce President Harlan Peyton, both from Spokane, and Mrs. Grace Farber, national chaplain of the Marine Corps Auxiliary. She presented a big, white English bulldog to the Depot as mascot to be known as Captain Lee in honor of her son, Lee, missing in action at Corregidor.

By May 30, 1944, there were, in the supply depot area, 12 general storehouses and five heavy material storehouses, 200 feet wide and 600 feet long. In addition to this inside storage, there was open storage that would accommodate approximately 2500 to 3000 carloads, accessible to railroad trackage.

The Spokane International Railroad provided access for the Depot to three of the major railroads centered in Spokane and acted as the delivering carrier for carload shipments via one of these railroads. For less than carload shipments, Depot trucks and local supplementary trucks were used.

Air service, too, was conveniently located in respect to the Depot site. Felts Field was only eight miles away—an airport large enough to accommodate any airplane then in use. Spokane Army Air Depot at Galena was ten and one half miles west of Spokane and assisted the Navy on occasion in transporting high priority air shipments to the California coast. Railroad tracks went inside the heavy duty warehouses.

Five of the warehouses on the Depot were used to store Medical Stores which included the 2938 different items from mouse traps to prefab buildings that made up a one-hundred bed hospital.

Landing craft for the Pacific Theater came into the Depot ready for overseas shipment.

Approximately 30 carloads a month of Lend Lease material arrived during the first year—huge diesel engines weighing 21 tons each, radio and electrical equipment, and chemicals—89 carloads in one peak month. And 52 carloads of Hi-Octane gasoline in transit for the USSR under the Lend Lease Program.

Personnel

The manpower shortage, prevalent in the industrial cities of the United States during the War, affected the Velox Depot also. Spokane was a critical labor area, and the Depot experienced a regular turnover of labor. Many workers, hearing tales of exorbitant salaries paid by industry, became dissatisfied with the Civil Service wage scale and separated themselves for better paying jobs. Many women left to join their husbands with the armed forces in other parts of the country.

Although both workers and the Depot itself were, in a way, only transients, work conditions were as fine as in any area business. Captain McDonald made certain all workers, civilian and military, had access to recreational facilities. Behind the Marine barracks was a ball diamond and grandstand. In the spring of 1943, as soon as the snow melted from the surrounding mountains, the personnel organized softball teams. Later on that first summer, tennis courts were built and flooded in the winter for ice skating.

At regular intervals, the military personnel drilled, bowled, exercised, and held target practice so that they were ready when the call to overseas duty came.

Assembling a shipment for the islands at a critical time during World War II.
Naval Supply Depot, Velox, 1944.

EXPANSION

During the first year and a half, the Supply Depot ran along quite leisurely. Among Thirteenth Naval District personnel, it was often called the "Velox Country Club." The seventeen warehouses were ample to take care of the material consigned "NSD Velox." The officers had time to see that the stores were stocked neatly, allowing large aisles and runways. In their spare time they planted victory gardens and beautified the grounds of the Depot.

Then, quite suddenly and unexpectedly in the spring of 1944, three major programs were hurled at the Velox Supply Depot. The amount of Bureau of Ships material for storage increased tremendously. Clothing and small stores, formerly not stocked at Velox at all, was designated for Velox to alleviate critical storage conditions at the Clearfield Supply Depot; and a new retail business, known as the BBB Program, became the largest program at the Depot.

In a three month period, the civilian payroll jumped from 542 employees at the end of May to 1212 employees as of August 31. Warehouses were chock full with stores stacked on loading ramps, along aisles and even along the streets. The cafeteria, garage, and garage annex were enlarged and twenty prefabricated warehouses were transferred from the Army to the Navy and erected at the Depot site.

A contract for six new warehouses was awarded to the Western Construction Company of Seattle July 1944.

At the height of the expansion period, Captain McDonald was detached and replaced by Captain John Ball (SC) USN. With over 1200 employees, the depot expanded overnight from a part-time-like activity to a full-time war activity.

BBB

BBB meant Basic Boxed Baseload. A BBB load consisted of the required base supplies, other than medicine and food, to provide for 10,000 men for a 60-day period after a beachhead in the Pacific had been secured. There were approximately 5000 general stores items, special clothing and small stores, ship's store and fountain and laundry supplies in each load—about 6000 items in all. When packed the load weighed approximately 3500 tons, valued at $41,500,000. Items handled varied from a small drill to soap and cargo nets.

All the facilities of the Depot were utilized in arranging for initial space for the procurement of equipment and supplies, and for the recruiting of personnel necessary to carry out the details of the BBB program.

By December, 1944, because of the increasing tempo of the war in the Pacific, the accent on military activity had diverted from the east coast to the west coast. The invasion of the Philippines had begun and the main islands of Japan had been bombed. The Naval Supply Depot saw another great increase in incoming and outgoing shipments. This called for more civilian employees and more military, more storage space, maintenance buildings, warehouses, enlarged parking areas, and an enlarged cafeteria. Within a six month period there were over 2000 employees at the Depot with a War Manpower Commission ceiling set at 2500. Recruiting was no small task.

In many cases the employees hired were untrained and inexperienced. A typing school, a school for supervisors, and a school to train materials handling equipment operators were set up at the Depot. Other workers, particularly laborers, were trained on the job. NSD Velox was granted the highest recruiting priority in the area except for the secret project at Hanford.

During the last quarter of 1944, the Depot did not confine its activities within its own walls. Officers from the Depot spoke at schools, community club meetings, and at gatherings for special occasions, especially Navy Day celebrations. In cooperation with the Naval Training Center, Farragut, Idaho, NSD furnished a company of Marines, a float, and eight representative vehicles for the Spokane Navy Day Parade.

It was the community's hope that the Supply Depot would be a permanent Valley installation. However, in 1958 the Navy left the Spokane Valley. In 1960 the Depot was purchased from the General Services Administration by a group of businessmen who converted it to an industrial park. They did not have the resources to make necessary improvements and found it difficult to attract tenants. Six months later Washington Water Power acquired the property and in 1962 successful development of the park was begun by the Pentzer Corporation, a subsidiary of Washington Water Power. Today (1994) the old Depot property is known as the Spokane Industrial Park.

Farragut, a Near Neighbor

[Spokane Valley Today, June-July, 1987]

I drove through the tranquillity of Farragut State Park last Sunday and tried to picture the area as it had been when I first saw it in 1943.

World War II was at its height and the gigantic Naval Training Station at Farragut, second largest in the U.S., bustled with activity. It occupied the entire 8000 acres that is now park. The six 5000-man boot camps on the station were being fully utilized. Nearby Farragut Village with its 500 apartments and five dorms for single men and women was fully rented to Navy personnel.

The base had six baseball diamonds, seven motion picture theaters, a laundry six times larger than any in nearby Spokane, supply depots the equivalent of six department stores, and an auditorium that seated 2500.

The Northern Pacific Railroad had built a spur into it and so did the Spokane International Railroad. At one point during the war, more passenger tickets were sold at Farragut than at any other Northern Pacific station in the U.S.

More than 13,500 workers built the massive Naval station. Many of them were from Spokane and the Valley.

Suddenly, early in the spring of 1942, the job of carving the installation out of the wilderness was begun. By September 15, at a cost of approximately $75,000,000, the base was ready for commissioning.

Just as suddenly, with the end of the war, Farragut Naval Training Station was decommissioned on June 16, 1946.

Then began the task of determining what should be done with what had been, during the war, the largest city in Idaho.

The most feasible suggestion seemed to be giving the site, in the form of a school, back to the GI's who had won the war.

There was no doubt that the beauty of the site would challenge that of any campus in the United States. Located in the Kaniksu National Forest of Idaho, the area abounded with elk, deer, game birds, and geese. Half a mile away, lay Lake Pend Oreille, the second largest lake totally within the boundaries of the U.S. It was bordered by towering mountains and pine and fir trees with some of Idaho's grandest peaks looking down upon it. Pack Saddle rose some 7200 feet, and Cape Horn some 6000 feet. An ideal spot it was for the war weary GI's to regain their civilian footing.

On October 14, 1946, Farragut College and Technical Institute opened its doors to veterans. With the colleges of the United States filled to overflowing with returning GI's, the decision to convert the training station into a college was received with rejoicing. 400 veterans, their wives, and co-eds from 43 states moved into the hospital areas and what had been Farragut Village. The charter for the school was granted by the state of Idaho.

From the first, financing was a problem. Although the necessary buildings were established and housing was not a problem, as it was in most colleges throughout the country, money was needed to pay the staff and maintain the facility. The school was to be financed solely from the GI educational allotment allowed military personnel after the war. It opened in October and the first payment from the government was not expected until January. An estimated $250,000 was needed to get the school going.

Shoshone and Kootenai counties contributed $100,000 of the needed funds. Veterans' organizations in Idaho and Washington and the Spokane Chamber of Commerce and private contributions made it possible for the school to open.

The students were fascinated with the site. They could often be seen meandering back to their dormitories with a creel of trout from the nearby mountain streams or a string of gleaming bass from the sparkling waters of Lake Pend Oreille. They hunted in the mountains and snapped scenic photos of the sunspotted peaks of the visible Cabinets, Selkirks, and Bitterroots.

But like all good things, the college came to an end. Financing was the problem. In the summer of '49 the school closed. Soon, the remaining buildings of the original Farragut Naval Training Station were demolished for scrap or sold. The site soon became Farragut State Park and once again reverted to wilderness.

It all rose out of nothing fast; and thankfully, its need ended so fast that the Farragut war experience has the illusive quality of a dream.

For those who were stationed there or went to school there from the crowded cities of the east, perhaps it was the one beautiful spot in the nightmare that is war.

"The War Is Over!"

[by Estella Hanson, Opportunity, used with permission.]

"The war is over! The war is over!" blasted the radio. People were going crazy with joy all over the Valley and City. Over and over they echoed the radio, "The WAR is OVER!"

I remembered Pearl Harbor Day. I was alone in the house with five-year-old Del and was carrying Lavonne. Would our family be disrupted? Would Japan take over our country? My heart thumped. I prayed in fear that day.

Now it was over. I stopped painting the outside window frames. I couldn't see. Tears streamed down my cheeks.

Del, his little sister now in tow, looked at me with solemn eyes. "Why are you crying, Mama? Aren't you glad?"

I hugged them both.

"It is just too wonderful. Let's go across the street and see if Grandma and Grandpa have heard the news."

We ran across the road. My mother was crying, too.

Myrt and Dad didn't get home until two hours later. Dad had been in the country and Myrt had to drive from Spokane.

"It was almost impossible to get from our warehouse on Main and Division to the Valley," Myrt said. "Flags were waving; fire crackers were sputtering and booming; spontaneous bands were marching up the centers of downtown streets playing 'America,' off-key. No one noticed. The air was filled with gladness, relief, and thankfulness. Strangers hugged and kissed.

"'Thank God! Thank God!' was the cry."

That night as we ate dinner with my parents, we gave thanks that loved ones now would come home. We talked of our friends and relatives in the service. Myrt's nephew, Bill, and his bride, Betty, who had married during his furlough between the South Pacific and the Aleutians, could now establish a real home.

"Will rationing end?" I asked. "Maybe no more lines for nylons," I said suddenly feeling guilty with joy.

"That was a small sacrifice," my mother answered soberly. And everyone was quiet, remembering .

Moving Forward

V-E Day, Victory in Europe, occurred May 8, 1945. V-J Day, Victory in Japan, occurred September 2, 1945. Those were dates of unprecedented joy, celebrated loudly on the streets of Spokane and the Valley but quietly in homes that had made the supreme sacrifice.

Those dates ended a period in Valley history—ended one era and began another.

The busy post-war years brought a new era of growth to the Valley. The Valley population jumped from an estimated 16,000 in 1940 to an estimated 45,000 by 1960. The Chamber of Commerce concentrated on becoming a force toward providing a rich, unified community life for the residents. It sponsored the first Miss Spokane Valley contest in 1955, followed the next year by the building of the first Valley Float. A State Information Booth at the State Line soon followed; then a county library, planning for parks and playgrounds, a Christmas lighting contest, the widening of Trent Road, a Valley hospital, a major shopping center, and school consolidation.

Chief among the problems that had to be addressed following the war was that of providing jobs for returning veterans. The Chamber of Commerce sponsored a post-war job planning committee for that purpose and fought a single-handed battle to prevent the Velox Naval Supply Depot from being dismantled. That facility became the Spokane Industrial Park, the largest operating industrial park in the Northwest.

Both Edgecliff Hospital and the aluminum plant remained active.

Road and bridge construction continued at regular intervals as needed and programs to make roadside areas less unsightly continued to occupy local committees.

Permits for the location of signs and advertising structures were examined as to location and size before being granted. There was a gradual weeding out of billboards in inappropriate locations.

Increased interest in the forming of zoning districts was manifested as the population increased. New districts were formed and many requests for zoning information and copies of the master zone ordinance were received and answered by the Planning Commission.

House numbering at East Valley was completed and all the areas east of the city of Spokane to the Idaho state line were covered, and all road and street intersections appropriately marked and proper street numbers furnished residents.

The Valley moved into the era of suburban/urban life.

TRANSPORTATION DOMINATES THIS VIEW OF THE VALLEY IN 1935.
The buildings in the background, center and left, are Felts Field. The Fancher Street overpass is under construction in the center of the photograph, spanning the Northern Pacific Railroad track. The Parkwater school is just below the Felts Field building on Fancher. The cluster of buildings at the far end of the newly constructed overpass are Jack's Diner to the left (west) of the Fancher and Trent crossing (later the Town and Country Restaurant) and Nelson's rental cabins to the right (east).

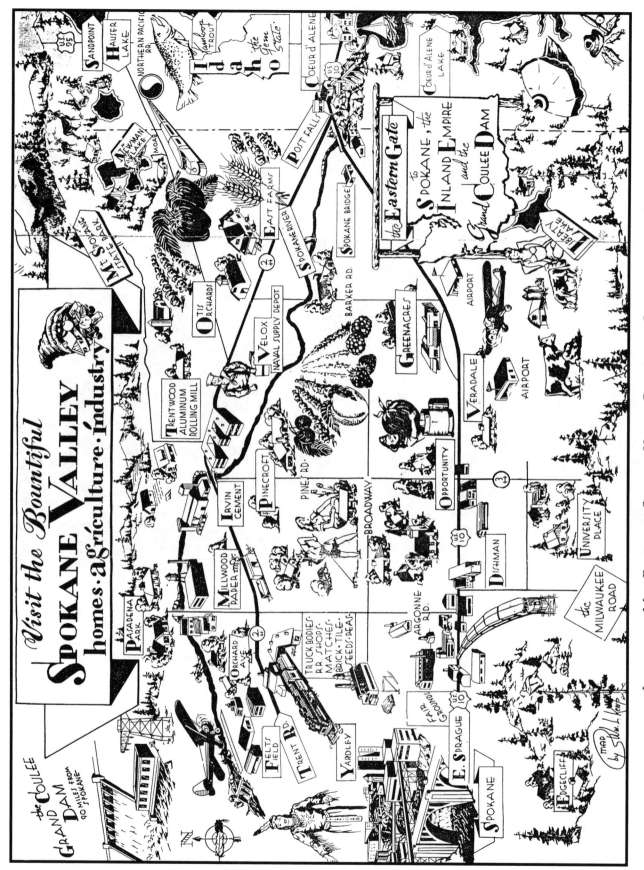

ILLUSTRATED MAP, PRINTED BY SPOKANE VALLEY CHAMBER OF COMMERCE IN THE '40S.
Used with permission. Courtesy of Erma Bates.

The Valley, 1945, as Author Says Good-Bye . . .

[From "Facts Concerning the Spokane Valley" published by Spokane Valley Chamber of Commerce, Dishman, Washington, 1945.]

The following towns and communities are represented in the Spokane Valley Chamber of Commerce through their own local Community or Commercial Clubs:

Dishman	Orchard Avenue
Greenacres	Otis Orchards
Irvin	Pinecroft
Millwood	Verdadale
Trentwood	University Place
Opportunity	Liberty Lake

LOCATION:
The Spokane Valley is situated in Eastern Washington, extending into Northern Idaho, 300 miles east of Seattle, 395 miles northeast of Portland and approximately 100 miles south of the Canadian border.

POPULATION:
1940 Census...........14,854
1946 Estimate to October 1...24,500
(Approximately 65% increase)

FORM OF GOVERNMENT:
County and township governed.
Millwood only incorporated town.

AREA OF VALLEY:
56.7 square miles to Idaho state line.

ALTITUDE AND CLIMATE:
Average elevation: 1734 ft.

Mean annual temperature: 48.6 degrees Fahrenheit
3 summer months avg: 57 degrees Fahrenheit
3 winter months average: 30 degrees Fahrenheit
Average annual rainfall: 15.79 inches
Sunshine average: 58% of possible
Average hourly wind velocity: 6.5 miles per hour
Average number of dense fog days: 17
(From 10 to 30 years average, United States Weather Bureau)

WATER SUPPLY:
Cold, pure drinking and domestic water from deep wells throughout the Valley. Water in abundance for irrigation purposes furnished by wells and gravity flow from water districts.

POWER AND LIGHT:
Washington Water Power Company
Bonneville Power Administration
Modern Electric Company

SANITATION:
Spokane County Health Department
Spokane Valley Garbage Collection

AMUSEMENTS AND RECREATION:
Large auditoriums in grade and high schools
3 motion picture theatres, including 700-car-capacity outdoor drive-in unit.
Swimming, in pools and at Liberty and Newman lakes
Two riding academies
Two large roller- rinks
Valley country Club
Bowling and Golf

Quick access to all Spokane facilities
Fishing in lakes, streams and river
Big game and upland game bird hunting within
thirty minutes' driving time
Total recreation area 3.5 square miles in Liberty
and Newman lake areas
3.5 acre undeveloped Pinecroft area

TRANSPORTATION:
Served by Great Northern, Northern Pacific, Union Pacific, Milwaukee, S.P. & S. and Spokane International Railways, U.S. Highway No. 10 and State Highway No. 2H, Interurban Bus service to all Valley points, connecting with transcontinental systems in Spokane, United, Northwest, and Empire Airline connections in Spokane.

FINANCIAL INSTITUTIONS:
Two commercial banks

TELEPHONES IN SERVICE:
4,002 telephones connected as of October 15, 1946
472 unfilled orders

INDUSTRIES:
21 manufacturing plants employing approximately 3,800 people. Annual industrial payroll approximately $4,400,000.

CHURCHES:
Nineteen, representing most leading denominations.

SCHOOLS:
The public school system consists of thirteen grade schools, three high schools, and one parochial school.

FIRE PROTECTION:
Five fully manned and equipped stations located at strategic sites throughout the Valley. Average loss per Valley resident for first six months of 1946 was 4% or about 50¢ per person.

POLICE PROTECTION:
Spokane County Sheriff Patrol
Washington State Patrol
Spokane County Merchants' Police Service

HOSPITALS AND CLINICS:
Four modern clinics and hospitals in Valley and quick access to Spokane's facilities.

HOMES:
Approximately 7,950, with 93.2% of these owner occupied.

TOURIST COURTS:
23 with 324 individual units

NEWSPAPERS:
Spokane Valley Herald
Spokane County News
Spokesman-Review
Spokane Chronicle
Washington Farmer

LODGES/FRATERNAL ORGANIZATIONS:
12

SERVICE CLUBS:
Kiwanis
Toastmasters
Spokane Valley Woman's Club
Veterans of Foreign Wars
Numerous Grange Organizations

WELFARE ORGANIZATIONS:
Community Welfare Federation
American Red Cross
Boy Scouts
Girl Scouts
Camp Fire Girls
Salvation Army

BUSINESS ASSOCIATIONS:
Spokane Valley Chamber of Commerce
Spokane Valley Retail Credit Association

. . .And God Speed

"Our hearts are filled with cheer as we look forward to the year 1946. We know there are many troubled spots over the globe, and many different problems to solve on our own home front. But we have an undying faith in the ability of our own people to make their adjustments for the new order and that things will get rolling early in the New Year toward abundant prosperity and the era of an enduring peace.

"Next year holds many opportunities for continued growth and expansion in the Spokane Valley, and in our own local affairs. We shall confidently hope that not too many of these opportunities will be missed and that by a united effort we shall all move forward toward these goals.

"Let's hope that the nation and the world will be able to find a common ground for understanding and good will and that the things for which the war was fought shall begin to materialize. This is wishing everyone the best of everything in the New Year to make our dreams come true.

"Forgetting the things that are behind, let us reach for the better things which lie ahead."

Editor Charles L. Vaughan, *Spokane Valley Herald*. December 28, 1945.

Bibliography

Brereton, Mildred, and Evelyn Foedish: *Memories of Liberty Lake*, printed and photographs reproduced by Leo Oestreicher of Leo's Studio, Spokane Valley, Washington , 1951

Coddington, Frederick L.: *Boyhood Years, School Years* (manuscript)

Cunningham, Eloise Laughlin: *Newman Lake Ladies Auxiliary and Civic Society*, May 1970 (manuscript)

Fahey, John: *The Inland Empire, D.C. Corbin and Spokane*, University of Washington Press, Seattle, Washington, 1965

Felts, Buell: *Editorials*, a memorial booklet prepared by his widow, Genevieve (Collins) Felts, privately printed after Buell's death, 1927

Galbraith, John Kenneth: *The Great Crash, 1929*, The Riverside Press, Cambridge, Houghton Mifflin Co., Boston, 1929

Glenrose Women's Club: "Glenrose Builds a Monument," January 1954 (manuscript)

Goetter, Patricia Smith: *Opportunity Presbyterian Church*, privately printed, Spokane, Washington, 1988

Goldsmith, Roberta: *Memories of Yesterday and Today*, Freeman, Washington, 1885-1985, privately printed, March 1, 1986

Jacklin, Arden: *Memories 1983, 1985, 1990*, (manuscript)

Jones, Aaron C.: *Inland the First Forty Years*, Inland Power and Light, Times Lithograph, Forest Grove, Oregon, 1977

Kister, Gene and Letty: *Fifty Years of Square and Round Dancing in the Spokane Area*, privately duplicated, Spokane, Washington, 1986

Lewis, William S.: "Reminiscences of Pioneers of the Inland Empire," a series of articles in the Sunday *Spokesman-Review*, Spokane, Washington, 1925

Mica Peak Women's Club: *Down Memory Lane with Mica Peak People*, privately duplicated, 1979

Moroney, Rita L.: *History of the United States Postal Service, 1775-1984*, U.S. Postal Service, Washington, D.C.

Mower, Lois: *Government in Spokane County*, Spokane League of Women Voters, 1969

National Rural Electric Cooperative Association: *People—Their Power, The Rural Electric Facts Book*, Washington, D.C., 1980

Nebel, Diane: "100 years of Tradition," Spokane Interstate Fair Program, Sept. 9-18, 1994, Century Marketing Communications for the Spokane County Parks and Recreation Department, Spokane, WA, 1994

Ness, Arthur B.: *History of Orchard Park Schools and West Valley High School*, Millwood, Washington, about 1950 (on file at the school, duplicated)

Pratt, Orville C. *The Spokane Valley*, privately duplicated, 1951

Price, Channon P., "Channon Price Remembers" (manuscript)

Sandberg, Robert A., *Autobiography*, privately printed

Scofield, W.M., *Washington's Historical Markers*, The Touchstone Press, Inc., 1967

Shideler, John C: *A Century of Caring*, Sacred Heart Medical Center, Spokane, Washington, 1985

Smith, Tom M: *History of the Spokane Valley Chamber of Commerce*, privately printed , October , 1977

Spokane County Planning Commission: *Governmental Units in Spokane County,* published by the Spokane County Planning Department, Spokane, Washington, 1955

Spokane City/County Historic Preservation Office: *Historic Resources Inventory*, Spokane, Washington.

Spokane County Medical Society: *Medical Bulletin*, Vol. 62, Number 3, Spokane, Washington, 1989

Spokane Valley Directory 1941-1942, published by the *Spokane Valley Herald*

Washington State Association of County Commissioners and County Engineers in cooperation with the State College of Washington: *The Book of the Counties*, 1953

West, Leon L.: *The Wide Northwest*, Shaw and Borden, Printers, Spokane, Washington, 1927